UK Taxation of Trusts

Tenth Edition

by

Ian Ferrier MA Barrister TEP

and

Matthew Hutton MA (Oxon) FTII AIIT TEP

Tolley Publishing

Published by Tolley
2 Addiscombe Road
Croydon
Surrey CR9 5AF England
020 8686 9141

Photoset by
Phoenix Photosetting, Chatham, Kent

Printed and Bound by
Hobbs the Printers Ltd, Southampton

© Reed Elsevier (UK) Ltd 2000
Reprinted March 2001

ISBN 07545 0706 8

Preface

The principal statutory development this year has been the FA 2000 attack on six capital gains tax avoidance arrangements using trusts, all outlawed from Budget Day 21 March 2000. Two of these relate specifically to onshore trusts, two to offshore trusts and one, which counteracts the traditional 'flip-flop' scheme, could be used with either onshore or offshore trusts. The interesting thing about the avoidance of this scheme is that it has been going for a good many years now (and indeed was most effective onshore only so long as trustees of a life interest trust enjoyed the favourable rate of 23%).

In terms of practice, trustees of discretionary and accumulation trusts continue to wrestle with the effect of the abolition of ACT. This means a certain amount of head scratching as to whether simply to accept the consequent increase in the effective rate of tax on distributions borne by higher rate beneficiaries (assuming no brought forward tax pool) or whether to try to take steps to get round this.

Offshore trusts have continued to receive hostile official attention, with no less than four additional anti-avoidance provisions in FA 2000. The Revenue's contentions regarding the treatment of interest-free demand loans to beneficiaries were upheld in *Billingham v Cooper ChD [2000] STC 122*.

We have reproduced the text of Inland Revenue's Statement of Practice, Extra-statutory concessions and press releases in the Appendices. This is by kind permission of HM Stationery Office.

We hope that this tenth edition of our book will keep readers up to date. We believe that we have taken account of all changes in the law down to the end of July 2000.

Ian Ferrier, London
Matthew Hutton, Chedgrave

September 2000

Contents

	Page
Abbreviations and References	xi
Table of Cases	xiii
Table of Statutes	xx

PART I: UK RESIDENT TRUSTS (Matthew Hutton MA (Oxon) FTII AIIT TEP)

1. Introduction	3
2. Types of Trust	6
General	6
Interest in possession trusts	9
Disabled trusts	10
Protective trusts	11
Accumulation and maintenance trusts	11
Discretionary trusts	14
Charities	15
Miscellaneous	16
Trusts and estates contrasted	17
Bare trustees	19
Trust Manual	19
3. Rights of Beneficiaries	20
4. The Settlor—Anti-avoidance Provisions	23
Income tax	23
Settlements on children	25
Capital gains tax	28
Inheritance tax	29
Miscellaneous	29
5. Trustees—Tax Liabilities and Compliance in Summary	31
Statutory obligations	31
Residence of trustees	33
Liability of trustees	33
Returns for income tax	35
6. Income tax	36
The basic and lower rates	36
Deductibility of expenses	37
Bank interest	38
Building society interest	38
The accrued income scheme	39
Enhanced scrip dividends	42
Scrip dividends	42
Foreign income dividends (before 6 April 1999)	43

Contents

	Page
The rate applicable to trusts	43
Payments to beneficiaries of accumulation and maintenance settlements where ICTA 1988, s 687 applies	46
Payments to beneficiaries of accumulation and maintenance settlements where ICTA 1988, s 687 does not apply	53
Payments to or for the beneficiaries of discretionary settlements	53
Payments to beneficiaries of fixed interest trusts	53
Taxation of land transactions	55
Miscellaneous	55

7. Capital Gains Tax — 57
- Occasions of charge — 57
  - Termination of a life interest — 57
  - Absolute entitlement — 59
- Deeds of variation — 61
- Hold-over relief — 63
  - Disposal following earlier hold-over (the half-gain rule) — 68
- Retirement relief — 69
- Main residence relief — 69
- Reinvestment relief — 70
- Enterprise Investment Scheme — 70
- Base values — 70
- Rates of tax and exemptions — 73
- Interaction of accrued income scheme etc. and capital gains tax — 74
- Appointments and distributions — 75
  - Demergers — 75
  - Connected persons — 76
- Miscellaneous — 77
- Variation of Trusts — 78

8. Inheritance Tax—Definitions — 80

9. Inheritance Tax—Interest in Possession Settlements — 84
- Potentially exempt transfers — 86
- Valuation — 87
- Administration — 88

10. Inheritance Tax—Accumulation and Maintenance Settlements — 89
- The potentially exempt transfer — 89
- Qualifying conditions — 89
- Exemption from charge on making a qualifying settlement — 89
- The use of accumulation and maintenance settlements — 90
- The charge to tax on failure — 94

11. Inheritance Tax—Discretionary Settlements — 97
- The ten-year charge — 97
- The ten-year anniversary — 97
- The amount which is chargeable — 98

	Page
The calculation of the tax	100
The ten-year charge (simple case)	100
The deemed chargeable transfer	100
The deemed cumulative total	101
The effective rate	101
The rate of ten-year charge	101
The ten-year charge where there are accumulations	102
The ten-year charge where there are related settlements	103
The ten-year charge where there is relevant and non-relevant property	104
The ten-year charge where property is added to the settlement	107
The ten-year charge where property changes character within the settlement	109
The ten-year charge where property becomes relevant property on death	110
Anti-avoidance measures	111
Property moving between settlements	111
Excluded property	112
Practical difficulties	112
Identification	112
Potentially exempt transfers	113
Gifts with reservation	115

12. Discretionary Settlements—The Proportionate Charge — 116
Introduction	116
The occasions of charge	116
Exemptions from proportionate charge	117
The amount chargeable	119
The rate of charge	120
Proportionate charge before first ten-year anniversary	120
The deemed chargeable transfer	120
The deemed cumulative total	121
Rate of charge	121
Proportionate charge between ten-year anniversaries	123

13. Discretionary Settlements Made Before 27 March 1974 — 125
The transitional charge	125
The proportionate charge	125

14. Inheritance Tax—Administrative Matters — 126
Determination of tax chargeable	126
Reliefs	129
Payment of tax by instalments	134
Liability for tax	136

15. The Use of Discretionary Settlements — 138
Avoiding aggregation	138
Fast-growing asset	139
Elderly people	140

Contents

		Page
	Married couples	141
	Having your cake	143
	Family companies	144
	Business property	147
	Future considerations	148
	Comparisons with accumulation and maintenance settlements	149
	Protection from foreign legislation	150
	Income tax planning	150
	The flexibility provided by a discretionary settlement	151
	Anti-avoidance	152
16.	**The Use of Non-Discretionary Settlements**	155
17.	**Charities**	159
	Introduction	159
	Exemptions on setting up charities	159
	Stamp duty	159
	Inheritance tax	159
	Capital gains tax	159
	Income tax	160
	Transfer of shareholdings to charities	160
	Tax exemptions for charities	161
	Anti-avoidance	162
	Time charities	165
	Inland Revenue administration	165
	Value added tax	165
	Disaster funds	166
	Miscellaneous	166
18.	**Self-Assessment**	168
	Commencement	168
	Notification of liability	169
	Payment of tax	169
	Estimates	170
	Penalties and interest	170
	Clearance	171
	Policy for trustees	171
	Miscellaneous	171
	The beneficiaries	171
	Trust income	172
	Points on completing the Trust and Estate Tax Return—SA900	173

PART II: OFFSHORE RESIDENT TRUSTS (Ian Ferrier MA BARRISTER TEP)

19.	**Residence, Ordinary Residence and Domicile**	181
	Introduction	181
	Basic concepts	181
	Residence	181

		Page
	Ordinary residence	183
	Domicile	184
20.	**Income Tax**	187
	Liability to UK tax	187
	Anti-avoidance	189
	Transfer of assets abroad	190
	Transactions in land	191
	Deduction of tax	192
21.	**Capital Gains Tax**	193
	Introduction	193
	Exporting trusts	194
	The pre-1981 provisions	194
	The 1981 provisions	195
	The tax in transition	197
	The 1991 provisions	197
	Exit charge	198
	Charge on settlor	200
	Supplementary charge	203
	Strengthening of 1981 provisions	203
	The 1998 provisions	204
	Transitional provisions	205
	Application	205
	The 2000 provisions	206
22.	**Inheritance Tax**	207
	Excluded property	207
	Settled property situated outside the UK	207
	The settlor	207
	Situation of property	208
	Reversionary interests	208
	Exempt gilts	209
	Domicile	211
	Reporting obligation	211
	Executors and trustees	212
	Enforcement—the Clore case	213
23.	**The Use of Offshore Trusts in Tax Planning**	214
	Protection and establishment of domicile	214
	The trust document and its contents	215
	The family context	216
	The security aspect	216
	The location of the trust	217
	Opportunities for non-domiciled individuals	218
	A sting in the tail	218

Appendices
A	Press Releases and Statements of Practice	220
B	Extra-Statutory Concessions	229

Contents

		Page
C	Checking Liabilities and the Tax Pool, etc. in 1997/98	231
D	Statements of Practice SP8/94 and SP7/81	235
E	Trustee Act 1925, ss 31–33	238
F	Inheritance Tax Act 1984, s 71	242

Index   244

Abbreviations and References

ABBREVIATIONS

ACT	= Advance Corporation Tax
AIM	= Alternative Investment Market
App	= Appendix
APR	= Agricultural Property Relief
BES	= Business Expansion Scheme
BPR	= Business Property Relief
CA	= Court of Appeal
CA(NI)	= Court of Appeal (Northern Ireland)
CGT	= Capital Gains Tax
CGTA 1979	= Capital Gains Tax Act 1979
Ch D	= Chancery Division
CIOT	= Chartered Institute of Taxation
CIR	= Commissioners of Inland Revenue ('the board')
col	= column
CJEC	= Court of Justice of the European Community
CRT	= Composite Rate Tax
CS	= Court of Session
CTO	= Capital Taxes Office
CTT	= Capital Transfer Tax
DTR	= Double Taxation Relief
EIS	= Enterprise Investment Scheme
ESC	= Extra-statutory Concession
FA	= Finance Act
FOTRA	= Free of tax to residents abroad
HL	= House of Lords
ICAEW	= Institute of Chartered Accountants in England & Wales
ICTA 1988	= Income and Corporation Taxes Act 1988
IHT	= Inheritance Tax
IHTA 1984	= Inheritance Tax Act 1984
IRPR	= Inland Revenue Press Release
KB	= King's Bench Division
para	= paragraph
PC	= Privy Council
PET	= Potentially exempt transfer
Pt	= Part
QB	= Queen's Bench Division
s	= section
Sch	= Sch [*4 Sch 2* = 4th Schedule, paragraph 2]
SI	= Statutory Instrument
SP	= Inland Revenue Statement of Practice
SpC	= Special Commissioners' decisions
SSCBA 1992	= Social Security Contributions and Benefits Act 1992
TCGA 1992	= Taxation of Chargeable Gains Act 1992

Abbreviations and References

TM	= Inland Revenue Trust Manual
TMA 1970	= Taxes Management Act 1970
UK	= United Kingdom
USM	= Unlisted Securities Market

REFERENCES

AC	= Law Reports, Appeal Cases
All ER	= All England Law Reports
JLR	= Jersey Law Reports
LR Sc & D	= Law Reports, Scotch and Divorce (HL)
STC	= Simon's Tax Cases
STC (SCD)	= Simon's Tax Cases, Special Commissioners Decisions
SpC	= Special Commissioners
STI	= Simon's Tax Intelligence
TC	= Official Reports of Tax Cases

Table of Cases

Administrators of the Estate of Caton (dec'd) v Couch, CA [1997] STC 970	7.29
Aikin v Macdonald Trustees Ex (S) [1894] 3 TC 306	6.2
Allan, Bosanquet v HL, [1985] STC 356	6.22
Appleby, Crowe v Ch D, [1975] STC 502	7.8
Archer-Shee, Garland v HL 1930, 15 TC 693	19.7
Attorney-General, Winans v HL, [1904] AC 287	21.3
Bailey v Garrod Ch D 1983, 56 TC 695	19.7
Baird's Executors v CIR, Lands Tribunal for Scotland, 1990 (1991) 09 EG, 10 EG 153	14.11
Bambridge v CIR HL 1955, 36 TC 313	18.7
Bank of Nova Scotia, US v 691 F.2d 1384 (1982)	21.16
Barclays Bank Trust Co v CIR SpC, [1998] STC (SCD) 125	14.6
Beckman v IRC [2000] STC (SCD) 59	14.6
Begg-McBrearty v Stilwell (Trustee of the G E Coke Settlement), [1996] STC 413	7.17
Berry v Warnett HL 1982, 55 TC 92	21.3
Billingham v Cooper [2000] STC 122	21.6
Bond v Pickford CA, [1983] STC 517	7.8; 15.22; App A
Bosanquet v Allan HL, [1985] STC 356	6.22
Botnar, CIR v Ch D, [1998] STC 38	4.6; 20.8
Brandenburg, CIR v Ch D, [1982] STC 555	22.9
Briscoe and Others, Hart v Ch D, [1978] STC 89	11.31; 15.23
Brodie's Trustees v CIR KB 1933, 17 TC 432	6.37
Brown, Jenkins v Ch D, [1989] STC 577	7.36
Brown's Executors v CIR, SpC 83 [1996] STC (SCD) 277	14.6
Brumby v Milner HL, [1976] STC 534	6.37
Buchanan, CIR v CA 1957, 37 TC 365	4.13
Bullock, CIR v CA 1976, 51 TC 522	19.6
Bulmer v CIR Ch D 1966, 44 TC 1	4.4
Butler v Wildin Ch D, [1989] STC 22	4.7
Carver v Duncan HL, [1985] STC 356	6.22
Caton dec'd Administrators of the estate of, v Couch, CA [1997] STC 970	7.25
Chase Bank (CI) Trust Co Ltd, Rahman (Abdel) v, 1983 JLR 1; 1984 JLR 127; 1985–86 JLR N–5; 1987–88 JLR 81; 1990 JLR 59, 136	23.3
Chinn v Collins HL 1980, 54 TC 92 1991 JLR 103	21.3
Cholmondeley and Another v CIR Ch D, [1986] STC 384	15.26
CIR v Baird's Executors, Lands Tribunal for Scotland, 1990 (1991) 09 EG, 10 EG 153	14.11
CIR, Bambridge v HL 1955, 36 TC 313	20.5

Table of Cases

CIR, Barclays Bank Trust Co Ltd v SpC, [1998] STC (SCD) 125	14.6
CIR v Botnar CA [1999] STC 711	4.6; 20.8
CIR v Brandenburg Ch D, [1982] STC 555	22.9
CIR, Brodie's Trustees v KB 1933, 17 TC 432	6.37
CIR, Brown's Executors v SpC 83 [1996] STC (SCD) 277	14.6
CIR v Buchanan CA 1957, 37 TC 365	4.13
CIR v Bullock CA 1976, 51 TC 522	19.6
CIR, Bulmer v Ch D 1966, 44 TC 1	4.4
CIR v Challenge Corp Ltd, PC [1986] STC 548	20.8
CIR, Cholmondeley and Another v Ch D, [1986] STC 384	15.27
CIR, Clinch v QB 1973, 49 TC 52	21.6
CIR, Congreve v 1948, 30 TC 163	20.5
CIR, Cunard's Trustees v CA 1945, 27 TC 122	6.37
CIR, Dawson v HL, 1989 62 TC 301	19.4
CIR v De Vigier HL 1964, 42 TC 24	4.10
CIR, Dreyfus (Camille & Henry) Foundation Inc v HL 1955, 36 TC 126	2.21; 23.4
CIR, Fitzwilliam (Countess) and others v HL, [1993] STC 502;	15.27; 21.3; 22.6
Ch D [1990] STC 65	15.27
CA, [1991] STI 158	15.27
CA, [1992] STC 185	15.27; 21.3
CIR, Frankland v CA [1997] STC 1450	12.7
CIR, Gray (surviving executor of Lady Fox) v CA, [1994] STC 360	14.11
CIR, Harding and another (exor of Loveday dec'd) v [1997] STC (SCD) 321	12.7
CIR, Hatton v Ch D, [1992] STC 140	15.27
CIR v Helen Slater Charitable Trust Limited CA 1981, 55 TC 230	17.9, 23.4
CIR, Howard de Walden (Lord) v CA 1941, 25 TC 121	20.5
CIR, Howarth's Executor v SpC [1987] STC (SCD) 162	5.12
CIR, Jones & Another (Bell's Administrators) v Ch D [1997] STC 358	7.25
CIR, Inglewood and Another v CA, [1983] STC 133	2.16
CIR, Lady Ingram, Exors of v HL [1999] STC 37	15.28
CIR, Levene v HL 1928, 13 TC 486	19.5
CIR v Levy Ch D, [1982] STC 442	4.4
CIR, Lloyds Private Banking Ltd v Ch D [1998] STC 559	15.6
CIR, Macpherson and Another v HL, [1988] STC 362	12.3
CIR v Matthew's Executors, CS [1984] STC 386	7.8
CIR v McGuckian, HL [1997] STC 908	4.17; 15.24
CIR v Mills HL, [1974] STC 130	4.14
CIR, Minden Trust (Cayman) Ltd v CA, [1985] STC 758	22.9
CIR, Montague Trust Co. (Jersey) Ltd v Ch D, [1989] STC 477	8.5; 22.9
CIR, Padmore v CA, 1989, 62 TC 352	21.7
CIR, Pearson and Others v HL, [1980] STC 318	2.12; 8.3
CIR, Pilkington v HL, [1964] AC 612	2.16
CIR v Plummer HL, [1979] STC 793	4.4
CIR, R v, ex p Fulford-Dobson QB 1987, 60 TC 168	19.4

Table of Cases

CIR *v* Portland (Duchess of) Ch D 1981, 54 TC 648	19.6
CIR, Ramsay (W T) Ltd *v* HL 1981, 54 TC 101	4.17; 21.3; App A
CIR *v* Regent Trust Co Ltd (Butt's 1970 Settlement Trustee) Ch D 1979, 53 TC 54	20.4
CIR *v* Richard's Executors HL 1971, 46 TC 626	7.29; App D
CIR, Royal Bank of Canada *v* Ch D 1971, 47 TC 565	21.6
CIR, Sheppard and Another (Trustees of the Woodland Trust) (No 2) Ch D, [1993] STC 240	17.15
CIR, Stanley *v* CA 1944, 26 TC 12	6.39
CIR *v* Stannard Ch D, [1984] STC 245	22.12
CIR, Strathalmond *v* Ch D 1972, 48 TC 537	21.11
CIR, Swales *v* Ch D [1984] STC 413	8.3
CIR *v* Universities Superannuation Scheme Ltd Ch D [1997] STC 1	17.15
CIR, Vestey *v* HL 1979, 54 TC 503	20.7; 23.7
CIR, Von Ernst & Cie SA *v* CA, [1980] STC 111	22.9
CIR, Walding & others (executors of Walding dec'd), *v* Ch D [1995] STC 13	14.6
CIR, Walton (executors of Walton dec'd), *v* CA [1996] STC 68	14.11
CIR, Whitney *v* HL 1925, 10 TC 88	20.1
CIR *v* Willoughby, HL [1997] STC 995	20.8; 23.8
Clark, Reed *v* Ch D 1985, 58 TC 528	19.3
Clarke, Figg *v* Ch D [1997] STC 247	7.6
Clinch *v* CIR QB 1973, 49 TC 52	21.6
Clore (deceased) (No 2), re, Official Solicitor *v* Clore and others Ch D, [1984] STC 609	19.7; 22.13; 23.2
Clore (deceased) (No 3), re, CIR *v* Stype Trustees (Jersey) Ltd and Others Ch D, [1985] STC 394	21.16
Clore's Settlement Trusts, re Ch D, [1966] 2 All ER 272	2.16
Collins, Chinn *v* HL 1980, 54 TC 92	21.3
Commissioner of Estate Duty, Kwok *v* PC, [1988] STC 728	22.5
Congreve *v* CIR 1948, 30 TC 163	20.5; 23.8
Couch *v* Administrators of the estate of Caton dec'd CA [1997] STC 970	7.25
Countess Fitzwilliam and Others *v* IRC, HL [1993] STC 502	15.26
Crossland *v* Hawkins CA 1961, 39 TC 493	4.14
Crowe *v* Appleby Ch D, [1975] STC 502	7.8
Cunard's Trustees *v* CIR CA 1945, 27 TC 122	6.37
Dawson *v* CIR HL, 1989 62 TC 301	19.4
Dawson, Furniss *v* HL, [1984] STC 153	15.27
De Vigier, CIR *v* HL 1964, 42 TC 24	4.10
Dixon, Robson *v* Ch D 1972, 48 TC 527	19.3
Dreyfus (Camille & Henry) Foundation Inc *v* CIR HL 1955, 36 TC 126	2.21; 23.4
Duncan, Carver *v* HL, [1985] STC 356	6.22
Edwards, Roome and Denne *v* HL, 1981; 54 TC 359	7.8; 19.4; App A
Eilbeck *v* Rawling HL 1981, 54 TC 101	21.3

Table of Cases

Ewart v Taylor Ch D 1983, 57 TC 401	21.3
Farmer v IRC [1999] STC (SCD) 321	14.6
Figg v Clarke Ch D [1997] STC 247	7.6
Fitzwilliam (Countess) and Others v CIR HL, [1993] STC 502	15.26; 21.3; 22.6
Ch D [1990] STC 65	15.27
CA, [1991] STI 158	15.27
CA, [1992] STC 185	15.27; 21.3
Fletcher, Yuill v CA 1984, 58 TC 145	20.9
Frankland v CIR, CA [1997] STC 1450	12.7
Furness v IRC [1999] STC (SCD) 232	14.6
Furniss v Dawson HL, [1984] STC 153	15.26
Furse (deceased) Ch D, [1980] STC 597	19.7
Gardner, Hoare Trustees v Ch D, [1978] STC 89	7.8; 19.8
Garland v Archer-Shee HL 1930, 15 TC 693	20.2
Garrod, Bailey v Ch D 1983, 56 TC 695	21.3
Gee, Wood and Others, re, v Staples and Others Ch D, [1948] 1 All ER 498	10.12
Government of India v Taylor HL, [1953] AC 491	23.5
Gray (surviving executor of Lady Fox) v CIR CA, [1994] STC 360	14.11
Gulbenkian's Settlement Trusts (No 2), re, Stephens and Another v Maun and Others Ch D, [1969] 2 All ER 1173	3.6; 11.17
HM Treasury, ex p Daily Mail and General Trust Plc CJEC, R v [1988] STC 787	21.7
Harding and another (exor. of Loveday dec'd) v CIR [1997] STC (SCD) 321	12.7
Hart v Briscoe and Others Ch D, [1978] STC 89	11.31; 15.22
Hart, Pepper v HL [1992] STC 898	20.7; 23.7
Hatton v CIR Ch D, [1992] STC 140	15.26
Hawkins, Crossland v CA 1961, 39 TC 493	4.14
Helen Slater Charitable Trust Limited, CIR v CA, [1981] STC 471	17.9; 23.4
Hoare Trustees v Gardner Ch D, [1978] STC 89	7.8
Howard de Walden (Lord) v CIR CA 1941, 25 TC 121	20.7
Howarth's Executor v CIR SpC [1997] STC (SCD) 162	5.12
Income Tax Special Purposes Commissioners v Pemsel HL 1891, 3 TC 53	2.21
Inglewood and Another v CIR CA, [1983] STC 133	2.16
Ingram and another (executors of Lady Ingram dec'd) v CIR, HL [1999] STC 37	15.28
Jenkins v Brown Ch D, [1989] STC 577	7.44
Jennings, Inchyra (Lord) v Ch D 1965, 42 TC 388	20.3

Table of Cases

Jones & Another (Bell's Administrators) *v* CIR, Ch D
 [1997] STC 358   7.29

Keeler's Settled Trusts, re, Ch D, [1981] 1 All ER 888   10.12
Kerr, Marshall *v* HL [1994] STC 638   4.18; 7.9; 16.9; 21.15
Kwok *v* Commissioner of Estate Duty PC, [1988] STC 728   22.5

Lawson *v* Rolfe Ch D 1969, 46 TC 199   20.3
Lee and Another, Sinclair *v* Ch D [1993] STI 844   7.39
Leedale *v* Lewis HL 1982, 56 TC 501   21.4
Levene *v* CIR HL 1928, 13 TC 486   19.5
Lewis, Leedale *v* HL 1982, 56 TC 501   21.4
Levy, CIR *v* Ch D, [1982] STC 442   4.4
Lloyds Private Banking Ltd *v* CIR Ch D, [1998] STC 559   15.6
Lowther, Page *v* CA, [1983] STC 799; 57 TC 199   6.47; 20.9

Macdonald Trustees, Aikin *v* Ex (S) [1894] 3 TC 306   6.2
McGuckian, CIR *v* HL [1997] STC 908   4.17; 15.25
Macpherson and Another *v* CIR HL, [1988] STC 362   12.3
Major, St Dunstan's *v* SpC [1997] STC (SCD)   15.7
Marshall *v* Kerr HL, [1994] STC 638   7.9; 16.9; 21.15
Matthew's Executors, CIR *v* CS [1984] STC 386   7.8
Maun and Others, re Gulbenkian's Settlement Trusts (No 2),
 Stephens and Another *v* Ch D, [1969] 2 All ER 1173   3.6; 11.17
Mills, CIR *v* HL, [1974] STC 130   4.14
Milner, Brumby *v* HL, [1976] STC 534   6.37
Minden Trust (Cayman) Ltd *v* CIR CA, [1985] STC 758   22.9
Montague Trust Co. (Jersey) Ltd *v* CIR Ch D, [1989] STC 477   8.5; 22.9
Moxon's Will Trusts, re Ch D, [1958] 1 All ER 386   2.16

Padmore *v* CIR CA, 1989, 62 TC 352   21.7; 21.11
Page *v* Lowther CA, [1983] STC 799; 57 TC 199   6.47; 20.9
Pearce *v* Young Ch D, [1996] STC 743   4.3; 4.6
Pearson and Others *v* CIR HL, [1980] STC 318   2.12; 8.3
Peay, Sansom and Another *v* Ch D, [1976] STC 494   7.33; 8.3
Pemsel, Income Tax Special Purposes Commissioners *v* HL
 1891, 3 TC 53   2.21
Pepper *v* Hart HL, [1992] STC 898   20.7; 23.7
Phillips, Young *v* Ch D 1984, 58 TC 232   21.3
Pickford, Bond *v* CA, [1983] STC 517   7.8; 15.23; App A
Pilkington *v* CIR HL, [1964] AC 612   2.16
Plummer, CIR *v* HL, [1979] STC 793   4.4
Portland (Duchess of), CIR *v* Ch D 1981, 54 TC 648   19.6

R *v* CIR, ex p Fulford-Dobson QB 1987, 60 TC 168   19.4
R *v* HM Treasury, ex p Daily Mail and General Trust Plc CJEC,
 [1988] STC 787   21.7
Rahman (Abdel) *v* Chase Bank (CI) Trust Co Ltd, 1983 JLR 1;
 1984 JLR 127; 1985–86 JLR N–5; 1987–88 JLR 81;
 1990 JLR 59, 136 1991 JLR 103   23.3; 23.8

Table of Cases

Ramsay (W T) Ltd v CIR HL 1981, 54 TC 101	21.3; App A
Rawling, Eilbeck v HL 1981, 54 TC 101	21.3
Reed v Clark Ch D 1985, 58 TC 528	19.3
Regent Trust Co Ltd (Butt's 1970 Settlement Trustee), CIR v Ch D 1979, 53 TC 54	20.4
Renton, Swires v Ch D, [1991] STC 490	7.8, 7.32
Richard's Executors, CIR v HL 1971, 46 TC 626	7.25; App D
Robson v Dixon Ch D 1972, 48 TC 527	19.3
Rolfe, Lawson v Ch D 1969, 46 TC 199	20.3
Roome and Denne v Edwards HL, 1981; 54 TC 359	7.8; 19.4; App A
Royal Bank of Canada v CIR Ch D 1971, 47 TC 565	21.6
Sansom and Another v Peay Ch D, [1976] STC 494	7.26; 8.3
Scrutton v Young, Ch D [1996] 743	4.3; 4.6
Sheppard and Another (Trustees of the Woodland Trust) v CIR (No 2) Ch D, [1993] STC 240	17.15
Sinclair v Lee and Another Ch D, [1993] STI 844	7.38
Singer and Others, Williams v HL 1920, 7 TC 387	5.7; 20.2
Stanley v CIR CA 1944, 26 TC 12	6.39
Stannard, CIR v Ch D [1984] STC 245	22.12
Staples and Others, re Gee Wood and Others v Ch D, [1948] 1 All ER 498	10.12
State of Norway's Application (No 1 & 2) HL, [1990] 1 AC 723	23.5
Stephens and Another v Maun and Others, re Gulbenkian's Settlement Trusts (No 2) Ch D, [1969] 2 All ER 1173	11.17
Stevenson v Wishart and Others (Levy's Trustees) CA, [1987] STC 266	6.37
Stilwell (Trustee of the G E Coke Settlement), Begg-McBrearty v [1996] STC 413	7.17
Strathalmond (Lord) v CIR Ch D 1972, 48 TC 537	21.11
Swales v CIR Ch D, [1984] STC 413	8.3
Swires v Renton Ch D, [1991] STC 490	7.8; 7.36
Taylor, Ewart v Ch D 1983, 57 TC 401	21.3
Taylor, Government of India v HL [1953] AC 491	23.5
Tucker (a bankrupt), ex p Tucker, re CA, [1988] 1 All ER 603	21.16
Turner, Wilson v [1883] 22 Ch D 521	2.16
Udny v Udny HL 1869, 1 LR Sc & D 441	19.6
Universities Superannuation Scheme Ltd, CIR v Ch D [1997] STC 1	17.15
US v Bank of Nova Scotia, 691 F.2d 1384 (1982)	21.16
Vestey v CIR HL 1979, 54 TC 503	20.7; 23.8
Von Ernst & Cie SA v CIR CA, [1980] STC 111	22.9
Walding & others (executors of Walding dec'd) v CIR Ch D [1995] STC 13	14.6

Table of Cases

Walton (executors of Walton dec'd) v CIR CA, [1996] STC 68	14.11
Warnett, Berry v HL 1982, 55 TC 92	21.3
Weston v IRC [2000] STC (SCD) 30	14.6
Weston's Settlements, re Ch D [1968] 1 All ER 720; CA, [1968] 3 All ER 338	21.2
Whitney v CIR HL 1925, 10 TC 88	20.1
Wildin, Butler v Ch D, [1989] STC 22	4.7
Williams v Singer and Others HL 1920, 7 TC 387	5.7; 20.2
Willoughby, CIR v HL [1997] STC 995	20.8
Wilson v Turner [1883] 22 Ch D 521	2.16
Wilson, Yuill v HL 1980, 52 TC 674	20.9
Winans v Attorney-General HL, [1904] AC 287	19.7
Wishart and Others (Levy's Trustees), Stevenson v CA, [1987] STC 266	6.37
Young v Pearce, Young v Scrutton, Ch D, [1996] STC 743	4.3; 4.6
Young v Phillips Ch D 1984, 58 TC 232	21.3
Yuill v Fletcher CA 1984, 58 TC 145	20.9
Yuill v Wilson HL 1980, 52 TC 674	20.9

Table of Statutes

1881 Customs and Inland Revenue Act
s 38(2)(A)   15.27

1925 Law of Property Act
s 175   3.5

1925 Settled Land Act
s 64   7.48

1925 Trustee Act
s 31	2.15; 2.16; 3.5; 3.6; 4.8; App C; App E
(1)	2.15
(2)	6.37
s 32	2.9; App E
s 33	2.154; App E
s 57	7.48
s 68(17)	2.4

1958 Variation of Trusts Act   7.48

1960 Charities Act
s 38   2.21

1965 Finance Act
s 42   21.1; 21.2

1970 Taxes Management Act
s 8A	18.22
s 9A	18.17
s 12B	18.17
s 13	5.7; 19.4
s 19A	18.17
s 28A	18.17
s 29	18.17
s 42	18.22
s 43	App A
ss 71–73	5.3
s 76	5.7
s 90	6.21
s 98	21.16
s 107A	18.22

1973 Education Act
s 2   17.21

1975 Finance Act
Sch 5   11.31; App A
para 6   22.9

1980 Finance Act
s 79   7.31

1982 Finance Act
s 108   App A
s 129   17.2

1984 Finance Act
s 64   7.34

1984 Inheritance Tax Act
s 2(3)	14.1; 14.10
s 3(1)	12.3; 22.2
(2)	22.2
s 3A	8.9; 11.35
(1)(*c*)	10.1
(2)	9.10
(3)	8.9
(4)(5)	14.2
(6)(7)	9.10
s 4	22.12
(1)	11.30
s 5(1)	22.2
s 6	19.6; 22.7
(1)	22.6
(2)	8.5; 12.5
s 7(2)	11.15
(4)	14.2; 14.9
s 10(3)	15.25
s 11	2.13; 2.16
s 15	4.8
s 18(2)	7.5
s 19(3A)	11.35
s 23	17.3; App A
s 24	12.8; App A
s 25	App A
s 40	App A
s 43	8.2
(2)	11.30; 15.6
(3)	22.6; App A
s 44(1)	22.4
s 44(2)	8.2; 11.34; 22.4

Table of Statutes

1984 IHTA		(4)	12.7
s 45	5.10	(5)	12.6
s 47	22.6	(6)	12.3
s 48	8.5; 22.2	(7)	12.5
(1)	9.5; 10.9; 16.11; 22.6	(8)	12.5; 22.10
(2)	22.6	(9)	12.4
(3)	11.28; 22.3; 22.6; 23.7	s 66	5.10; 11.10
		(1)	11.15; 11.16
(4)	11.33; 11.34; 22.7; 22.8; 22.9	(2)	11.17; 11.20
		(4)(*b*)	2.20; 11.20; 12.9
(5)	11.33; 11.34; 22.9	(*c*)	11.19; 12.9
(6)	11.34	(5)	11.12
s 49	2.20; 5.10; 22.6	(*a*)(*b*)	2.20; 11.29
		(6)	11.12; 11.14
(1)	5.10; 9.1; 9.3; 9.11	s 67	5.10; 11.24
s 50	5.10	(1)–(3)	11.23
(1)	9.4	(6)(7)	11.29
(3)	9.4	s 68	5.10; 12.9
(6)	App A	(1)	12.9; 12.14
s 51	5.10	(2)	12.14
s 52	5.10; 14.6	(3)	12.15
(1)	9.2; 9.4; 9.11; 16.5; App A	(4)	12.13
		(5)	12.9; 12.12
s 53	5.10	s 69	5.10
(1)	22.2	(1)	12.16; 12.17
s 54	5.10	(2)(3)	12.19
ss 54A, 54B	9.7; 9.8; 11.22	(4)	12.16
		s 70	2.22; 5.10; 17.16; App F
ss 55–56	5.10	(6)(8)	10.15
s 57	5.10; 9.10	s 71	2.16; 5.10; 6.25; 10.2; 10.10; 10.15; App A; App F
s 58	2.20; 5.10		
(1)	22.2	(1)	2.15; 2.16
(*b*)	10.17	(*a*)	App A; App B
(*f*)	2.20	(*b*)	6.25
s 59	2.20; 5.10	(2)	2.15; 2.17
s 60	5.10; 11.4	(3)	10.15
s 61	5.10	(4)	7.17; 10.5, 10.15
(1)	11.4	(5)	10.15
(2)	11.5	(6)	10.3
(3)(4)	11.4	(7)	10.10
s 62	5.10; 11.18	(8)	2.18
s 63	5.10; 8.7	ss 72–74	5.10
s 64	5.10; 11.7; 11.16; 11.17	s 75	5.10; 12.8
		s 76	5.10; 17.3
s 65	5.10; 11.29; App A	ss 77, 78	5.10
(1)(*a*)	10.17; 12.2	s 79	5.10
(*b*)	12.2; 15.14; App A	(8)(9)	11.9
(2)	12.9		

Table of Statutes

1984 IHTA

s 80	5.10; 11.5; 11.18; 11.22; 11.28; 11.30; 11.32
s 81	5.10; 11.31; 11.32
s 82	5.10; 11.28; 11.32
s 83	5.10; 11.6; 11.27; 11.30; 22.12
ss 84, 85	5.10
s 86	2.20; 5.10
s 87	2.20; 5.10
s 88	2.14; 5.10
s 89	2.13; 5.10
s 90	5.10; 10.12
s 91	5.10; 22.12
ss 92, 93	5.10
s 98	15.2
s 103(1)	11.8; 14.6
s 105(1)(*b*)	9.3
(1A)	9.3
(1ZA)	14.6
(3)	14.6
(4)(b)	14.6
ss 107, 108	14.6
s 112	14.7; 15.9
s 113A	7.31; 14.7
(2)	14.9
(3)(3A)	14.7
(3)(b)	14.7
s 113B	14.6; 14.7
s 115(1)	11.8
s 117(a), (b)	9.1
ss 124A, 124B	14.7
s 124C	14.6
s 131	10.14; 15.3
s 141	14.10
s 142	7.9; 15.7; 16.9
(1)	7.9; 10.13
(2)	11.6
s 144	7.9; 7.15; 12.7; 16.9
s 160	11.7
s 161	14.14; 17.6
s 162	11.7
(4)	11.9
s 165	7.22
ss 178–189	7.25
s 186A	7.25
s 186B	7.25
ss 190–198	7.25
s 191	7.25
s 199	App A
(2)	14.2
s 201	14.17
s 204	5.12
(1)(2)	22.12
(5)–(8)	14.2
s 215	14.1
s 216	5.10; 14.1; 22.11
s 216(1)	10.4; 14.2
(6)	14.2
s 217	14.1
s 218	5.10; 14.1; 14.4; 22.11
(3)	14.4
s 219	14.1
(1)(1A)(3)(4)	14.4
s 220	14.1
ss 221–223	14.1; 14.5
ss 224, 225	14.1
s 226	14.1; 14.2
(3)–(3B)	14.2
s 227	14.1; 14.13; 14.14
(1)(3)	14.16
(4)	14.15
ss 228, 229	14.1; 14.14
ss 230–232	14.1
s 233	14.1; 14.3
(3)	6.2
s 234	14.1; 14.13; 14.14
s 235	14.1; 14.3; 14.20
s 236	14.1
s 237	14.1; 14.17
s 238	14.1; 14.18
s 239	14.1; 14.18
ss 240–244	14.1
s 245	14.1
s 245A	22.11
ss 246–261	14.1
s 267	8.5; 12.5; 19.6; 19.7; 22.10; 23.1
s 268	9.4; 11.18; 15.4; 15.25
s 272	2.21; 14.6; 15.15; 22.12
Sch 1	11.8
Sch 2 para 1A	11.36
para 3	12.18

Table of Statutes

1984 **IHTA**		s 65(4)	19.6; 23.7
Sch 3	12.8; App A	(5)–(9)	23.7
Sch 4	2.20	s 66	20.3
para 16	12.8	s 192	19.6
Sch 6 para 2	9.2; 9.3; 10.9	s 202	17.5
Pt III	11.34	s 209	App A
Pt VI	11.9	ss 213, 218	7.38
Pt VIII	14.1	s 219	6.23
		s 233(1A)	20.4
1984 Trusts (Jersey) Law	23.3	s 235	17.15
		ss 246A–246Y	6.20
1985 Enduring Powers of Attorney Act		s 249	App A
		s 256	5.4
s 3 para 3	2.7	s 278	App B
1985 Finance Act		ss 334–336	19.3
s 86	20.6	s 339	17.8
		s 348	6.24; 6.27; 6.32; 6.43
1986 Finance Act	15.15		
s 58	21.8	s 349	6.24; 6.27; 6.43
s 102	4.1; 7.9; 8.8; 11.37; 15.6; 15.8; 15.27	s 349(1)	6.32
		s 350	18.24
(1)	15.27	ss 352 *et seq.*	6.2
(4)	11.37	s 364	6.2
s 103	15.27	s 379A	5.5
Sch 19 para 1	8.9	s 416	4.10; 21.14
46	8.9	s 417	21.14
Sch 20	4.1; 7.9	s 476(5)(*b*)	App C
		s 481	20.10
1986 Insolvency Act	2.23	s 505	17.9
s 423	2.23; 23.6	(1)	17.8; 17.9
		(2)	17.8
1987 Finance (No 2) Act		s 506	17.9
s 96	8.9; 9.10	(1)	2.21
Sch 7 para 1	11.22	s 573–576	14.12
		s 631	7.32
1987 Reverter of Sites Act	17.21	ss 660A–G	4.2; 4.6
		ss 660A–678	4.1
1988 Income and Corporation Taxes Act	16.12	s 660A	4.6; 6.22
		(6)	4.3
s 1	5.4	B	4.7; 4.8; 4.9; 18.24
s 1A	20.7; 20.10		
s 18	20.2	(4)	4.5
Schedule D		(5)	4.7
Case V	6.2	s 660D	6.22
Case VI	6.47	s 660G	4.3; 4.9
s 24(1)(3)	6.47	(3)	4.5
s 34	6.23; 6.47	ss 677–682A	4.2
s 42A	5.11	s 677	4.10
s 47	19.5	s 678	4.10
s 59	5.3; 18.24; 19.4	(1)	4.10

Table of Statutes

1988 ICTA		s 721	6.5; 6.13
s 686	2.6; 5.4; 6.1; 6.2;	(2)	6.16
	6.20; 6.21; 6.22;	ss 722–728	6.5
	6.23; 6.25; 6.27;	s 730	4.17
	6.28; 6.29; 6.36;	s 739	4.17; 20.7; 20.8;
	6.37; 6.40; 15.21;		21.6; 23.8
	18.22; 20.4; 20.5;	(1A)	20.8; 23.8
	App C	s 740	20.7
(1A)	6.21	s 741	20.8
(1AA)	6.21; 6.22;	s 745	21.6
	16.7	s 761	6.27; 6.40; 7.35
(2)(*a*)	2.20; 6.23;	s 764	5.4
	6.25; 20.4; 20.5	s 765	21.7
(*b*)	6.22	s 767A–C	2.23
(2AA)	6.22	s 776	6.47; 20.9
s 687	6.10; 6.20; 6.21;	(2)(ii)	6.47
	6.22; 6.24; 6.25;	(5)(*a*)	20.9
	6.27; 6.28; 6.29;	s 788	21.11
	6.31; 6.32; 6.33;	s 790	20.6
	6.34; 6.35; 6.36;	s 832(1)	6.21; 17.9
	6.37; 6.40; 18.24;	s 835	6.23
	20.5	Sch 20	17.9
(1)(2)	6.32	Pt XV	App A
(1)	App B	**1988 Finance Act**	7.1
(2)	6.29; App B	**1989 Finance Act**	7.45
(3)	6.20; 6.27	ss 110, 111	19.4
s 689A	20.7; 20.10	s 124	5.18; 7.31
s 689B	6.22	s 151	6.49
ss 695–702	2.4; 2.6; 5.9;	Sch 11 para 5	6.27
	18.19	**1990 Finance Act**	
s 698(3)	App A	s 25	17.5
s 700(5)	18.21	s 126	2.20
s 701(3A)	18.19	**1991 Finance Act**	
s 701(9)	App A	s 121	2.20
ss 703–709	17.15	**1992 Taxation of Chargeable**	
s 705(2)	17.15	**Gains Act**	
s 710	6.5; 7.34	s 2(1)	7.1; 21.1
(2)–(4)	6.5	(2)	5.6
s 711	6.5	s 3(3)	7.32
s 712	6.5; 6.8	(7)	7.32
s 713	6.5	s 4	20.9
s 713(1)	6.13	s 10	7.28; 21.10
s 714	6.5	s 10A	21.13
s 715	6.5	s 12	19.6
(1)	6.5	(1)	23.7
(4)	6.5	(2)	23.7
ss 716–719	6.5	s 13	21.6
s 720	5.4; 6.5	s 16(2A)	7.40; 18.1
(5)	6.10		
s 720(6)	6.23		

Table of Statutes

1992 TCGA	
s 17	7.30; 7.38
(2)	7.38
s 18	7.39
(1)(2)	7.30
(3)	7.30; 7.39
s 19	17.7
s 37	7.35
s 38	App D
(1)(b)	7.29; App D
(2)(b)	7.25
s 49(1)	14.14
s 60	2.28; 7.7; App A
(2)	7.8
s 62	7.9
s 62(1)	7.25
(4)	2.5; 7.9
(6)(b)	7.9
(6)(7)	4.16; 7.9
s 64(1)	App D
s 65(1)	7.41
(4)	5.18
s 67	7.31; App B
s 68	2.6; 5.2; App B
s 69	2.6; 5.2; 19.4; 21.1; 21.8; App A; App B
s 70	2.6; 7.46
s 71	2.6; 7.4; 7.8; 7.9; 7.38; 10.11
(1)	7.3; 7.6; 7.42; 15.22; App A
(2)	7.8; 7.40; 7.42
(3)	7.8
s 72	2.6; 7.4
s 73	2.6; 7.4
(1)(a)	7.6
s 74	2.6; 7.5; 16.3
s 75	2.6
s 76	2.6; 16.11; 21.6; 21.19
(1)	7.47
(1A)	7.47; 16.11
(1B)	16.11
(2)	7.2
s 76A	7.47
s 76B	7.15A
s 77	4.1; 4.2; 4.11; 7.9; 7.15A; 7.28; 9.11; 14.12; 21.12
(2)	4.11; 21.12
(6)(a)	4.17
s 78	4.11; 21.12
(3)	21.12
s 79A	7.8
s 79B	21.21
s 80	7.20; 21.9; 21.11
s 81	21.9; 21.11
s 82	21.9; 21.11
s 83	7.20; 21.9; 21.10; 21.11
s 84	21.9; 21.11
s 85	16.11; 21.21; 21.6
(1)	21.11
(2)–(9)	21.11
s 86	7.9; 7.25; 7.28; 9.11; 21.12; 21.16
(1)(c)	21.15
(4)	21.12
s 86A	21.13
s 87	7.9; 18.24; 21.5; 21.6; 21.19; 21.17
(2)	21.12
(3)	21.12
(7)	21.5
(9)	21.5
s 88	21.6; 21.18; 21.19
s 89	21.6
s 90	21.6
s 91–95	21.6; 21.9; 21.17
s 96	21.18; 21.21
(5)	21.21
s 97(1)(6)	21.6
s 98	21.6
s 107	App A
s 107A	7.41
s 119	7.34
s 127	App A
s 141	App A
s 142	App A; 15.9
ss 146, 147	23.5
s 152	7.11; 21.10; 21.11
s 163	10.12
s 164	7.24
ss 164A–164N	7.27
s 165	5.15; 7.5; 7.15; 7.16; 7.18; 7.31; 10.12; 12.15; 14.7; 14.12; 15.15; 16.13; 21.11

Table of Statutes

1992 TCGA	
s 165(2)	7.11
(3)	7.11
(4)	7.11
(6)	7.11
(10)	7.31
s 166	7.19
s 167	7.19
s 168	5.13; 5.14; 5.15; 7.20
s 169	21.8
ss 185–187	21.7
s 222	7.25
(5)(a)	7.25
ss 223, 224	7.25
s 225	7.25; 7.26
s 251	7.19
s 256	17.8; 17.9
(2)	17.21
s 257	17.4
s 258	7.14
s 260	5.15; 7.5; 7.15; 7.16; 7.18; 14.7; 15.15
(2)(a)(d)	6.25; 7.15; 7.17
(3)	21.11
(7)(8)	7.31
s 261	7.19
s 272	7.25
s 274	7.29
s 281	7.21
s 286	7.30
(3)	7.26; 7.39
s 288(1)	7.20
Sch 1 para 1, 2	7.32
Sch 4 para 1, 2, 9	7.23
Sch 4A	7.47
Sch 4B	7.15A; 21.21
Sch 4C	21.21
Sch 5	21.9; 21.12
para 2	21.15; 21.19
para 3–5	21.15
para 6	21.15
para 8	21.15
para 9	21.14; 21.19
para 10	21.16
Sch 5A	21.16
Sch 5B	7.28
para 17	7.28; 14.12
Sch 6	7.11
Sch 7	7.11; 16.13
(1)(a)	7.11
(2)	7.12
(7)	7.13

1992 Finance Act

s 27	17.5

1992 Finance (No 2) Act   **17.6**

Sch 15	
paras 8, 9	14.6

1992 Charities Act   **17.9; 17.20**

s 52	17.14

1993 Charities Act   **1.7; 17.6; 17.9; 17.20**

s 3	2.21
s 10	17.14
s 25	17.8

1993 Finance Act

s 67	17.5
s 79	20.4
s 118	App A
s 200	14.5
s 208	19.3
Sch 6 paras 2, 3	20.4
Sch 7	7.33

1994 Finance Act

Sch 16	6.20

1994 Social Security Incapacity for Work) Act   2.13

1995 Finance Act   1.2; 2.4; 4.2; 4.11; 7.24; 7.42

s 86	20.10
s 113	7.41
s 114	7.41
s 128(3)	20.7; 20.10
s 154	14.6
s 155	14.6
Sch 17(13)(14)	6.22

1995 Law Reform (Miscellaneous Provisions) Act   2.8

Table of Statutes

1996 Finance Act
s 73	20.7, 20.10
s 154	8.5; 22.8; App B
s 158(3)	6.16
s 199	7.42
s 200	19.10
Sch 6(13)	5.4
Sch 6(16)	20.7; 20.10
Sch 28(7)(8)	8.5, 22.8
Sch 38	7.42
Sch 39(5)	7.4

1996 Trusts of Land and Appointment of Trustees Act 15.6

1997 Finance Act
s 81	20.8; 23.8
s 94	14.6
Sch 3(7)	6.23
Sch 7	18.24

1997 Finance (No 2) Act
s 31	6.1
s 32	6.28
Sch 4	6.28

1998 Finance Act 7.24; 10.12; 16.3
s 74(1)	14.12
s 120	16.1
s 127	19.3; 21.13

s 128	21.19
s 129	21.13
s 130	21.19
s 131	21.19
s 132	21.19
s 143	14.21
s 161	8.5
Sch 13	14.12
para 18	7.43
Sch 22	21.20
Sch 23	21.20

1999 Finance Act 4.7; 7.8
s 64	2.28
s 71(2)	7.8
s 75	7.8
s 104	15.28

2000 Finance Act 1.2; 7.15A; 7.47; 10.12; 21.21
s 38	17.5
s 46	17.8
s 89	7.11
s 90	7.47
s 91	7.15A
s 92	7.8
s 94	21.21
s 95	21.21
s 96	21.21
Sch 25	21.21
Sch 26	21.21

STATUTORY INSTRUMENTS

1987/1130	Inheritance Tax (Double Charges Relief) Regulations	11.37; 15.27
1989/1297	Taxes (Interest Rate) Regulations	14.3
1990/2231	Income Tax (Building Societies) (Dividends and Interest) Regulations	20.10

Part I:
UK Resident Trusts

by
Matthew Hutton MA (Oxon) FTII AIIT TEP

Chapter 1

Introduction

1.1 Given the present tax rates, those who use trusts are generally more concerned about inheritance tax than other taxes. With a few exceptions, there is not a lot of difference between the burden of income tax on trust income and on the income of an individual. Similarly with capital gains tax even though 34% is the trust rate. However, inheritance tax is a different matter. The occasions when tax is charged can be diminished and the rates can be less.

1.2 In this country the capital taxes are a political football. This is quite understandable as the inheritance of over-large sums does excite comment, criticism and envy. The relative importance of income tax, capital gains tax and inheritance tax is shown in the latest projections for 2000/01:

	£ bill
Total Inland Revenue net receipts	143.8
of which	
Income tax	95.9
Corporation tax	33.8
Petroleum revenue tax	1.2
Capital gains tax	3.4
Inheritance tax	2.3
Stamp duties	7.2
	143.8

The number of taxpayers who suffer income tax is counted in tens of millions, whilst those who suffer inheritance tax are numbered in tens of thousands.

The amount held in discretionary settlements has to be a guess but the latest report shows that £245 million had been assessed in 1997/98 (as opposed to £167 million in 1996/97). That would be due to the ten-year charge. It was a gross figure before liabilities, reliefs and exemptions. No statistics are available as to the importance of accumulation and maintenance settlements.

Anything to do with income tax is going to affect the Treasury's cash flow. Inheritance tax and, for that matter, capital gains tax, are Cinderella taxes but they do have considerable emotive value and can cause press comment. They are therefore highly susceptible to political change. The

1.3 *Introduction*

lifetime exemptions for small gifts (£250), wedding presents (£1,000/£2,500/£5,000) and the annual exemption (£3,000) have not been increased for many years. During the passage of *FA 1995*, a new clause which would have improved these exemptions was rejected. The Minister of State in the debate, thought them to be redundant in view of the size of the nil rate band. (Hansard Standing Committee D, 14 March 1995, col 726). The Labour government must wish to reinforce the capital taxes but so far the only substantive structural change has been in capital gains tax. Meanwhile, of course, the importance of stamp duties continues to increase, now contributing more to the Inland Revenue than the combined total of capital gains tax and inheritance tax. *FA 2000* has seen a number of statutory reversals of anti-avoidance arrangements.

1.3 The number of taxpayers in a tax paying family can be artificially increased. The trading community regularly incorporate companies and so add taxpayers to their numbers. The private capitalist can create settlements and each of these can be a separate taxpayer with its own income tax return, inheritance tax rates and so on. Potentially exempt transfers (PETs) are really intended to encourage gifts to individuals. However, so that children can rank as possible donees, gifts to accumulation and maintenance settlements also rank as potentially exempt transfers. Therefore, this class of settlement is the standard settlement used to swell the number of taxpayers in one taxpaying family, with the nil rate band discretionary settlement as a close second.

Intending donors *should* use their opportunities while they are available as there must be a political question mark over the (PET) regime and the generosity of the present rates of business and agricultural property reliefs (BPR/APR). The estate owner can use this very generosity as an excuse for retaining assets which qualify for relief. To the authors the existence of these reliefs is an argument for the use of settlements whilst the PET should be a spur to generation skipping in one form or another. It makes better sense to go through the window when it is open rather than wait for it to be shut and then attempt to wriggle through.

1.4 Accumulation and maintenance settlements are approved donees for PETs. Whatever the tax climate, they are ideal for families with most of their capital in an asset which should not really be fragmented. Let the beneficiaries' interests remain settled for life and the senior members of the family provide the trustees, and there can be no better vehicle for shares in the family company or the landed estate. Interest in possession settlements will serve for adult donees but they probably indicate the lack of business training of the beneficiary more than anything else.

1.5 Discretionary settlements of any great size are not now made (except to receive property qualifying for BPR or APR) because gifts to them are chargeable transfers. The fact that a chargeable transfer can attract holdover relief is in their favour and this adds to the attractions of nil rate band discretionary settlements. Old discretionary settlements should be jealously preserved as they will almost certainly shelter substantial sums. The improved valuation reliefs for inheritance tax should increase the number of settlements of land and unquoted shares.

1.6 The use of trusts to manage and protect capital seems to have been connected with tax saving for hundreds of years. About 30 years ago the cellars were being tidied up in Somerset House and correspondence dating from 1690 was found. There was not a great amount but what there was was privately reprinted in what must have been a very limited edition. The correspondence discloses that people were using trusts to save tax even then. If you adhered to the wrong religion you paid more tax so that trustees were being appointed where land was valuable and trustees of the right religion were available.

The complex and ever changing nature of the capital taxes, coupled with the ingenuity of those who draft trust deeds will, together, ensure that settlements, in one form or another, will help save taxes for another hundred years at least. If there is a cloud on the horizon at all it must be connected with the European Union. Voices are raised in favour of the harmonization of taxes. Trusts are really an Anglo-Saxon creation and are not really known in Europe. However, VAT which is a European tax is still not harmonised, so there is not much chance for harmonisation in other quarters.

1.7 This book sets out to explain the taxes assessed by the Inland Revenue on family settlements wherever they reside.

It is not a book on tax planning as such, but it is intended to be helpful and to explain the most usual situations fully. It does not deal with the very few points where Scottish law requires attention. One difficulty for Scots readers may be the references to the *Trustee Act 1925* which, of course, has no application in Scotland. There is a similar problem in the limited application to Scotland of the *Charities Act 1993*.

Chapter 2

Types of Trust

General

2.1 Every professional adviser working with trusts must be able to distinguish between the various types of trust and to understand the rights of beneficiaries. Different tax consequences attach to each different sort.

2.2 There is no practical difference between a trust and a settlement. It is only the manner of creation which distinguishes the two. A settlement can only come into being when there is a settlor. A trust can arise in many ways and, often enough, without a trust instrument (e.g. in an intestacy, there are statutory trusts).

2.3 The commonest types of documentation are wills and settlement deeds. These are referred to as trust instruments.

2.4 A will speaks from death. That is to say that it is construed as if it had been written on the date of the testator's death. If the will contains settled legacies, importance attaches to a transitional period called the administration period. The executor's appointment is retrospective. The grant of probate validates any previous acts of the executor. However, the beneficiaries have no legal entitlement to their legacies etc. until the executor gives his assent or transfers the gift: until that point, they have merely a 'chose in action', that is a right to have the estate properly administered and in course of time their entitlement made over to them.

An executor is not a trustee. It is customary for a will which gives settled legacies to appoint the same people as executors and trustees. It is not always easy to see which they are at any given moment. This can be important in terms of general law as executors and trustees have different powers. Having said this, the *Trustee Act 1925, s 68(17)* extends the meaning of trustee, to include a personal representative. However, the functions are quite different. A personal representative also includes an administrator of an intestate estate.

The distinction is also important for tax. The executor has to assume control of the assets, pay debts, taxes and so on. Whilst this is going on, the estate is said to be in course of administration. During this period the provisions of *ICTA 1988, ss 695–702* apply for the purposes of income tax. Those sections attempt to bridge the gap between the general rules of executorship (which sometimes take a different view of what is income and what is the amount due to the income beneficiary) and the income tax rules. Changes made by *FA 1995* moved the calculation of the beneficiaries' income more or less onto a receipts basis. This can be quite important where there has been a deed of variation. These deeds have no effect for income tax until they are executed and under the old rules this left an untidy area between the date of death and the date of the deed where the income for tax and the income awarded by the deed might differ. This element of untidyness has largely gone under the receipts basis. Now, if a deed seems likely, it would be sensible to hold back any payments of income until the deed has been executed. As soon as the executor sees clearly what there is in the residue, the administration period comes to an end and, to the extent that there are settled legacies, he becomes a trustee. As regards taxation, these remarks apply equally to an administrator. There are usually problems where there is a discretionary settlement in a will, equal to the nil rate band for inheritance tax. The problems are to do with identification. Which of the deceased's assets form part of the settlement at any particular time and at what value? It is those assets which have been appropriated, valued for the purposes of the administration at the date of appropriation (albeit for inheritance tax at their value at date of death).

2.5 In the context of taxation it is more logical to date an inheritance back to the date of death rather than to the date of assent and so, for instance, *TCGA 1992, s 62(4)* ensures that a specific legacy will generally date back to the death, so that the assent is not a disposal for capital gains tax purposes.

2.6 There can be planning points in choosing the moment when an executor becomes a trustee and, obviously, there is some room for manoeuvre as to when that takes place. It will usually be up to the executors to decide: the self-assessment literature contains no guidance on the issue. This is not just a matter of the application of *ICTA 1988, ss 695–702*. The capital gains tax exemptions and loss reliefs are different. Time limits for assessment are different. There can be no assessment under *ICTA 1988, s 686* (the additional tax on discretionary and accumulation settlements) until the executors become trustees. *TCGA 1992, ss 68–76* apply only to trustees. It would not be easy to provide a complete list of the planning possibilities, because they depend upon the family, type of asset etc.

2.7 A settlement will normally be constituted by a deed. One reason is that a deed validates a transaction which would otherwise fail for lack of consideration. An oral declaration by the settlor can create a settlement. In the offshore tax havens, trusts are often constituted by a declaration of trust by the trustees who have already received the capital to be settled. This means that a settlement can be made without the settlor being physically present. Where the settlor lives in a country which has not yet emerged into a genuine democracy, with a balanced economy, this can be a great help as it obviates the need for journeys to the offshore jurisdiction which would attract attention. However, in most cases where UK practitioners are concerned, there will be a trust instrument, either a settlement deed or a will. Occasionally, by reason of intestacy, there will

2.8 Types of Trust

be a settlement with no trust instrument. Sometimes there will be a will with a deed of variation. There are still UK trusts executed before the coming into force of the *Trustee Act 1925* and, here and there, there may be imported trusts where the true law of the trust is not that of the UK. There have been stories about a Prince Edward Island trust which may be run from London. That territory was once a tax haven. However, it came to an end by being merged into Newfoundland which, in turn, became part of Canada. In general, the UK practitioner is more likely to be looking at a post-war English settlement, made by deed or by will.

The *Enduring Powers of Attorney Act 1985, s 3(3)* carries over to all trusteeships (unless expressly amended). That is to say, that an attorney, by virtue of his appointment, will be able to take over the donor's trusteeships. This result was not really intended. The purpose of the clause was to cover houses, etc. held on trust for sale (e.g. a tenancy in common). The section is to be repealed by the *Trustee Delegation Bill* once enacted.

An accountant who prepares a working epitome of the trust instrument should ask the solicitor who drafted the document to confirm that the epitome is correct. The annual trust accounts may usefully summarise that epitome.

2.8 A post-war trust instrument will normally be based on a standard precedent and so should be comprehensible to a modern practitioner. Occasionally, some legislative change causes a problem. For instance, when the *Family Law Reform Act 1969* reduced the age of majority to 18, it enacted that the age of majority should be taken to be 21 when construing documents dated before 1 January 1970. This can still be of importance. For instance, a modern variation of such a trust, perhaps an appointment made by the trustees of a discretionary trust, is made under the new law with 18 as the age of majority whilst the original instrument is under the old law. See 7.17 below.

Another example of a problem solved by recent legislation is the effect of divorce on the entitlements of children under the will of the first of the ex-spouses to die. Before 1 January 1996, the gifts to the children could fail if the will made them contingent on the prior death of the former spouse and he/she was still alive. The entitlements of the children would, in effect, pass to the Crown. That problem was solved by the *Law Reform (Miscellaneous Provisions) Act 1995* under which the ex-spouse is treated as having pre-deceased the testator for all purposes.

2.9 Trust instruments commonly include dispositive powers (i.e. powers which are not merely administrative). Two common powers of this sort are as follows.

(a) *Appointment.* This is a power to declare fresh trusts within the framework of the main trust instrument. It is a power to fill in blanks left by the settlor, as it were. So, a discretionary trust will always contain powers to appoint funds in favour of a beneficiary or a class of beneficiaries selected by the trustees. The result is usually a sub-trust. It is not a separate trust (unless the deed of appointment makes it one). It is a fund within the trust designated for its own beneficiary(ies).

(b) *Advancement.* This is a power to hand over capital to a beneficiary. If the trust instrument is silent, then *Trustee Act 1925, s 32* (see Appendix E) will apply to permit the advancement of up to one half of the presumptive share of the favoured beneficiary. A modern trust instrument normally permits advancement of the whole. Conditions may be imposed. Advancement is not a casual payment. It is some substantial preferment, something to give a start in life or to consolidate a beneficiary's position once a start has been made. To pay for education is advancement. So is the handing over of a substantial block of shares. To pay living expenses is not. Note generally that capital cannot be advanced under the statutory power (whether or not extended) unless the beneficiary in question has a right to capital, whether or not contingent. That is, if the beneficiary is only an income beneficiary, an express power to pay capital to him is required in the deed (as otherwise there is no such power).

2.10 Reference is sometimes made to trusts which are resulting, implied or constructive. This really means reading into a trust something which is not already written there or finding that a particular transaction results in a trust. Resulting, etc. trusts do occur in family settlements where there is a defect in the draftsmanship. For instance, a fixed interest (i.e. not discretionary) trust might have successive interests for life, but, because the draftsman omitted a page, no beneficiary is named to receive the capital on the death of the last life tenant. There is then a resulting trust for the settlor. He gave away everything except for the right to receive the capital, so he must have retained that right. Needless to say, whatever tax planning was intended will have been defeated if there is a resulting, etc. trust for the settlor.

2.11 The types of trust normally encountered in a professional practice are:
 (i) interest in possession trusts;
 (ii) accumulation and maintenance trusts;
 (iii) discretionary trusts;
 (iv) charities.

There are numerous other types of trust ranging from bare trusts through superannuation schemes to employee share ownership trusts. The bare trusteeship involves no tax consequences because the transactions of the trustee are imputed to his principal. The others are specialist situations which are beyond the scope of this book.

Interest in possession trusts

2.12 An interest in possession trust is one with fixed interests in income. Normally there will be a life tenant or an annuitant. The commonest may be will trusts giving the income to the widow for life and

2.13 Types of Trust

the capital to the children upon her death. There will be one or more beneficiaries currently entitled to income, subject only to the due payment of tax and expenses.

The right to income may be defeasible. That is to say that the right can be brought to an end. Common cases of defeasible interests are as follows.

(i) Income is left to a widow during widowhood. Not only death, but also re-marriage could bring her interest to an end.

(ii) A class gift has been made, one member of the class has become entitled to an interest in possession in his putative share and the class is enlarged. An obvious illustration is where capital is left to 'such of my grandchildren as attain the age of 25, if more than one in equal shares'. There are three grandchildren, one over 18 with an interest in possession in one-third and two others under age. A fourth grandchild is born. The interest in possession is now in one-quarter and not in one-third, i.e. the interest in possession in one-twelfth (owned by the grandchild over 18) has come to an end.

(iii) An overriding power to accumulate income which has not been invoked. That is to say, the trustees cannot withhold income from the life tenant once they have received it, but at some future time they could exercise the overriding power.

(iv) The trustees have power to revoke a gift of income or have power to appoint capital to a non-income beneficiary.

In all these cases the fact that the right to income is defeasible does not prevent the trust being an interest in possession trust, so long as the defeasance has not taken place. The phrase 'interest in possession' is not defined in any statute but has been explored in *Pearson and Others v CIR HL, [1980] STC 318*: it may be taken as meaning 'present right to present enjoyment'.

An Inland R]evenue statement issued on 12 February 1976 confirms this view and has been reproduced as Appendix A to their explanatory booklet IHT16 issued in August 1996. Before that the statement was reproduced in their IHT1 (now out of print).

Disabled trusts

2.13 It is usual to consider a disabled trust as a type of interest in possession trust because it is so treated for inheritance tax purposes. As a consequence, to set up a disabled trust is to make a PET. There may be cases where it is a disposition for maintenance of the family and, as a consequence, exempt. *[IHTA 1984, s 11]*.

Disabled trusts are rare because other, more usual, types of trust can do their work equally well. Such a trust must benefit a disabled person, who is one either

(i) incapable of looking after their own affairs by reason of a mental disorder within the meaning of the *Mental Health Act 1983*; or

(ii) in receipt of an attendance allowance or a disability living allowance by virtue of entitlement to the care component at the highest or middle rate, under the *Social Security Contributions and Benefits Act 1992*. For an attendance allowance the disability has to be such as to require supervision or attention in connection with the person's bodily functions. It is not enough to qualify for either allowance—the disabled person must actually receive it. Incapacity benefit was introduced by the *Social Security (Incapacity for Work) Act 1994*. However, the attendance allowance continues. The principal difference is that attendance allowance is only paid to those over 65.

The trust will be discretionary but will be required to benefit the disabled person to the extent of half the benefits arising, at the very least.

Such a trust will be treated for inheritance tax as an interest in possession trust and the disabled person as the income beneficiary, even though there may be power to accumulate income. [*IHTA 1984, s 89*].

Nowadays this type of trust seems to be not quite as useful as an interest in possession settlement, a transfer to which is a PET, or a true discretionary trust to which transfers are kept within the nil rate band. It is something of a rarity.

Protective trusts

2.14 Next there is the protective trust. The standard definition is in *Trustee Act 1925, s 33* (see Appendix E). It is traditionally a trust for a spendthrift. The spendthrift is the life tenant. If he takes any steps to sell, mortgage or anticipate his rights, those rights are brought to an end (as, indeed, if he becomes bankrupt) and the trust becomes discretionary. He and his family are the objects of the discretion. These trusts were popular in Victorian times. Latterly they enjoyed a brief spell of popularity when it was found that some inheritance tax schemes could be based upon them. This popularity came to an end on 12 April 1978 when new tax rules took effect.

These trusts are now treated for inheritance tax as interest in possession settlements, the principal beneficiary being the individual with the deemed interest in possession. [*IHTA 1984, s 88*]. This analysis continues for inheritance tax (but not capital gains tax or income tax) purposes even after the trust has become discretionary.

Accumulation and maintenance trusts

2.15 Accumulation and maintenance settlements are defined for inheritance tax purposes in *IHTA 1984, s 71(1)(2)*. This follows closely the statutory trusts for infants in the *Trustee Act 1925, s 31* (see Appendix E). The general scheme is that the trustees manage the infants' capital, spending income upon them if it is desirable and saving it for them (i.e. accumulating) if there is no reason to spend it. Therefore there is no interest in possession. Perhaps because this is the classic way of providing for infants, when CTT was enacted these settlements were kept

2.16 *Types of Trust*

within the 'interest in possession' rules rather than being included with discretionary trusts. On 24 September 1975 an Inland Revenue Press Release made it clear that any settlement within the *Trustee Act 1925, s 31(1)* would be an accumulation and maintenance settlement. The Inland Revenue booklet IHT16 contains on pages 22 and 23 an explanation of these trusts and the manner in which they are taxed.

2.16 The first conditions which must be fulfilled for a settlement to be within the protection of *section 71* are:

(a) there is no interest in possession in the settlement (i.e. at the time when the settlement is tested);

(b) the income from the settlement is to be accumulated so far as not applied for the maintenance, education, or benefit of a beneficiary; and

(c) one or more persons will become beneficially entitled to the settled property or to an interest in possession in it before attaining a specified age not exceeding 25 years.

[*IHTA 1984, s 71(1)*].

In most cases, it should be obvious whether condition (a) is satisfied.

Condition (b) requires a trust to accumulate. A mere power to accumulate is not enough. A settlement would be within this condition if the trusts of income required either the whole of the income to be disbursed or, alternatively, the whole income to be accumulated. An accumulation settlement with power to maintain could satisfy the test. The words 'maintenance, education or benefit' are lifted from *section 31* of the *Trustee Act 1925* (see Appendix E) and are used in the same sense as in that Act. 'Maintenance' and 'education' also appear in *IHTA 1984, s 11* (dispositions for maintenance of family etc.) and presumably have the same meaning. There are cases on trusteeship (e.g. *Wilson v Turner, 1883 22 Ch D 521*) which show that the automatic payment of income to the parent is not within these words. Some assessment of the situation is necessary and annual review should take place. 'Benefit' generally signifies the improvement of the material situation of the beneficiary. Again the trustees must consider whether a particular application of funds will benefit the beneficiary (*re Moxon's Will Trusts, Ch D [1958] 1 All ER 386*). 'Benefit' is a word with a wide meaning and has been found to include resettlement (*Pilkington v CIR, HL [1964] AC 612*) and the making of a charitable donation (*re Clore's Settlement Trusts, Ch D [1966] 2 All ER 272*) where that was expected of the beneficiary. The standard administrative powers would take a settlement outside *section 71* if they could divert income. The most obvious is a power to insure lives out of income. This is not maintenance or education etc., and it is not accumulation. Therefore this power would prevent condition (b) being certain and the settlement would be outside *section 71*.

Condition (c) contains the word 'will'. This means 'must'. Provisions which could defeat the beneficiaries from obtaining an interest in

Types of Trust **2.17**

possession, etc., on attaining the specified age mean that the settlement fails the test (see *Inglewood and Another v CIR, CA [1983] STC 133*). Put another way, the only thing which the beneficiaries have to do to qualify is to survive to the specified age. Provided they reach that age, nothing should disqualify them. Provided the age has been made clear, it has been specified. See also ESC F8 (reproduced in Appendix B).

If the trust instrument is silent, it is likely that *section 31* of the *Trustee Act 1925* would apply and the age at which the beneficiaries would be entitled to an interest in possession would be 18. This would save the status of the settlement. The beneficiaries need not become beneficially entitled to the capital. It may remain settled for the rest of their lives. The settlement would still qualify because a beneficiary takes an interest in possession at or before the age of 25. It is possible to have an accumulation and maintenance settlement with several beneficiaries where powers are given to decide their shares or to vary them. However, if such a settlement is to qualify under *section 71* the consequence of using such a power must be that benefit accrues to some member or members of the class of beneficiaries who is or are also under the age of 25. It may be that only one of a class of children or grandchildren actually benefits from income or capital at or before the age of 25. The Board issued a Press Notice on 19 January 1976 to this effect (see SP E1 reproduced in Appendix A). It is possible to have an accumulation and maintenance settlement where at age 25 each child takes a life interest but at age 26, etc., the trustees can vary their shares. Any such variation would be an occasion of charge and tax would be calculated as if the beneficiary had made a transfer of value. This will usually be a PET (see 9.10 below).

2.17 Having satisfied the conditions mentioned in 2.16 above, either of the following alternative tests must then be satisfied, i.e.

(*a*) not more than 25 years have elapsed since the creation of the settlement or, if it has been some other sort of settlement and has been converted into an accumulation and maintenance settlement, not more than 25 years have elapsed since it became such a settlement; or

(*b*) all the persons who are or have been beneficiaries, are or were grandchildren of a common grandparent. Where a grandchild has died before attaining a vested interest, then his children, widows or widowers may take his place as beneficiaries. [*IHTA 1984, s 71(2)*].

The only problem with condition (*a*) (the 25-year test) will be the ascertainment of the day on which the 25 years start to run. This must be a particular day and, bearing in mind that one may be dealing with a trust which commenced a long time ago, considerable research into family histories may be needed to determine the members of a class etc. Settlements depending on this test are rare. Condition (*b*) (the one generation test) has simpler problems. If the trust instrument mentions as beneficiaries 'children or remoter issue of X' then it must fail the condition even though only grandchildren of a common grandparent do, in fact, benefit. The fact that a deceased beneficiary is replaced by one or more of his dependants does not mean that the dependant(s) take a share in the

2.18 Types of Trust

settlement which is related to or derived from the share to which the deceased might have become entitled. Therefore reasonable powers to deflect wealth for the benefit of such a victim of misfortune are permissible. 'Common grandparent' settlements are the usual ones.

2.18 The *section* is quite generous in that illegitimate children, adopted children and stepchildren are treated in the same way as legitimate children of the full blood. [*IHTA 1984, s 71(8)*].

Discretionary trusts

2.19 Discretionary trusts have been a favourite tool of the tax planner for many years. They were well used as estate duty saving trusts because, of course, there was no taxation of gifts under that tax except for gifts made during the seven years prior to death or those where there was some reservation of benefit.

2.20 Although commonly referred to as discretionary trusts, the statutory definitions are not so concise. That for income tax is short. It is in *ICTA 1988, s 686(2)(a)*–'income ... is payable at the discretion of the trustees....'. The section goes on to exclude charities, pension schemes and so on.

For inheritance tax, discretionary trusts are included in the general class of settlements without an interest in possession. It is necessary to look for 'relevant property', which is settled property in which there is no 'qualifying interest in possession'. [*IHTA 1984, s 58*]. A qualifying interest in possession is one to which an individual is entitled or one which the individual has sold to a reversionary interest company. [*IHTA 1984, s 59*]. Having, in effect, defined a settlement without an interest in possession, *section 58* then lists those which are not to be caught. They are the standard favoured trusts:

(*a*) charities;

(*b*) accumulation and maintenance trusts;

(*c*) protective trusts where the failure or determination occurred before 12 April 1978;

(*d*) certain trusts for disabled persons set up before 10 March 1981;

(*e*) employee trusts within *IHTA 1984, s 86*;

(*f*) maintenance funds for historic buildings, within *IHTA 1984, 4 Sch*;

(*g*) pension funds and superannuation schemes;

(*h*) trade or professional compensation funds (such as that established by the Law Society);

(*j*) newspaper trusts (such as that which owns *The Guardian*), within *IHTA 1984, s 87*;

(*k*) football club trusts, to the extent that their capital represents pools payments for ground improvements [*FA 1990, s 126*]; and (*l*) sports and games trusts, to the extent that their capital represents the reduction in pools betting duty from 40% to 37.5% [*FA 1991, s 121*].

Finally, 'relevant property' does not include excluded property (see 8.5 and 22.2 below). [*IHTA 1984, s 58(1)(f)*]. Therefore *section 58* when it refers to 'relevant property' is referring to property, not being excluded property, which is contained in a discretionary or accumulation trust. Nonetheless, there is a trap where a discretionary trust, established by a non-UK domiciliary, contains both UK situs and non-UK situs property. The latter would be excluded property. However, its existence in the settlement, and specifically its value immediately after the settlement commenced, is taken into account in computing the rate of tax either on exit or at each ten-year anniversary (see *IHTA 1984, s 66(4)(b)* and *s 68(5)(a)*). It is therefore essential that, if a non-UK domiciliary is to make a settlement of UK situs property, that settlement should not be tainted in any way with excluded property.

Apart from the usual settlements of shares and will trusts, it is quite possible to hold life policies on discretionary trusts. The extent of legislation on discretionary trusts in the IHTA 1984 is necessary once the Act has taxed chargeable transfers made by an individual and then gone on to tax property subject to an interest in possession as if it belonged to the income beneficiary. [*IHTA 1984, s 49*]. It also covers the situation where a trust is part discretionary and part not. A moderately common illustration is a will trust where there may be a settled legacy of £234,000 (the nil rate band) on discretionary terms and an interest in possession of the residue given to the widow.

Charities

2.21 A charity is, for many practitioners, a trust which is registered under *Charities Act 1993, s 3*. The *Charities Act* has very limited application outside England and Wales and not all charities are registered anyway. However, registration is prima facie evidence that the trust is charitable. The Inland Revenue will apply their own tests and decide separately whether to accord charitable status. The basic tests were laid down in the *Pemsel* case (*Income Tax Special Purposes Commissioners v Pemsel, HL 1891, 3 TC 53*) as follows.

(*a*)　The relief of poverty. This need not be general and the beneficiaries may come from a designated class.

(*b*)　The advancement of religion. This need not be for the public benefit in layman's English. Those who fashioned the law believed that it is good for mankind to have and practise a religion. Therefore sects which demand absolute obedience from their adherents and shut out strangers will qualify. A contemplative order does not advance religion and so is not charitable. However, if there is an element of its work which is for the public benefit, it may qualify (see Decisions of the Charity Commissioners vol. 3, *The Society of the Precious Blood*).

2.22 Types of Trust

(c) Education. Therefore virtually all independent schools are charities. So are youth organisations such as the Boy Scouts. Museums and libraries come under this heading.

(d) Other purposes beneficial to the community. These must not benefit a clique or class. Many worthy causes fail because they are too narrowly based to benefit an important part of the community.

For the purpose of applying tax exemptions, a charity is defined as 'any body of persons or trust established for charitable purposes only'. [*ICTA 1988, s 506(1); IHTA 1984, s 272*].

The only other statutory definitions of charity are in the *Charitable Uses Act 1601* and the *Recreational Charities Act 1958*. The first was repealed by the *Mortmain and Charitable Uses Act 1888*, but in that Act the preamble to the *1601 Act* was preserved and this in turn was repealed by the *Charities Act 1960, s 38*. The *Pemsel* classification is based on the *1601 Act* and it is in fact used as the definition of charity and in defining charitable purposes. The *1958 Act* ensures that facilities for recreation, provided in the interests of social welfare, and certain miners' welfare funds are charities. It covers village halls and women's institutes. It is, therefore, very limited. Over the years there have been attempts to provide a better definition of charity but it seems to have been too difficult. Our partners in Europe have nothing which is strictly comparable and problems can result (see 2.24 below).

It is necessary that the charity be founded in the UK. It may benefit people overseas but, to benefit from our tax exemptions, it must be founded here. (*Dreyfus (Camille & Henry) Foundation Inc v CIR, HL 1955, 36 TC 126*).

2.22 A charity will normally exist in perpetuity, i.e. it is not required to be wound up after any specific period, although the trustees may effectively wind it up by giving everything away. However, it is possible to have a charity which has a definite life, say 10 years. Such a trust is known as a 'time charity'. The authors are not sure any exist, but the draftsman of the *IHTA 1984* had to contemplate the possibility. Had he not done so there would have been a considerable loophole. Hence *IHTA 1984, s 70*.

Miscellaneous

2.23 Although not strictly to do with tax there have been developments in recent years which can affect estate planning. These include the following.

(a) *Insolvency Act 1986* which permits the court to set aside transactions at an undervalue (e.g. gifts into settlement) within the five years prior to bankruptcy. In the two years prior to the bankruptcy any such transaction can be set aside. In the rest of the five-year period the donor must have been insolvent when the gift was made or have become insolvent as a result. Note also the overriding provision in *section 423* of that Act which allows a court to set aside a transaction at an undervalue made at any time if satisfied by the trustee in bankruptcy that it was made with the dominant motive of putting assets beyond the reach of creditors.

(b) Where there has been a change of ownership of a company and the company cannot pay its corporation tax during the three following years it is possible for the tax to be charged upon the outgoing shareholders. [*ICTA 1988, s 767A–C*].

Trusts and estates contrasted

2.24 A distinction must be drawn between estates and trusts. Trusts can arise in a variety of ways. They can arise because of legislation, for example under the rules of intestacy. So too, where assets are misappropriated, the holder is trustee for the rightful owner. A firm's clients' account is held in trust for the clients whose balances are held in that account. The purchaser of goods under a Romalpa (or retention of title) clause can be a trustee. Therefore, the standard legal definition is very wide:

'A trust is an equitable obligation, binding a person (who is called a trustee) to deal with property over which he has control (which is called the trust property) for the benefit of persons (who are called beneficiaries or *cestuis que trustent*), of whom he may himself be one, and any one of whom may enforce the obligation. Any act or neglect on the part of a trustee which is not authorised or excused by the terms of the trust instrument, or by law is called a "breach of trust"' (Underhill).

This definition appears in TM 1010, slightly foreshortened.

This is not the only definition. A very narrow definition is to be found in the Hague Convention on the Recognition of Trusts: 'The term "Trust" refers to the legal relationships created—*inter vivos* or on death—by a person, the settlor, when assets have been placed under the control of a trustee for the benefit of a beneficiary or for a specified purpose'. Bearing in mind that the purpose of the Convention is to ensure that this method of holding property is accepted in jurisdictions where trusts are not acknowledged, this definition will do. The purpose is to prevent such occurrences as the French authorities claiming death duties because the trustees of a UK settlement have bought a flat in Paris for the use of a beneficiary and one trustee has died.

2.25 In a professional office a trust will be somewhere between these two definitions, probably being a settlement by deed, by will, by gift *inter vivos* or a statutory trust in an intestacy. As can be seen, an estate can spawn a trust. This is of considerable importance for income tax purposes from 6 April 1995. We now have two different sets of rules for beneficiaries' income according to whether the income is that of an estate

2.26 *Types of Trust*

in course of administration or is trust income. The beneficiaries of an estate are taxed more or less on a receipts basis, the income falling into the year of receipt (see 18.19 and 18.20 below). However, apart from accumulation and discretionary settlements, beneficiaries of trusts are taxed on a 'see through' basis. That is to say that the income of the trustees is apportioned through to the beneficiaries. The fiscal year of the income is the year in which the trustees receive it or are assessed upon it, not the year of payment to the beneficiary.

2.26 Therefore it now becomes important to know when an estate is in administration and when a will trust commences. Taking the second question first, the will trust comes into existence once its capital has been appropriated. This may happen in whole or, through interim distributions, in part. If an estate is in course of administration and there is a settled legacy for infants, the executors may well feel safe in putting a few thousand pounds into investments designated as part of the infants' legacy. That brings into existence the trust for the children. Later the balance of the legacy may be added and that, too, will become subject to the trusts of the settled legacy. So, once there is trust property separately identified and managed, there is a will trust. It can exist alongside the estate in course of administration and the executors can be trustees of the settled legacy. The first question can now be considered. When does the administration period come to an end? Once the residue of the estate has been ascertained and all due debts and taxes paid or quantified, the administration is complete. At one time, a good rule of thumb was the time when the corrective account was filed. However, where the spouse exemption prevents there being a charge to inheritance tax the original account is little more than a statistic for government and it seems highly likely that corrective accounts are not always filed. Estates under £210,000 (broadly) do not require an Inland Revenue account anyway, as 'excepted estates'. 'Administration period' is discussed in TM App 2, App B but with no greater clarity.

There can be times when, with an estate not now in course of administration, there may appear to start a fresh administration period. This would happen if some asset were discovered, perhaps shares in a company overlooked because dividends had not been paid for many years, perhaps some benefit from another estate. Even more like a fresh administration period would be the death of a life tenant with consequent inheritance tax, the possibility of statutory apportionment, payment of legacies and so on. However, once the original administration period came to an end the estate ceased to be in course of administration. If there is settled estate then that is a trust and it cannot change into an estate in course of administration just because some new asset turns up or some event causes tax to be paid, etc.

2.27 This problem of definition where there are changes can also arise where a beneficiary disposes of an interest, for instance, the life tenant of a settled estate might wish to benefit her young grandchildren and they may be the remaindermen but with their interests settled until age 25. Were the life tenant to surrender say half her life interest so as to accelerate the interest of the grandchildren then there would be one settlement held on the trusts of the will and within that settlement there would be the life interest fund and the grandchildren's fund. For capital gains tax purposes there would be one taxpayer, the trustees of the settlement. For income tax purposes there would be two settlements, because the gift by the grandmother would be a separate settlement (until the interests of the grandchildren vest absolutely) with a 34% tax rate, whilst the life interest fund would pay tax at 10%/20%/22% (10%/20%/23% for 1999/2000).

Bare trustees

2.28 As has been said (para 2.11) the actions of a bare trustee are the actions of his principal. The trustee may be assessed but not for CGT which is dealt with in the name of the principal and at his tax district. This approach is confirmed by *TCGA 1992, s 60* (see 7.7 below). The most common form of bare trust may be the portfolio of shares held by a stockbroker's nominee company for his client. The next commonest may well be assets in settlements where the beneficiaries are entitled to them but, for some reason or other, the actual transfer has been delayed. Parents have sometimes set up bare trusts for their infant children. Generally the intention would be to recover tax on the infant's personal allowance and use his exemptions and lower rates. However, this device was countered by *FA 1999, s 64* in relation to trusts established, or capital transferred to existing trusts, on or after 9 March 1999. From that date, income will be treated as the parent's, subject to the existing £100 *de minimis* limit. Any gains of the trust will benefit from the infant's annual capital gains tax exemption, whenever the trust was set up. Problems are more likely to arise in the field of administration rather than tax. If there is income and a tax recovery there must be cash and somebody must manage it. If the gift of capital was made by a parent then, in order to avoid assessment on the parent, the income must be accumulated.

It is to be hoped that the principal does not die in infancy and that the trustee's investment policy is approved. Because an infant lacks contractual capacity it is not usually desirable to put shares, etc. into his name. Perhaps the company registrar would not notice but, for example, an infant should not transfer shares, nor take up a 'rights' issue. Banks will open savings accounts for minors but the facility of a cheque book is generally denied. In a book of this sort it is not sensible to attempt a list of the administrative problems of bare trusts for infants, but the reader can see that there are problems.

Trust Manual

2.29 The Inland Revenue Trust Manual includes at paragraph 6 of Appendix 2 a good explanation of trusts of various sorts, the manner in which they are created and so on. Most of what is said is already in this book.

Chapter 3

Rights of Beneficiaries

3.1 The interests of the beneficiaries can be:

(i) a mere *spes*;

(ii) vested;

(iii) contingent;

(iv) in possession;

(v) in reversion.

The differences can be important for tax purposes.

3.2 A mere *spes* is a hope, the right to be considered as a beneficiary which one sees in a discretionary settlement. This cannot form part of the beneficiary's estate and is not subject to the capital taxes. Its existence may trigger anti-avoidance legislation, e.g. if the settlor or spouse has such an interest.

3.3 A vested interest is one to which a person is entitled for the time being. It may be defeasible. Sometimes a vested interest which is defeasible looks very like a contingent interest. A vested interest can be in possession or in reversion. Vested in possession means that the beneficiary is entitled to the current enjoyment of the income from the capital. Put simply he is the life tenant or is the annuitant. Vested in reversion means that, although the beneficiary has a right which forms part of his estate, there is some prior right. For instance, a simple trust: 'to my widow for life and, upon her death, to our children in equal shares'. Here the widow has a vested interest in possession and each child has a vested interest in reversion. An adult child can transfer such an interest whilst it is still in reversion: there will be good inheritance tax reasons for so doing (see 9.5 below).

3.4 A contingent interest requires the beneficiary to satisfy a pre-condition. Therefore, the gift in the illustration in 3.3 above would have quite different consequences if it were: 'to my widow for life and, upon her death, to such of our children as are then living, in equal shares'. This formula gives each child a contingent interest. Should their mother wish to release her life interest she could only assign it to her children. They would then receive the income during her lifetime (called an interest 'pur autre vie') and the capital would be divided among the survivors at her death.

Rights of Beneficiaries **3.6**

A further illustration is: 'To my son for life with remainder to his children at 25 and subject thereto to my daughter'. The son has a vested interest in possession. His children have contingent interests because any who does not reach the age of 25 gets nothing. The daughter has only a contingent interest because she gets nothing if any of her nephews and nieces attain the age of 25.

3.5 The interests of the beneficiaries must be clearly understood when considering exposure to the capital taxes. As has been indicated some interests are more easily given away or re-settled. Furthermore, the income for tax purposes of someone enjoying the income of a contingent gift can differ from that of someone with a vested interest. The most common case where this causes confusion is where there is a trust for children at age 25 and some are over 18 and therefore by reason of *Trustee Act 1925, s 31* are in receipt of income (subject to an overriding accumulation period). The trust instrument can overrule *section 31* but, if it does not, then a child who has only a contingent interest is entitled to the income of his putative share at age 18. This is so even if the share is revocable.

A popular type of accumulation and maintenance settlement is for 'such of the beneficiaries as attain the age of 25, if more than one in equal shares' and with a power to accumulate income up to that age. In such a case the child who is over 18 can receive the income but only if the trustees choose not to accumulate it (given that there is still a permitted accumulation period, see 3.6). Occasionally one sees an old will which provides for capital to go equally among a class of children but so that no child shall receive his share until age 25. This is not a contingent gift, all that happens is that vesting is deferred. From the age of 18 the child is entitled to his income. Where a gift is not immediate but is to take effect at a future time or is contingent, then there is always a question as to who gets the income in the meantime. This income is known as the intermediate income. The rules are complicated. To some extent they depend on case law but there are rules contained in *Trustee Act 1925, s 31* and *Law of Property Act 1925, s 175*. The upshot is that all future and contingent gifts carry the intermediate income unless:

(*a*) the settlor or testator has expressed a wish to the contrary (e.g. to accumulate); or

(*b*) the gift is a deferred or contingent pecuniary legacy; or

(*c*) the gift is a deferred residuary gift of personalty (i.e. not "realty" viz real property).

Trustee Act 1925, s 31 (as amended) is reproduced in Appendix E.

3.6 Modern precedents generally give a power to accumulate income. This power is given by *Trustee Act 1925, s 31* in relation to children's trusts, viz the income of the share of a child who is under 18. There is no implied power to accumulate and therefore if the trust instrument is silent and *section 31* does not apply, accumulation cannot

3.6 Rights of Beneficiaries

take place. The periods of accumulation are limited. Twenty one years is a standard period. Accumulations are income which the trustees have resolved to use as capital (though a distribution from accumulations can be treated as income in the hands of the beneficiary: see below). Sometimes they have no option and the income is bound to be accumulated. The point in time when money changes from being undistributed income into an accumulation is never easy to decide. Sometimes it becomes obvious from a transaction, because, say, income has been used to purchase an investment. At other times it will depend upon the behaviour of the trustees. For instance, if accounts are made up to 5 April 2000 and no positive steps were taken during the year to accumulate, then it is unlikely that the trustees will consider the matter until the autumn. Thus it might be possible to say in December 2000 that the trustees had resolved not to distribute the income of 1999/2000 and that that was when accumulation took place. That is not conclusive, of course. Dilatory trustees could easily defer the decision for months. In the end they must make their minds up because they have a fiduciary duty. Very occasionally, income can be undistributed for years and still not be accumulated. This can be seen from the *Gulbenkian* case (see 11.17 below). There are tax consequences because:

(*a*) in a children's trust, the accumulations can typically be applied by the trustees as income if the income of the trust fund is inadequate and they then become income of the current year;

(*b*) once the children become entitled to the accumulations otherwise than as augmentation of income, they receive them as capital;

(*c*) the ten-year charge for inheritance tax is levied on accumulations in a special way. It is not charged at all on undistributed and unaccumulated income. The Inland Revenue expects trustees to have made their minds up within the year next following the accounting year concerned.

The above said, the advent of self-assessment, requiring (in the normal case) submission of returns and payment of tax, on or before the 31 January following the end of the tax year, has encouraged the timely turning of the trustees' minds to the issue of accumulation among others. While there will always be exceptions, it is likely that the decision whether or not to accumulate will have been taken within nine months less five days after the end of the tax year.

Chapter 4

The Settlor—Anti-avoidance Provisions

4.1 Even though property has been successfully settled it is still possible for tax referable to either the property or income from it to fall upon the settlor. Given a modern precedent correctly used by the family solicitor who is not driven to daring draftsmanship by the provocative wishes of the settlor, this should not happen. The principal dangers are, of course, a trust caught for income tax by *ICTA 1988, ss 660A–682A*, for capital gains tax by *TCGA 1992, s 77* or for inheritance tax as a gift with a reserved benefit under *FA 1986, s 102, 20 Sch*. See also Chapter 21 below for the capital gains tax charge on certain settlors of non-resident trusts. Conversely, the anti-avoidance provisions outlined below apply to the UK resident settlors of non-resident trusts as much as resident trusts.

Income tax

4.2 The anti-avoidance sections operating up until 5 April 1995 were of great age, some having been brought forward, more or less intact, from the days of surtax. *FA 1995* replaced these with sections *660A* to *660G* and *677* to *682A*. There are no exceptions for settlements made in some distant period: the new sections operate whenever the settlement was made. The influence of the CGT rules *(TCGA 1992, s 77)* is visible. The target is now the settlor who retains 'an interest' (as defined).

The old test was whether the settlor had divested himself of the settled property. The new sections are much easier to understand than the old. The disappearance of tax effective deeds of covenant for individuals may have made the draftsman's task easier. There is now a general provision for the reimbursement of the settlor's extra tax by the trustees (*s 660D*).

4.3 For income tax purposes the definitions of 'settlor' and 'settlement' are extremely wide. *ICTA 1988, s 660G* defines 'settlement' as including 'any disposition, trust, covenant, agreement, arrangement or transfer of assets'. These are the words used in the old *section 670* which was the widest of the definition sections. These definitions should ensure that the shadow settlor (i.e. he who provides funds indirectly) is picked up. Nevertheless *section 660G(2)* specifically targets the person who provides funds indirectly and those who make reciprocal arrangements for the making of settlements. TM 4004 and 4711 more or less repeat this.

4.4 The Settlor—Anti-avoidance Provisions

The settlement of a nominal sum followed by the making of loans to trustees on other than fully commercial terms will encourage the Inland Revenue to apply the settlements legislation (TM 2155).

A recent case illustrates the width of the section. Two husbands ran a profitable company and owned all the shares. They caused the share capital to be reorganised so that their wives had preference shares entitling them to 30% of the company's profits and virtually nothing else. This was a 'settlement' as defined by *section 681(4)*. This definition has been carried forward into *section 660G* (*Young v Pearce; Young v Scrutton*, Ch D *[1996] STC 743*). The problem in those cases was that what was given was 'substantially a right to income' within *section 660A(6)*: had the shares given to the wives been, say, a separate class of non-voting ordinary shares with rights to capital on a winding up, the appeals would have succeeded (see 4.6).

4.4 These sections are only intended to attack settlements where bounty is given. (*CIR v Levy*, Ch D *[1982] STC 442*); (*CIR v Plummer*, HL *[1979] STC 793*); (*Bulmer v CIR*, Ch D 1966, 44 TC 1). Therefore, commercial transactions are not open to attack.

4.5 Income has its usual meaning for tax purposes although extended to include offshore income not otherwise assessable. [*ICTA 1988, ss 660B(4), 660G(3)*].

4.6 Section 660A treats settlement income as that of the settlor unless it derives from property in which he has no interest. He is deemed to have an interest in property if it or any property derived from it could be applied for his benefit or the benefit of his spouse. Derived property is defined (*s 660A(10)*) quite straightforwardly. It does include income as well as capital. Subsections ensure that those who are not currently spouses can be ignored, as can interests in property derived from insolvency, premature death of beneficiaries and so on.

A settlement by one spouse on the other is caught if the gift does not carry the right to the whole of the income or if the gift is of property which is really a right to income. This is a logical consequence of the separate taxation of husband and wife and the resultant possibility of moving income from a higher rate to a lower rate taxpayer. The case of *Young v Pearce* and *Young v Scrutton* is relevant (see 4.3 above). Allocations of pension rights are not affected, nor are settlements related to divorce or separation, nor trading payments, nor charitable covenants. If a settlement is caught and the settlor then takes remedial action so that he no longer has an interest, his liability ceases from the end of that tax year (i.e. not retrospectively). It will be clear that it is quite safe to use a discretionary settlement where the surviving spouse can benefit after the death of the settlor. This can be important where the settlor is the breadwinner and his death will reduce the family's income.

A cautionary tale can be found in *CIR v Botnar*, CA *[1999] STC 711*. Mr Botnar had made a settlement in Liechtenstein. He was excluded from benefit but there was a clause in the settlement deed which permitted capital to be transferred to any other trust fund. Therefore, it became possible for Mr Botnar to benefit as a beneficiary of that other trust fund. The income of the settlement was, accordingly, assessed upon him.

Settlements on children

4.7 Following on from the attack on settlements where the settlor retains an interest, settlements are caught where income is used to benefit an unmarried infant child of the settlor (see also 4.8 below for the *FA 1999* anti-avoidance rules). This is not really different from the old rules. It is the income paid to or for the benefit of the child which is caught and treated as income of the settlor. Income accumulated is safe, although if it is drawn down later and used as income it will be caught. Parental settlements which do accumulate are, of course, liable to the 12% or 14% (11% or 14% for 1999/2000) additional tax under *section 686* (see 6.21 below). The biggest danger here is of a parent joining in an 'arrangement' and so becoming a settlor without knowing. Then, income is spent on his infant children and *section 660B* is triggered. There is a *de minimis* relief where the income of the infant children does not exceed £100 p.a. per child *(section 660B(5))* and this is available to each parent's settlement, separately.

Those advising on deeds of variation should bear this problem of settlements on infant children in mind, because it is not unknown for parents to re-direct legacies from themselves to their children without appreciating that in so doing they have become 'settlors' for income tax purposes. Believing that the income is from, say, grandfather's estate, they allow it to be spent on their own infant children and are caught. Not unnaturally the Inland Revenue are interested in cases where money moves to an unmarried infant child of the settlor. This includes capital payments as well as income (TM 2226).

It is never clear where the borderline is to be found. The case of *Butler v Wildin*, Ch D [1989] *STC* 22 illustrates this. Two brothers wished to benefit their infant children who had money which had come from their grandparents. The money was invested in a £100 company which had a development site and this became valuable. The purchase of the site was financed by a bank loan guaranteed by the brothers. The brothers gave their services to the company free of charge. This scheme was held to be an 'arrangement' (i.e. a settlement for *section 660G* purposes). However that was a High Court decision. The case went to the Court of Appeal but was settled by agreement. Therefore there is no report of the case except in the High Court. It is thought that the High Court might have been overruled had the case proceeded.

Bare trusts of income

4.8 A single 'bare trust' for a child might be a trust of income only or also a trust of capital. In the latter case the capital as well as the income belongs absolutely to the child and he can call for it on attaining the age of 18. In either case, the income belongs absolutely to the child and, though it may be paid to him or applied for his benefit while under the age of majority, more usually the income will be retained by the trustees until the child is old enough to give a valid receipt, that is on attaining the age of 18.

4.9 The Settlor—Anti-avoidance Provisions

Until 9 March (Budget Day) 1999, *section 660B* did not apply to such income which was not paid out and the child was due a refund based on his personal allowance in most cases. Income from trusts established, or from capital added to existing trusts, on or after 9 March 1999 is now assessed upon the parent settlor, subject to the £100 *de minimis* limit. This applies whether or not the income is paid out, though the settlor has a statutory right of indemnity for the tax from the trustees. The rule is not retrospective, insofar as income from pre-9 March 1999 settlements continues to benefit from the old rule. Although the Budget Day Press Release referred to 'bare trust', in the sense of capital belonging absolutely to the beneficiary (subject to his infancy), the new anti-avoidance provision seems to apply (as well as the old rule) also in the case where the right is to income only and not also to capital. In the latter case, viz under a life interest settlement, it is of course important that *Trustee Act 1925, s 31* is excluded.

Discretionary payments of income

4.9 Where a discretionary or accumulation settlement has shares in a family company, this may affect dividend policy. The company will be paying mainstream corporation tax on its profits and thus (up to and including 1998/99) could use the Advance Corporation Tax (ACT) on a dividend. The tax credit to the trustees was 20%. The trust rate was 34% so that if the income was likely to be accumulated there was a disincentive to distribution by the company. This has changed with effect from 1999/2000 when the tax credit is reduced to 10% and ACT is abolished. There will be a small difference in the additional tax paid by the trustees (an extra 15% as compared with 14%), but there will be a big difference in that the tax credit will be a non-repayable 10% and the input to the tax pool will be much less than the 34% deductible from a beneficiary. As a result 1998/99 was the last year for large dividends (without what can now be a significant additional income tax charge). See 6.24 to 6.41 below.

Waiver of dividends

4.10 If all the shareholders who are *sui juris* waive their dividends from a family company and the result is an increase in the dividend to trustees, it must be obvious to them that this will be so. Therefore, the waivers are arrangements and the individuals making them are settlors. [*ICTA 1988, s 660G*]. If the trustees then make payments to or for infant unmarried children of one of these settlors and these can be connected to the waiver, *section 660B* can cause the 'parent settlor' to be assessed.

There is no inheritance tax problem. The waiver of a dividend is not a transfer of value if made within twelve months before the right to the dividend has accrued. [*IHTA 1984, s 15*]. A waiver before then would almost certainly be a disposition because there would be a fall in value of the donor's estate.

Capital sums

4.11 *Sections 677* and *678* must not be ignored. They are aimed at settlements from which capital sums reach the settlor or settlor's spouse,

The Settlor—Anti-avoidance Provisions 4.11

having been funded from trust income. Originally, the abuse consisted simply of borrowing money from the accumulated income of the family settlement. As strategies were caught by legislation, the schemes became more sophisticated, culminating in the settlement owning shares in a company which accumulated its income and made loans to the ruling family. Nowadays, such loans are highly unlikely. Both company law and tax law work against them.

It is easiest to look first at the simple case where there is no connected company. It is the payment of a 'capital sum' to the settlor or his or her spouse which actuates the *section*. A 'capital sum' means a loan, a repayment of a loan or any other payment not being income and not paid for full consideration. In such a case, the first comparison is of the capital sum and the undistributed income of the trust. If the capital sum is less than the income which has not been distributed, the capital sum will be assessed on the settlor. If the capital sum is greater, the undistributed income is assessed. Then running totals are kept so that every year when there is income which is within the total of capital sums that, too, is assessed. It is the income which is the real target, not the capital sum. A case which shows how easy it is to fall within the *sections* is that of *CIR v De Vigier, HL 1964, 42 TC 24* where, in order to take up a rights issue, the trustees borrowed from Mrs De Vigier, the settlor's wife. Within the year, the trustees had repaid the loan. The trust had income and Mr De Vigier was assessed. This is an easy trap to fall into, even now, nearly 30 years after the House of Lords decision. The amount of the repayment will be assessed on the settlor to the extent that it falls within the income available up to the end of that tax year or the following ten years. The charge to tax will be on the relevant amount grossed up at 34% (though with a 34% tax credit). This means that £1,000 is grossed up to £1,515.10, producing a tax liability of £90.91 for a higher rate taxpayer (who has no right of reimbursement for the tax from the trustees, as he does elsewhere in the settlement code).

The extension of this anti-avoidance legislation to the case where there is a company involved requires that:

(*a*) the trustees hold shares in a company (or are participators in any other way);

(*b*) the company is a close company (or would be if UK resident) or is controlled by such a company [*ICTA 1988, s 682A(2)*];

(*c*) a capital sum is paid to the settlor by the company; and

(*d*) a capital sum etc. is or has been paid to the company by the trustees.

[*ICTA 1988, s 678(1)*].

The various payments must fall within the same period of five years. Payments by or to an associated company (within *ICTA 1988, s 416*) are caught as if they were made by or to the company concerned. The likeliest trigger for *section 678* nowadays is some simple transaction like that in the *De Vigier* case above.

4.12 *The Settlor—Anti-avoidance Provisions*

Capital gains tax

4.12 Because of the alignment of the rates of income tax and capital gains tax in the Finance Act 1988 it became necessary to protect the Inland Revenue from settlements where the settlor or his spouse could benefit from the resultant capital gains tax anomalies. Plainly the damage to the Revenue was there whether the settlements were new or old. Therefore the anti-avoidance legislation aimed at UK resident trusts [*TCGA 1992, s 77*] applies regardless of when a settlement was made. (See Chapter 21 below for anti-avoidance provisions affecting non-resident trusts.) There will be far less interest in this type of operation now that trustees pay the 34% rate of capital gains tax whatever the type of trust. Nevertheless, the section still operates to impose an additional 6% in settlor-interested cases where the settlor is a higher rate taxpayer: bear in mind that if he is no more than a basic rate taxpayer the application of s 77 brings an advantage. The first year in which it applies is 1995/96. The legislation applies when:

(i) trust property or derived property will or may benefit the settlor or spouse; or

(ii) there is a benefit to the settlor or spouse which is derived directly or indirectly from the settled property or derived property.

[*TCGA 1992, s 77(2)*].

There are situations where avoidance is not seen (as with the corresponding income tax code: see 4.6) and these are listed in *section 77(3)–(7)*.

Once a settlor is caught by *TCGA 1992, s 77*, the capital gains of the trustees are assessed upon him and not on the trustees. The rules have been made tighter by *FA 1998, 21 Sch* which enacts the changes in *TCGA 1992* needed to accommodate taper relief. Therefore there are computational matters:

(A) the net gains, after deducting trustees' losses for that and earlier years, are assessed on the settlor, subject to his annual exemption;

(B) the rate of tax is that of the settlor, and could thus be as high as 40%; (or as low as 10%, from 2000/01);

(C) the trustees' annual exemption cannot be used to reduce the gain.

[*TCGA 1992, s 77(1)*].

Taper relief is given in the calculation of the trustees' gain which is to be assessed upon the settlor. The settlor's losses cannot reduce the settlement gains assessed upon him but his annual exemption will be used against them.

The settlor has a right of recovery against the trustees. [*TCGA 1992, s 78*]. This does not compensate him for the use of his exemption or losses.

If the trust has net losses for a fiscal year, these are not transferred to the settlor but are carried forward to offset subsequent gains made by the trustees.

The likeliest situations for these provisions to apply are where the trustees have the spouse as an object of their discretion (there was a short period during which inheritance tax plans produced such settlements) or can add the spouse as a beneficiary (although this is acceptable once the settlor is dead, so that widows or widowers can safely be added). There will also be settlements caught because capital may revert to the settlor on failure, perhaps when the remainderman has died.

One feature which seems unfair relates to settlements which contain separate funds or sub-settlements. If there is only one fund where the settlor or spouse may benefit, that is enough to bring the whole settlement within the legislation and so the settlor can be assessed on gains from which he is totally excluded.

Inheritance tax

4.13 The inheritance tax charge on gifts with reservation operates on a death. Where property is settled, the charge is made upon the trustees. Therefore, although gifts *inter vivos* which are gifts with reservation can affect the estate of the settlor, the charge on trusts is discussed in later chapters (see 8.8, 11.37, 15.6, 15.8 and 15.27 below).

Miscellaneous

4.14 A will is not a settlement (*CIR v Buchanan, CA 1957, 37 TC 365*) but a deed of variation may be.

4.15 There was a period when the question of paying the debts of the settlor seemed to be a trap where the trustees paid the capital taxes on making the settlement. It has always been possible for the trustees to pay the inheritance tax or capital gains tax occasioned by the making of the settlement. These taxes are the taxes of the settlor. However, he can make a settlement of assets subject to them. The risk of the trustees being attacked for having paid the capital taxes of the settlor receded when Inland Revenue Statement of Practice SP1/82 was published. (See Appendix A).

4.16 As has been explained in this chapter, shadow settlors have been caught. *Crossland v Hawkins, CA 1961, 39 TC 493*, and *CIR v Mills, HL [1974] STC 130* both illustrate this point. The Revenue consider that a loan to trustees on especially favourable terms would be a settlement.

4.17 A settlor must be living at the time income is assessable if it is to be deemed to be his. Gains arising to the trustees in the year of the settlor's death are not assessed on him. [*TCGA 1992, s 77(6)(a)*].

4.18 Where the donor of a deed of variation continues to enjoy the redirected property, it is not treated as a gift with reservation for inheritance tax. It is deemed to be a gift by the deceased not by the true donor. For CGT, *TCGA 1992, s 62(6)* applies but this deems the gift to have been made by the deceased only for the purposes of that section (i.e. in

4.19 The Settlor—Anti-avoidance Provisions

relation to a deemed disposal on death). If the original beneficiary has an interest in a settlement which results from a deed of variation *section 77* applies and the trustees' gains are assessed on him. (*Marshall v Kerr, HL [1994] STC 638* and see 7.9).

4.19 A tax saving scheme where trusts were used and the right to dividends sold for what appeared to be a capital sum was considered in *CIR v McGuckian, HL [1997] STC 908*. The shares in an Irish company were settled in a Guernsey trust, of which the income was payable to Mrs McGuckian. The Guernsey trustee sold the rights to any dividend payable in 1979 to an English company in exchange for a capital sum. Following this transaction a dividend was paid. In 1986 an assessment was made under what is now *ICTA 1988, s 739*. The question was raised as to whether, in view of *section 730*, *section 739* could be relevant. The authorities could not make an assessment under *section 739* as the six years had passed. Their Lordships found that if one applied the *Ramsay* approach then *section 739* could be applied to the real transaction.

Chapter 5

Trustees—Tax Liabilities and Compliance in summary

5.1 Each tax has its own approach to trusts and trustees.

Statutory obligations

5.2 The simplest approach is that of capital gains tax. *TCGA 1992, s 68* defines settled property as any property held in trust where the trustee is not a nominee or bare trustee. Then, in *section 69*, trustees are introduced. That section lays down that trustees are to be treated as a single and continuing body of persons. Therefore, retirements and appointments of new trustees do not of themselves give rise to disposals.

5.3 Income tax simply requires income to be assessed upon the person who receives it (with exceptions where caught by anti-avoidance legislation). This can be seen in:

ICTA 1988

section 59   relating to tax under Schedule D which is to 'be charged on and paid by the persons receiving or entitled to the income'.

TMA 1970

section 71   which states that 'every body of persons shall be chargeable to income tax in like manner as any person is chargeable under the Income Tax Acts'.

section 72   which makes the trustee of an incapacitated person assessable and chargeable to income tax.

section 73   which makes parents and guardians liable for the income tax liabilities of infants.

Other sections can be found which repeat this general rule, namely, that whoever is the recipient of income is assessable. It is this general rule which makes trustees assessable and there is no separate code for them.

5.4 Trustees are not 'individuals'. Therefore, except in the case of a bare trustee or the receiver etc. for an incapacitated person, there can be

5.5 Trustees—Tax Liabilities and Compliance in summary

no personal allowances. The lead section for the chapter in *ICTA 1988* on personal reliefs is *section 256* which starts 'an individual who makes a claim . . .'. Similarly, the higher rate tax is only imposed on the income of an individual. [*ICTA 1988, s 1(2)*]. Therefore the general rule is that trustees are assessable at the starting, lower and basic rates of 10%, 20% and 22% (for 1999/2000, 23%) on the full amount of their statutory income: special rules apply to dividend income from 1999/2000 (see below). There are special provisions charging an extra 14% or 12% (for 1999/2000, 11%) on the income of discretionary and accumulation settlements (see 6.21 below), on items assessed upon trustees under the accrued income scheme (see 6.5 below) and also under the rules relating to offshore roll-up funds and relevant discounted securities. [*ICTA 1988, ss 686, 720, 764; FA 1996, 13 Sch 6*]. Where dividends are received with a 10% tax credit (20% before 6 April 1999) an additional 25% (14% before 6 April 1999) will be charged on discretionary and accumulation settlements. The 34% rate can also apply to cases where trustees have shares in a company which buys them back (see 6.23 below).

5.5 Non-personal reliefs and losses may be claimed by trustees (e.g. trading losses, capital allowances, relief for interest paid). Schedule A business losses (see *ICTA 1988, s 379A*) can be carried forward.

5.6 Similarly, CGT losses can be carried forward. [*TCGA 1992, s 2(2)*].

5.7 Income can be mandated to the income beneficiary and then the trustee should report to his Inspector of Taxes, giving the name, address of the beneficiary and so on. The result will be that the income will not be assessed on the trustee. Where the income is not taxed at source the beneficiary should self-assess. Naturally there will be no relief for trust expenses (TM 3091). The legislation is in *TMA 1970, ss 13, 76*. Occasionally, this may alter the amount of tax (as in *Williams v Singer and Others, HL 1920, 7 TC 387* where UK trustees mandated US income to a non-resident beneficiary). This fits with the general rule that it is the recipient of income who is assessable.

5.8 It is possible for trustees to suffer a deficiency of income in a given year, perhaps because of exceptional expenses. If these are properly chargeable against income then the consequence may be that the beneficiary has no trust income that year and may well have a reduced income in the following year. Any such deficiency can be carried forward to reduce the statutory income of the next year (TM 3260).

5.9 Statutory and equitable apportionments will not normally affect trustees. They do appear in estates in course of administration; usually where there is an intestacy, and, of course, the consequences are blended into the income tax system by *ICTA 1988, ss 695–702* which cause the income for tax purposes to be related to that for executorship.

5.10 The inheritance tax approach is straightforward because the tax is on chargeable transfers and deemed chargeable transfers. There is a separate group of sections [*IHTA 1984, ss 49–93*] dealing with settled property. *Sections 49–57A* deal with property subject to interests in possession and they operate on the basis prescribed by section 49(1) that the income beneficiary is deemed to be the owner of the settled property underlying his interest for the purpose of calculating the tax. *Sections 58–69* deal with settlements without interests in possession and enact the ten-year charge and the proportionate charge which is levied when property ceases to be within the discretionary regime. *Sections 70–93* deal with favoured trusts (accumulation and maintenance, newspaper trusts etc.) and administrative matters. *IHTA 1984, s 216* requires occasions of charge to be reported by trustees as well as others. Therefore, there is no need for inheritance tax to define trustees. There is a definition of non-resident trustees in *section 218* but that relates to the report which is required by any professional person, other than a barrister, who has been concerned with the making of a settlement whose settlor is domiciled here, but where the trustees are not or will not be resident in the UK. There is also one other definition, in *section 45*, which covers what must be an exceptionally unusual situation, by saying that if there is settled property without trustees then the person managing the property is deemed to be a trustee.

Residence of trustees

5.11 The question of the residence of the trustees is very important, because liability to tax can depend upon residence to some extent. This is dealt with in Chapter 19.

Under the Non-resident Landlord's Scheme the rent paid to such a Landlord bears tax by deduction at source, unless a certificate has been obtained from the Inland Revenue authorising the payment of rent gross. [*ICTA 1998, s 42A*]. The problem stems from the scheme's definition of residence (in terms of 'usual place of abode') which is different from other definitions.

Liability of trustees

5.12 An invitation to act as a trustee requires very careful consideration. The first issue is personal liability. The general rule is that a trustee may be indemnified out of the trust assets for any liabilities which fall upon him as a trustee. Plainly if the trust investments were to fall sharply in value at a time when there were really large tax liabilities, the trustee might find that the trust capital was insufficient. This would leave him with a liability to be discharged out of his own capital. For inheritance tax this problem is resolved by *IHTA 1984, s 204*. That *section* applies equally to personal representatives and trustees and restricts their liability to the value of the capital of the estate or trust. The section first

5.13 *Trustees—Tax Liabilities and Compliance in summary*

limits the liability to 'so much of the property as he has actually received etc.' and then adds the value of any property which might have been available but for his neglect or default. The other taxes have no similar provision. A case on liability recently went to the Special Commissioners – *Howarth's Executor v CIR, Sp C [1997] STC (SCD) 162*. The executors were Mr Stephen Howarth, Mrs Susan Howarth and an employee of the family's solicitors. The testatrix died in 1985 and the executors were due to pay CTT, as it then was, over 10 years. Assets were transferred to beneficiaries following an election to pay tax by instalments on qualifying property and Mr Howarth duly paid the instalments of tax down to October 1994. He was made bankrupt in May 1995. Notices of determination were issued by the Inland Revenue so as to enable them to collect tax from the solicitor's employee. As a defence it was said that the Revenue should have registered a land charge on the deceased's property. That would have protected the employee from the problems which arose as a result of the sale of the property without payment of the outstanding tax. The Special Commissioner found that no charge need have been registered and that, as the tax is a personal liability of the executors (on a joint and several basis), the determination was valid.

5.13 The next major liability into which someone could walk by accepting a trusteeship is to be found in *TCGA 1992, s 168*. This is the section providing for the re-capture of a held over gain where the donee/transferee has become non-resident. In the context of trusts this means that the trustees have passed assets to a beneficiary, subject to a claim for hold-over. The danger exists for the remainder of the year of assessment during which the transfer took place and for the next six fiscal years. [*Section 168(4)*]. If the transferee's job takes him temporarily away from the UK and he returns within three years, there should be no charge. [*Section 168(5)*]. The assessment is made upon the transferee and is therefore at his tax rates. Should he fail to pay within twelve months of the due date, the transferor is liable. [*Section 168(7)*]. He has a right of recovery from the transferee. [*Section 168(9)*]. If the transferee, whilst resident in the UK, has disposed of all or some of the assets on which hold-over relief was claimed, then the gains thereon are not caught again by *section 168* to that extent.

5.14 The potential liability under *TCGA 1992, s 168* can be guessed with sufficient accuracy for most people. The gain held over is capable of exact calculation. The guesswork is as to the transferee's rate of tax in a future year. Most people would allow for a 40% rate and evaluate the risk to the trustees accordingly. It is possible to cover this risk by insurance but there may be a limited number of underwriters in the market.

5.15 For many gifts made after 13 March 1989, CGT hold-over relief was abolished by *FA 1989, s 124*. The main exceptions are gifts of business property and gifts constituting a chargeable lifetime transfer (excluding a potentially exempt transfer which becomes chargeable) for inheritance tax. [*TCGA 1992, ss 165, 260*]. For trusts other than discretionary trusts, which involve chargeable lifetime transfers, the possibility of a clawback charge under section 168 will thus become less relevant.

5.16 Where migration of a trust is possible, then the whole question of indemnities takes on a different aspect and competent legal assistance is required. See Chapter 21 for the capital gains tax charge on a trust becoming non-resident.

5.17 Other latent liabilities can surface on a premature death. They will be a consequence of a potentially exempt transfer. For instance if the settlor of a discretionary trust had first made a potentially exempt transfer, then set up the trust and then died within seven years of the potentially exempt transfer, it is almost certain that there would be an inheritance tax charge on the trustees (see 11.35 below). Another example is that of a life tenant who surrenders his interest, so making a potentially exempt transfer, who dies within seven years. There is then a charge upon the capital which supported his life interest.

5.18 From 6 April 1996 the term 'relevant trustees' is to be used to signify those trustees who hold office, when income arises or in the year of assessment when a capital gain arises. Trustees who are subsequently appointed are also 'relevant trustees'. It is the relevant trustees who are responsible to the Inland Revenue and are liable for tax, interest and penalties. [*TCGA 1992, s 65(4)*]

Returns for income tax

5.19 As regards income tax, a trustee will file his returns with one of the specialist districts, of which there are now five: Edinburgh, London, Manchester, Nottingham and Truro. At one time all tax districts dealt with the trusts resident in their area.

When a new settlement is made, it is good practice to register it with the Inland Revenue in the appropriate Trust District. The Inland Revenue no longer require to see a photocopy of the trust deed and details of the trust are supplied on the non-statutory form Trusts 41G. This will initiate a reference and therefore the issue of self-assessment returns year by year.

Chapter 6

Income Tax

The basic and lower rates
6.1

1998/99 and earlier years

Income receivable by trustees is, in the main, taxed at 20% or attracts a 20% tax credit. This covers income from stocks and shares and interest from building societies and banks. Any income taxable by direct assessment, e.g. rental income, bears tax at 23%. If a tax recovery is possible then this tax or tax credit can be repaid. A foreign income dividend (see 6.20 below) carries a 20% tax credit which cannot be repaid. This does not make the shares any less satisfactory as an investment as the companies concerned tend to distribute more now that they can pay foreign income dividends. Scrip and enhanced scrip dividends (see 6.18 and 6.19 below) are similar. 1998/99 was the last year for foreign income dividends and can perhaps be expected largely to be for scrip dividends. The abolition of ACT brings this about. Foreign dividends received through a UK paying agent generally suffer a foreign withholding tax and UK tax totalling 20%. Were a recovery possible only the UK tax could be repaid. There are one or two countries which do not fall into line with this, e.g. Irish dividends are susceptible to UK tax and nearly all the Irish tax can be recovered. There are exceptional cases where the 34% rate can apply to an interest in possession trust (see 6.23 below).

Unit trusts can act as a conduit for these various types of distribution as can any fixed interest trust. The tax voucher issued with the distribution should show what it is that is being distributed.

From 1999/2000

From 6 April 1999 the tax credit on dividends (and other qualifying distributions) is reduced to 10% which is not repayable. Although this is bad news for trustees who reclaim tax (e.g. charities) the general run of trustees are not affected because at the same time the Schedule F ordinary rate of 10% is introduced (*F(No 2)A 1997, s 31*). For those within *s 686* (i.e. discretionary and accumulation settlements), however, the change has been adverse (see 6.28 below). It is only the tax credit on dividends which has changed, so income from bank deposits, rents and anything except shares carries on as before. We continue to await introduction of the Scottish Variable Rate.

Income Tax **6.2**

Deductibility of expenses

6.2 There will be expenses which are deductible from Schedule A and Schedule D income in the ordinary way, but trust management expenses have to be paid out of the net taxed income. They reduce the amount of tax when calculating the additional charge on accumulation and discretionary trusts (see 6.21 below). They have to be allowed for when calculating the income of a beneficiary of any other trust. Sometimes the result can look wrong as in *Aikin v Macdonald Trustees, Ex (S) (1894) 3 TC 306* where trustees taxed on income from foreign possessions on a remittance basis could not obtain relief for their UK expenses which did, in part, relate to that income. However, in general, the results seem correct. The expenses of an accumulation or discretionary trust are not available to the beneficiaries, whether by way of income distribution or as capital when accumulations are paid out, and so income used to pay those expenses does not suffer any additional tax.

In a trust which is not discretionary etc., the trust management expenses which are properly chargeable to income are deducted from the net trust income to arrive at the net income of the beneficiary. This can then be grossed up to find the beneficiary's statutory income. The grossing up may be at 10%, 20% or 22% (23% for 1999/2000), as illustrated in Appendix C. In TM 3260 there is a detailed explanation which makes the point that expenses connected with the trust fund as a whole are chargeable against the capital (see also 6.22 (ii) below). If income were to fail then the trust management expenses would create a deficit. That can be carried forward to the next fiscal year (TM 3260).

Appendix C contains an example of the manner in which the incomes of beneficiaries with discretionary and vested interests in income are calculated, and provides a practical illustration of the manner in which expenses affect the statutory income of beneficiaries. This example is on the traditional basis (i.e. does not follow the Inland Revenue form) and illustrates a practical method of checking the Inland Revenue's calculation. This can be beneficial for a higher rate taxpayer and unsatisfactory for one with a very small income. In 1999/2000 trustees would have received four categories of income. Expenses are treated as paid out of income in the following order (ICTA 1988, s 698B):

(i) dividends carrying a non-repayable 10% tax credit and scrip dividends etc. where tax is not to be repaid;

(ii) foreign dividends assessed under Case V of Schedule D;

(iii) other savings income bearing tax at 20%;

(iv) income chargeable at 23%.

Where the beneficiary is non-resident there are special rules (see 20.7 below). The payment of interest by trustees is often misunderstood. There will be a few cases where tax relief is given. The general rules in *ICTA 1988, s 352 et seq.* apply. These include *s 364* under which personal representatives can obtain tax relief on interest on a loan to pay inheritance tax. Unfortunately it only relates to a loan which is used to obtain a grant in respect of personal (i.e. not real) property, and then only for twelve months, and not to subsequent borrowings. The fact that no tax relief is available does not change the nature of the interest paid, it is still an expense. Interest on tax paid late is attacked by *TMA 1970, s 90* and *IHTA 1984, s 233(3)*. Both sections are similar and prevent any deduction for such interest in a tax computation. Although not strictly a matter for trustees it is interesting to see the consequences in estates generally. The first case is an estate in course of administration where there is a limited interest (i.e. a life tenant). In that case the income of the beneficiary is based on the amounts paid to him. As the interest will have reduced the money available for him it will make his income less. The second case is an estate in course of administration where there is an absolute interest. In such a case the personal representatives keep two running totals, one being the payments made, the other the residuary income (i.e. the income for tax purposes). The payments made are income to the extent that they are within the residuary income. The interest on tax cannot be deducted from the residuary income and so does not reduce the income. The third case is an interest in possession trust where the interest paid is an expense. The fourth case is a discretionary or accumulation trust where that which is needed for *section 686* is the amount of income not used for expenses. The interest is an expense and so affects the figure for *s 686*. For 1999/2000 the form is the self-assessment form: the words in the Guide (pages 18 and 19 re box 13.19) are clear although there is no specific reference to interest on tax.

If income is mandated to the life tenant then the trustees cannot deduct expenses from it; they will have to pay them from capital.

Bank interest

6.3 The last vestiges of Case III disappeared on 6 April 1996 for most trustees. Before then accumulation and discretionary trusts received bank interest without deduction of tax. The tax rate is 20%. Where there are no UK resident beneficiaries interest can still be paid gross (see 20.6 below). In such a case the term 'beneficiary' extends only to people who, at the time the definition is applied, are identified as beneficiaries. People who might become beneficiaries can therefore be ignored. Those settlements where individuals are beneficially entitled to the interest will have tax deducted by the bank. In such cases the assessable amount is the interest actually arising in the year. Interest from the National Savings Bank will be received gross.

Building society interest

6.4 Building society interest is subject to deduction of tax, in like manner to bank interest. There is a procedure for interest to be paid gross where the beneficiaries are non-resident (see 20.10 below).

Income Tax **6.7**

The accrued income scheme

6.5 Trust law requires the cost of securities bought cum interest to be paid out of capital and the proceeds of sale to be a capital receipt. The accrued income scheme (see *ICTA 1988, ss 710–728*) does not work like that. Securities are defined [*ICTA 1988, s 710(2)–(4)*] and include loan stocks of governments, public and local authorities and companies, which are interest-bearing as well as, from 25 July 1991, certain qualifying building society shares. Shares, national savings certificates, zero coupon bonds, and certificates of deposit are excluded. There is a *de minimis* exemption for individuals, disabled trusts and personal representatives (securities of £5,000 nominal value) [*ICTA 1988, s 715(1)*], but there is no such exemption for other trustees. The aim of the accrued income scheme is to ensure that each person pays income tax on the interest on securities which accrues during his period of legal ownership. Therefore, tax is charged on an accruals basis and by reference to legal, rather than beneficial, ownership. (See also 6.13 below.) Although income tax aspects of offshore resident trusts are dealt with in Chapter 20 it must be worth saying that non-resident trustees will generally escape the accrued income scheme [*ICTA 1988, s 715(1)(f)(g), (4)*].

6.6 The scheme came into operation on 28 February 1986. When trustees purchase interest-bearing securities cum interest on or after that date, they are deemed to have purchased the interest which had accrued by the settlement day for the transfer. The accrued interest is called the 'rebate amount'. A gift to trustees produces the same result.

6.7 Similarly, when the trustees sell cum interest they are deemed to have received the accrued interest as income. This is known as the 'accrued amount'. There should be no problem in discovering the accrued interest as it is shown on the stockbrokers' contract note for transactions in fixed interest securities. The accrued amount is assessable upon the trustees. Relief is given in respect of the rebate amount, either against the next interest received from that security or against the accrued interest on sale, whichever comes first. The relief can be given in a different year of assessment from that in which the purchase is made.

Example 1

25 May 1999
    Purchase £10,000 10% Treasury Stock 2003.
    Accrued interest therein is £216 (8 March to 25 May).

8 September 1999	£
Interest–gross	500
Relief for accrued interest in the purchase	216
Income for tax purposes	£284

6.8 *Income Tax*

Example 2

25 May 1999
Purchase as in Example 1.

25 June 1999
Investment is sold.

	£
Accrued interest	
On sale 110 days	301
On purchase 79 days	216
Assessable (Sch D, Case VI)	£85

6.8 The words 'settlement day' are defined. [*ICTA 1988, s 712*]. For Stock Exchange transactions, there should be no problem as government stocks are normally for settlement on the day following the transaction. For dealings in eurosterling, settlement falls three days after the transaction; for domestic loan stocks and debentures, it is five days after the transaction. If the transaction is not through The Stock Market then 'settlement day' means:

(*a*) the due date for payment if the transaction is for cash; or

(*b*) the date of transfer in any other case.

6.9 If there is a beneficiary entitled to income (perhaps a beneficiary of an accumulation and maintenance settlement who is over 18) trust law accords him the whole of the interest received. Therefore most trustees would give the income plus the tax recovery to the income beneficiary in *Example 1*. Others believe that if they are to pay tax on accrued income out of capital (see 6.10 below), they should retain the recovery on the rebate amount. The two treatments may be compared:

(i) The trustees receive:

	£
Gross interest	500
less tax	100
Net	£400

Recovery of tax on rebate amount

£216 @ 20%   = £43

(ii) If the beneficiary receives the tax recovery as well as the interest, he has £443.

(iii) If the trustees withhold the recovery, he has £400.

It is a matter of indifference to the Inland Revenue whether one method is used or the other. The statutory income is £284 gross (see *Example 1*) either way. Where interest is mandated to the life tenant and relief is due against an interest payment, that relief is given to the life tenant by the Inland Revenue.

6.10 Where trustees are assessable upon the accrued interest on sale, they suffer tax at 34% (i.e. the rate applicable to trusts or, now, in accordance with subsection (1AA)) regardless of the type of settlement (i.e. there need be no power to accumulate or exercise discretion and there may be a life tenant). [*ICTA 1988, s 720(5)*]. Because trust law requires the proceeds to be received as capital, this tax will be paid out of capital. It is only when *ICTA 1988, s 687* applies and causes it to form part of the tax pool (see 6.27 below) that the tax can reappear as tax on the income of an individual. The rate is 22% (for 1999/2000, 23%) for an estate in course of administration.

6.11 The charge on the accrued amount is not really a charge on income. It is only a charge on income accrued and that is capital so far as trustees are concerned. Therefore, the accrued income does not become part of the income of the income beneficiary and he receives no credit for the tax paid thereon. Occasionally, someone may benefit from a discretionary trust and the tax voucher he is given will include the tax assessed on the accrued amount but this will be very rare.

6.12 Were it possible for trustees to deal in loan stocks only at a time when no interest had accrued they could avoid the conflict between trust and tax law. This must be impractical.

6.13 A further problem for trustees is that, although the prime purpose of the scheme is to deal with sales cum interest, it is enacted in relation to transfers. [*ICTA 1988, s 713(1)*]. A gift into settlement, an appropriation, a conversion of securities, the change from being a personal representative to being a trustee and the retirement and appointment of trustees are all technically within the charge (subject to the £5,000 *de minimis* limit in certain cases: see 6.5 above). Following representations, it is clear that a change of trustee will usually be ignored by the Inland Revenue. If the change of trustees takes the trust offshore, however, that will be caught. There is no transfer when a beneficiary becomes entitled absolutely as against the trustees, perhaps on fulfilling a contingency or on the termination of a life interest. This is because the legal ownership does not change. Thereafter, the trustees are bare trustees and the transfer to the beneficiary is then exempt. However, the transfer to a beneficiary in any other case is within the legislation. The coming to an end of the administration period will change the personal representatives into trustees. That, too, is an occasion of charge. Prior to 6 April 1996, a death caused a deemed transfer, no longer, however (see ICTA 1988, s 721).

6.14 One oddity of which settlors should be aware is that they will be charged on the accrued income when they give securities away. They will not be reimbursed the resultant tax if the donees are trustees.

Another oddity is that even though the income might escape tax, the accrued amount is still assessable. Therefore a gift of securities to a

6.15 *Income Tax*

charity would produce an assessment on the donor. The sale by trustees of exempt gilt edged (FOTRA) securities where the life tenant is non-resident also produces an assessment.

6.15 When making a transfer without going through the Stock Market, a trustee must bear in mind that the fact that the security has gone ex-div is irrelevant except to The Stock Exchange. The transferee will be entitled to the next interest payment on a private transfer, so that the transferor is handing over a stock carrying the accrued interest.

6.16 Personal representatives have a limited ability to avoid an assessment on accrued income if they transfer securities in specie to a legatee shortly after the death of their deceased: 'shortly after' means in the same interest period as that in which the death occurred. [*ICTA 1988, s 721(2)*]. Again, there is no equivalent relief for trustees. This subsection was amended by *FA 1996, s 158(3)* but the effect is unchanged.

6.17 Occasionally, the allowance on a rebate amount is stranded. If trustees purchase a security cum div. and, before the next interest is due, that security becomes one to which a beneficiary is absolutely entitled, nobody is entitled to the allowance.

Enhanced scrip dividends

6.18 Enhanced scrip dividends were popular in 1993/94 but since then have in practice come to an end. They are unlikely to be seen after 5 April 1999 because they were a device which helped dividend-paying companies to escape ACT. They were dealt with fully in previous editions of this book.

Scrip dividends

6.19 Scrip dividends are still quite common although these, too, have generally lost their tax attractions since 5 April 1999. The shareholder accepts shares in lieu of his cash dividend. The scrip and the cash amount are of much the same value. Trustees would not accept a scrip dividend unless they had power to accumulate and wished to add to an existing holding without dealing costs. The scrip dividend is a device to sidestep ACT. After the abolition of ACT (5 April 1999) pension funds will probably be happy to receive scrip dividends. A tax credit is given but is notional and non-repayable. Debt is cheaper to service than equity so that companies may be expected to stop making scrip dividends available. Quite a few companies are buying back shares so as to pass money out to shareholders, cutting down the number of shares and perhaps incurring interest if their gearing goes up. Some leading Irish companies continue with scrip alternatives. In due course there may be capital gains tax but that can be deferred as long as the investment is retained. These issues are not suitable if there is a life tenant.

Foreign income dividends (before 6 April 1999)

6.20 Details of the tax treatment of foreign income dividends appear in *ICTA 1988, ss 246A–246Y*, having been introduced by *FA 1994, 16 Sch*. These relate to dividends paid on or after 1 July 1994. The tax consequences for trustees are similar to those for a scrip dividend. There is a notional tax credit of 20% on the gross equivalent of the dividend grossed at 20%. It is notional and no repayment can be made. Tax under *section 686* will be at 14%. This is a consequence of *section 246D(4)*. Only the 14% enters into the tax pool under *section 687* [*section 687(3)(aaa)*]. The foreign income dividend disappeared on 6 April 1999 as part of the repeal of ACT.

The rate applicable to trusts (or, from 6 April 1999, the rate applicable in accordance with subsection (1AA))

6.21 The reduction of the tax credit on dividends which was introduced in 1993 caused an alteration in the manner in which discretionary settlements and those with a power to accumulate are charged. In 1992/93 and earlier years there was an additional rate of 10%. In 1993/94 and subsequent years a new term was introduced by *ICTA 1988, s 686(1)*, namely 'the rate applicable to trusts'. This is 34% (*s 686(1A)*). It therefore results in a charge of 14% on 20% income and of 12% on 22% income (or, in 1999/2000, 11% on 23% income). The trustees give income beneficiaries a tax voucher showing tax at 34%. [*ICTA 1988, s 687*]. To the extent that income flows through to beneficiaries this will be tax neutral where they have a low enough income to recover the tax or a high enough income to pay 40%. Those whose marginal rate is 22% (or, for 1999/2000, 23%) can find that 2% (or, in 1999/2000, 3%) has been lost, in that they could have received bank and building society interest direct or as life tenants of a fixed interest trust and they would have had no extra tax to pay. As it is, any 20% income received by the trustees suffers an extra 14% in their hands and the recovery by the beneficiary is only 12% (or, in 1999/2000, 11%). Where dividend income is accumulated the extra tax is 14% and that seems reasonable. From 6 April 1999 the extra tax (called 'the rate applicable in accordance with subsection (1AA)') became 25% in relation to Schedule F dividend income (so as to accommodate the reduction of the tax credit to 10%) and otherwise 34%.

Where a discretionary settlement is set up by a will, there will be a period during which the administration of the estate takes place. During this period the settlement has not been created and therefore *section 686* does not apply. However, when the administration period ends and income becomes that of trustees rather than executors, there will be a charge. In most cases the same people will be both executors and trustees, though the two capacities are different.

6.22 *Income Tax*

6.22 There are exceptions to the charge which brings the total up to the rate in accordance with subsection (1AA) and no assessment is made upon the following.

(i) Income which is that of the settlor for tax purposes. [*ICTA 1988, s 686(2)(b)(ii)*]. Therefore, for instance, where the settlor or his spouse is an object of the discretion and the income is treated as his under *ICTA 1988, s 660A*, there is no additional tax. Whilst it is the settlor's income for tax purposes and will be reported in his income tax return, the trustees must still record the income in their self-assessment. There is a power of recovery [*ICTA 1988, s 660D*], so that where the settlor does not receive the income from the trustees but is assessed upon it, he may recover tax thereon from the trustees. Where income is deemed to be that of the settlor because it is paid to or for his infant unmarried children (or arises under such a settlement from funds provided on or after 8 March 1999) it does not suffer the rate applicable to trusts (or in accordance with subsection (1AA)). [*ICTA 1988, ss 686(2)(b)(ii)* as amended by *FA 1995, 17 Sch 13*].

(ii) Income used to defray the expenses which are properly chargeable to income. [*ICTA 1988, s 686(2AA)*]. In deciding what is so chargeable, general law is applied rather than income tax law and any special provisions of the trust instrument are ignored. This was particularly relevant in two cases, heard together, *Bosanquet v Allan*; *Carver v Duncan, HL [1985] STC 356*, when life assurance premiums were, by reason of special clauses in the trust deed, chargeable to income and the trustees sought to have the income needed to pay the premiums excused from tax under what is now *section 686*. They were unsuccessful. By contrast, interest paid by trustees which is not deductible for tax is an expense properly chargeable to income. The income used for such a payment is, therefore, not assessable under *section 686*. See 6.2 above. Professional costs can only be treated as expenses if properly chargeable to income: this is a problem area. The expenses are set against net income in a particular order (as prescribed by section 689B):

(1) UK dividends and deemed income where a scrip dividend has been received or where a company has written off a debt;

(2) foreign dividends;

(3) savings income at 20%;

(4) 22% (or, for 1999/2000, 23%) rate income.

In other words the balance of income left is that which is probably most useful to the beneficiary.

In general accountants automatically charge fees, etc, against income in the accounts. Supported by the instructions in their standard charging clauses, the banks do the opposite. Solicitors are generally somewhere in the middle. The Inland Revenue view is quite modest in so far as they have a view. The authors have heard mentioned a figure as low as 10% of the income. The amount of the expenses can have a significant effect on the additional tax, thus:

	23% income	20% income
Gross	100	100
Tax	23	20
Net	77	80
Additional rate	11	14
Net for beneficiary, etc.	£66	£66

If in each case 50% of the net income had been used to pay expenses, there would be a corresponding reduction in the additional tax as follows (though with a very substantial effect on the beneficiary's income):

Net	77	80
Expenses	(38.5)	(40)
Additional rate	(5.5)	(7)
Net for beneficiary, etc.	£33	£33

(iii) Income which is the income of some person other than the trustees before it is distributed. [*ICTA 1988, s 686(2)(b)(i)*]. Therefore, the income of an infant's legacy is outside the charge provided the gift to the infant is outright. In such a case the trustees act as managers of the capital and income but the infant is the owner of the income and were he to die it would form part of his estate. If the gift is contingent in any way then it is not within this protection.

6.23 The income which is to be charged to bring the total up to the rate in accordance with subsection (1AA) is as follows:

(i) Income which is to be accumulated or which is payable at discretion. [*ICTA 1988, s 686(2)(a)*]. Income is viewed in the normal sense, i.e. the general law applies and not the definition in *ICTA 1988, s 835*. Therefore items which are truly capital but which are deemed to be income for tax purposes are excluded from the charge. One obvious example is a premium on a lease lasting for no more than 50 years, part of which would be income for tax by virtue of *ICTA 1988, s 34* but is not income for trust purposes.

A similar analysis applied before 5 December 1996 in relation to the proceeds of sale of shares bought by a company from trustees which are not subject to capital gains tax under *ICTA 1988, s 219*. In a situation where the proceeds of sale are treated as income for tax purposes, the qualifying distribution represented by the excess over the nominal value is now treated as *section 686* income [*FA 1997, 7 Sch 3*]. As from 6 April 1999 such a distribution now therefore suffers the additional 25% to make the tax rate up to 34%.

6.24 *Income Tax*

There are exceptions for charities, pension funds and cases where the settlor is assessed on the income. The legislation applies to interest in possession trusts as well.

(ii) Amounts assessed under the accrued income scheme (whether or not a discretionary or accumulation and maintenance settlement). [*ICTA 1988, s 720(6)*].

Mention has been made (see 6.22 above) of the order in which expenses are deemed to have been paid from net income.

Payments to beneficiaries of accumulation and maintenance settlements where ICTA 1988, s 687 applies

6.24 When a payment is made under a discretionary power and it is income of the recipient for tax purposes, *ICTA 1988, ss 348, 349* do not apply. Instead the payment comes within *section 687*. The net payment is grossed up at 34% (i.e. the rate applicable to trusts) and a tax voucher can be given for that tax. Such a payment may be from a discretionary settlement or it may be from an accumulation and maintenance settlement.

6.25 Payments to or for the beneficiaries of accumulation and maintenance settlements where their shares of income have not vested must be made pursuant to a discretionary power, because, by the terms of such a settlement the income must be '... accumulated so far as not applied for maintenance, education or benefit of a beneficiary'. [*IHTA 1984, s 71(1)(b)*]. The application of the income is therefore at the discretion of the trustees until the beneficiary becomes entitled to the income of his share. Once a beneficiary is entitled to his income the charge under *section 687* does not apply, as there is no discretion. The charge under *section 686* (see 6.21 to 6.23 above) upon the income of the settlement which the trustees must hand over to such a beneficiary will also disappear. This is because it is no longer 'income which is to be accumulated or which is payable at the discretion of the trustees'. [*ICTA 1988, s 686(2)(a)*]. The manner in which this is eliminated from the income of a settlement where there are still beneficiaries not yet entitled to their income is shown in the example in Appendix C where the incomes of Alice and Belinda are excluded from the extra charge.

The beneficiaries of accumulation and maintenance settlements commonly achieve a vested interest in their income at the age of 18. However, there are times when the draftsman of the trust instrument can retain a power of accumulation until a later age which is not more than 25 years. Those concerned with the making of such settlements should bear in mind *TCGA 1992, s 260(2)(d)* which permits hold-over of a capital gain for capital gains tax purposes if capital goes to a beneficiary of an accumulation settlement without an intervening right to income within *IHTA 1984, s 71* (see 7.15 below).

6.26 Where a payment is made to or for a beneficiary of an accumulation and maintenance settlement (i.e. one whose share of income has

Income Tax **6.28**

not vested) it must be for his 'maintenance, education or benefit'. Where significant sums are involved this must put some limit upon the amount which can be expended although the authors have never heard of a case being challenged by the Inland Revenue.

6.27 Where such a payment is made, an assessment under *section 687* is made upon the trustees to collect the 34% to the extent that it is not covered by the tax pool. The tax pool for 1999/2000 comprises:

Current input:
 (i) balance from 1998/99;
 (ii) 34% (i.e. the rate applicable to trusts) of the gross income charged under *section 686*, including tax on charges under the accrued income scheme;
 (iii) 15% of scrip dividends (i.e. the notional 10% does not get into the tax pool);
 (iv) 15% of any non-qualifying distribution. It is not obvious how something like, say, a bonus in redeemable preference shares can be taxed under *section 686* in the first place, so this must be a rarity; and
 (v) 34% of the assessments under *ICTA 1988, s 761* (offshore income gains) and *FA 1996, 13 Sch* (relevant discounted securities).

Input from prior years will be taxed at the rate applicable to trusts and earlier versions thereof on items (ii) to (v) above, plus two-thirds of the net undistributed income at 5 April 1973 plus tax on development gains (repealed 1985).

[*ICTA 1988, s 687(3)*].

There is provision for double tax relief to flow through so that the beneficiary can report taxed overseas income to the extent that it is included in a payment to him.

The tax pool and *section 687* are necessary because *ICTA 1988, ss 348, 349* (the provisions authorising the deduction of tax at source) do not apply. Therefore different machinery for deduction of tax is needed and that is contained in *section 687*. In older cases the tax pool should prevent any assessment being made on the trustees. This is a point which trustees should consider before making a distribution, because over the years there does tend to be a mismatch between the tax pool and the distributable cash. In the past tax pools have tended to cover a larger distribution than the accounts permitted. That is changing (see 6.28 and 6.29 below).

6.28 *Section 686* was considerably altered by *F(No 2)A 1997, s 32*. This has effect from 6 April 1999. The tax credit on a dividend is now 10% rather than the previous 20%. Dividends received by trustees who are within *section 686* are taxed at the Schedule F ordinary rate (i.e. 10%) and the Schedule F trust rate is 25% rather than the 34% which is the rate applicable to trusts. At the same time *section 687* was amended

6.29 *Income Tax*

by *F(No 2)A 1997, 4 Sch*. The amendment ensures that the 10% tax credit on dividends does not enter the tax pool although the extra 15% which makes it up to the Schedule F trust rate does go into the pool.

Of course, income which is not dividend income continues as before and the 34% thereon will go into the tax pool. This may affect the trustees' view of their investment portfolio. If only the 15% goes into the tax pool where dividends are received, should they buy debentures or gilts which attract the 34%? If the stock market rises the capital growth may cover the difference.

6.29 There is, from 6 April 1999, a problem over payments to beneficiaries which are within *section 687*. The 34% has to be deducted from them and then compared with the tax pool to see if any further tax is due. Any existing *section 687* trusts will have a tax pool from the past and they may be unaffected for a while. However, a new trust or one with a small tax pool would be caught if it relied on dividend income (on which only 15% enters the pool) to fund payments from which 34% is deducted. This can be seen:

	£	£
Dividend received by trustees		90.00
Add tax credit		10.00
Gross income		100.00
Section 686 tax thereon at 25% Schedule F trust rate:		
Met by tax credit	10.00	
Paid by trustees	15.00	
		25.00
		£75.00

However, £75 cannot simply be distributed to the beneficiary. The tax credit has met part of the trustees' own liability under *section 686* but cannot be used to frank the tax under *section 687* which they are liable to deduct on making the distribution.

	£	£
Net income of trust		75.00
Liability at 34% under *section 687* on gross payment of £90 to beneficiary	30.60	
Met by trustees' payment above	(15.00)	
Remaining liability of trustees		(15.60)
Available for distribution to beneficiary		59.40
Grossed up under *section 687(2)* at 34%		30.60
Gross income of beneficiary		90.00
Tax thereon at 40% (of which £30.60 met by trustees)		(36.00)
Net income of beneficiary		£54.00

It should be noted that this does not affect an accumulation settlement. That will pay the additional 15% but no more. It is only the discretionary settlement, invested in equities and making income payments to beneficiaries, which is caught.

6.30 The income tax return for trustees of accumulation and maintenance and of discretionary settlements is the standard Self Assessment Trust and Estate Return with its Guide and Tax Calculation Guide. This is explained in Chapter 18.

6.31 If there is an assessment under *section 687*, there can be no set-off against a future year. That is to say that, if tax on the distributions of income in 1999/2000 exceeds the total of the tax credits of that year, etc., together with the tax pool brought forward from 1998/99, then there will be a *section 687* charge and the fact that there may be accumulated income in 2000/01 does not give rise to a recovery of the tax so charged in 1999/2000. In fact, the new regime applying from 6 April 1999 means that, whatever the level of distributions, tax pools in hand at the end of 1998/99 can never be augmented (except in relation to non-dividend income) and will simply be run down through distributions of income over the years.

6.32 The tax pool can still act as a reservoir of income.

Example: (post 1992/93 and pre 1999/2000)

	Cash £	Tax pool £
Year 1 Net dividend	800	200
Further tax	140	140
	660	340
Distribution	(132)	(68)
	528	272
Year 2 Distribution	(132)	(68)
	396	204
Year 3 Distribution	(132)	(68)
	£264	£136

This is because *section 687(1)* rules out the use of *ICTA 1988, s 348* and *s 349(1)*, and *section 687(2)* makes the payment income of the beneficiary of the year of payment. It is the date of payment to the beneficiary, not the date of receipt by the trustees, which decides the year in which the income becomes that of the beneficiary.

Tax pools have been used as reservoirs against the advent of a suitable beneficiary. For instance, if in the illustration all possible beneficiaries were adult higher rate taxpayers in years 1 and 2 and in year 3 a child were added to the class, the trustees might accumulate in years 1 and 2 and distribute something in year 3, so giving to the new beneficiary income of years before he was born. The fact that tax rates change from year to year does not affect the balance brought forward in the tax pool, although a tax pool based on dividend income will as from 1999/2000 be run down. In view of the 1999/2000 provisions mentioned in 6.28 and 6.29 above, the last year for a special dividend, intended to feed distributions of future

6.33   Income Tax

years, was 1998/99. As a matter of caution the income to be paid out should not have been accumulated (see 6.39 below).

6.33   The lowering of tax rates means that much of an old tax pool may never be used. For several years, the sum of the basic and additional rates was 45%. The last such year was 1987/88. Therefore, in that year trustees might have received:

	£	£
Net dividend	730	
With tax credit of		270
Additional rate tax	180	180
leaving net cash	£550	
and a tax pool of		£450

If, in 1999/2000, this net cash were distributed as income it would appear on form R185 as:

	£
Gross	833
Tax @ 34%	283
Net	£550

If there were no other transactions the tax pool would be:

	£
B/fwd	450
Used 1999/2000	283
Balance c/fwd	£167

However, all the income would have been distributed so that this balance is useless.

Trustees should expect there to be a mismatch between the undistributed income and the tax pool under *section 687* after only a few years.

6.34   The repeal of the investment income surcharge in 1984 had a considerable effect upon the use of the tax pool in an old accumulating settlement. Such a settlement will inevitably have a large tax pool. In 2000/01 the single person's personal allowance is £4,385 and the first £28,400 of taxable income is charged at 10%, 20% or 22%. Therefore, apart from ensuring that infant beneficiaries have £4,385 gross each, there is an incentive, in the form of a 12% tax recovery, to top up all beneficiaries' incomes by trust distributions to say £32,750 gross if this does not strip the tax pool to the point of producing a *section 687* assessment. Some tax reliefs and allowances are now at a rate of only 10% (for 2000/01). This only slightly reduces the possibility of tax planning by raiding the tax pool. Distribution to infant beneficiaries is not normal if the settlement is parental as this would bring *ICTA 1988, s 660B* into play. Perhaps there will be cases where the parent has losses and would welcome a tax recovery by virtue of *section 660B*. However, this is outside the authors' experience. When planning distributions, account will be taken of the rules which apply after 5 April 1999. These could point to a more gradual use of any existing tax pool.

6.35 Stripping the tax pool is important in the years before an accumulation and maintenance settlement ceases to be such. The tax pool exists only so long as *section 687* applies to payments made by trustees and as the changeover from an accumulation and maintenance settlement to a life interest settlement or a series of absolute interests takes the trustees out of *section 687*, the tax pool will then disappear and with it the possibility of recovering the 12% etc.

6.36 The disappearance of the tax pool is not gradual. If the trust is within *sections 686* and *687*, the tax pool is there. Once it ceases to be within those sections (as for instance an accumulation and maintenance settlement once all beneficiaries are over 25), there is no tax pool. One oddity is that if there are several beneficiaries of an accumulation and maintenance settlement, the fact that one of them attains 25 does not reduce the tax pool. Had there been separate settlements, one for each beneficiary, the total of the tax pools would have been less.

6.37 For *section 687* to apply there are only two tests.

(*a*) Is the payment made by trustees in the exercise of a discretion?

(*b*) Is the sum income of the recipient for tax purposes?

Trustees generally have a power to advance capital and any such advancement would satisfy the first test. The Inland Revenue may then consider the possibility of the money being the income of the beneficiary. The cases which are of general application are *Brodie's Trustees v CIR, KB 1933, 17 TC 432* and *Cunard's Trustees v CIR, CA 1945, 27 TC 122*. In both cases there was a 'topping up' provision which could be used for the maintenance of the usual standard of living of the beneficiary. Therefore, trust capital was converted into income.

The case of *Stevenson v Wishart and Others (Levy's Trustees) CA, [1987] STC 266* concerned a discretionary settlement. The trustees had the usual dispositive powers. They gave away the entire income of the trust to charity for a short period of years. They then appointed capital to a lady aged over 90. In this way they expended £109,000 of capital on her medical expenses and nursing home fees. Anybody with capital might reasonably meet such expenses from it so that, although used for the maintenance of the beneficiary, the money was not income in her hands. Therefore, there was no *section 687* assessment upon the trustees.

The provisions of the trust instrument in *Brodie* and *Cunard* did not permit the use of capital save as a support for income. Therefore *section 687* is much less a danger to trustees than was thought to be the case before *Stevenson*. Indeed, the *Stevenson v Wishart* principle might be useful in a case where trustees want to avoid the adverse impact of the new tax regime for dividends on distributions to a higher rate beneficiary, where

6.37 *Income Tax*

there is no available tax pool. They could accumulate the dividend income for several years and then, using powers in the trust deed, appoint the accumulated income as capital to the beneficiary. Provided the circumstances are not such that the Inland Revenue could legitimately treat the distribution as income in the hands of the beneficiary, such a strategy should be effective.

There have been cases where employees benefited from capital settled for them. If the trustees distribute surplus capital to beneficiaries who can only receive it because of their employment, it becomes income in their hands, i.e. it forms part of the emoluments of their employment (*Brumby v Milner, HL [1976] STC 534*). Any reader referring to this case should bear in mind that *ICTA 1988, ss 686, 687* originated in the Finance Act 1973 and that the events in *Brumby v Milner* took place earlier. The winding up of settlements for employees can easily produce double taxation, i.e. the realisation of investments gives rise to a capital gains tax charge and the distribution of the net proceeds is received as income and is thus taxable under *section 687*.

Where income is used to fund payments which will be emoluments taxable under Schedule E, concession A68 provides for the tax deducted to be set against the tax pool. This prevents double taxation for income tax.

The Trust and Estate Tax Return Guide for 1999/2000 deals on page 21 in discussing boxes 14.1 to 14.15 with payments made on the exercise of the trustees' discretion which were income of a beneficiary. It says 'In general, payments out of trust capital or accumulated income are not to be regarded as the income of a beneficiary, irrespective of the purposes for which they are made and should not therefore be included'. The official view is that where a payment is made out of capital or accumulations it can only be income in the hands of the beneficiary if it is a 'topping up' payment as in *Brodie* and *Cunard* or if it is paid as an annuity. Traditionally a relaxed view is taken as to when accumulation takes place. Normally this would be left for the trustees to decide. Therefore, if the trustees carried forward undistributed income for a year or two without accumulating it, there should be no argument: in practice, however, especially under self-assessment, they are likely to make a decision in the autumn following the end of the year of assessment. This official view is at odds with the *Trustee Act 1925, s 31(2)* (see Appendix E) which contemplates accumulations being drawn down as income. It is based on the characterisation of the money in the hands of the trustees although *section 687* refers to its character in the hands of the recipient ('income of the person to whom it is paid'). The *Finance (No 2) Act 1997* severely restricts the use which companies can make of franked investment income which they receive. This extends to cases where dividends received by discretionary settlements are used to fund distributions to companies (*section 27* introducing a new *section 687A*). The new section operates on and from 2 July 1997. In practice the most likely situation which is affected is one where trustees wish to benefit a charitable company.

Payments to beneficiaries of accumulation and maintenance settlements where ICTA 1988, s 687 does not apply

6.38 Payments of income to beneficiaries of accumulation and maintenance settlements (rather than payments on their behalves) must be to adult beneficiaries. In general they will be beneficiaries entitled to the income of their share or putative share by reason of attainment of the age of 18 or some higher age specified in the trust instrument. The beneficiary's statutory income will depend upon his entitlement to capital. This is a 'see through' situation and the tax voucher given to the beneficiary should show special types of income separately e.g. income with foreign tax deducted or interest on a National Savings Bank account. Indeed, the current versions of forms R185 (Non-discretionary trust) and R185 (Estate Income) show separately different classes of trust income, less expenses, according as there is untaxed income, Schedule F ordinary rate income (e.g. UK dividends), other non-repayable taxed income (e.g. stock dividends), lower rate income (e.g. bank or building society interest), basic rate income (e.g. rents) and foreign income where UK tax at less than basic rate has been deducted.

6.39 Advancements of capital to adult beneficiaries with a vested interest in income may be made without income tax consequences. Payment over of accumulations upon majority, etc., is a capital payment (*Stanley v CIR, CA 1944, 26 TC 12*).

Payments to or for the beneficiaries of discretionary settlements

6.40 As has been explained in 6.21 and 6.24 above, trustees of discretionary settlements are within the scope of *ICTA 1988, ss 686, 687*. Where an income payment is made, the principles explained in 6.27 to 6.37 above apply with the proviso that the tax pool cannot disappear as in 6.35 and 6.36. This is because the discretionary settlement never changes into another type of settlement merely by the effluxion of time as does an accumulation and maintenance settlement. So long as payments can be made at discretion, *sections 686* and *687* will apply. Therefore the tax pool continues as long as the discretionary trust lasts, except in relation to dividend income up to and including 1998/99 where it will be gradually drawn down (see 6.32).

6.41 When payments are made by the trustees of a discretionary settlement, the question whether they constitute income in the hands of the recipient is highly relevant (see 6.37 above).

Payments to beneficiaries of fixed interest trusts

6.42 Where there is a vested interest in income the beneficiary will either be a life tenant or an annuitant. In both cases the payment of

6.43 *Income Tax*

income is nearly always quite straightforward. The trustee pays over the appropriate income and gives a tax voucher for the year showing the gross income, tax at basic or lower rate (or, from 1999/2000, the 10% rate) and the net sum to which the beneficiary is entitled. The payment of income to a life tenant may be in the year following the year of receipt. The details on the voucher will be those of the year of receipt. This is a transparent situation. The income of the trustee is not his; it is the income of the beneficiary, subject only to necessary outgoings. This transparency does not mean that capital sums which are deemed to be income of the trustees become income of the income beneficiary. Therefore, premiums assessed under Schedule A, charges under the accrued income scheme, etc., although income of the trustees in the fiscal sense, do not become income of the life tenant, etc. The transparency extends to foreign beneficiaries where there is income which is exempt to them. So the trustees will arrange for interest on exempt gilts (FOTRA) to be received gross and they will pay this over to the non-resident without paying or deducting tax.

6.43 An annuitant receives his annuity under deduction of tax. So far as the trustees are concerned, the annuity is a charge on income, or, if income is insufficient, on capital. Tax is deducted under *ICTA 1988, s 348* to the extent that the annuity is out of income. *ICTA 1988, s 349* applies to the extent that it is not out of income. In a case where, in 1998/99, the only income received by the trustees was dividend or interest, they would have deducted tax at 23% on paying the annuity. The dividend or interest will have suffered 20% tax and the 3% difference would be assessable directly on the trustees. This remains the position for an annuity paid out of interest during 1999/2000 and future years. However, there is on the face of it a problem with dividend income. FICO have confirmed that the trustees are given credit for the 10% non-repayable tax credit, though there will of course be an additional 12% (or, for 1999/2000, 13%) liability in the trust.

6.44 In trusts created by wills, it is not uncommon to see a 'top up' clause. This is a clause requiring the trustees to make payments out of capital if income is inadequate. Often the words in the trust instrument are imprecise, perhaps saying no more than that capital may be paid to a beneficiary if income is not sufficient for her to maintain her normal standard of living. This brings into question the character of the payment. This has already received attention (see 6.37 above).

6.45 It is common to see a right to occupy a property. The occupation itself has no income tax consequences, at least with UK trusts, i.e. there is no assessment of a notional income. Payments of rates and outgoings by the trustees are income of the beneficiary and the sums paid out are net sums. The gross equivalent will form part of the beneficiary's income.

6.46 Payments to beneficiaries with less than a vested interest have already been touched upon and the treatment of management expenses has been considered in 6.2 above.

Taxation of land transactions

6.47 Premiums on leases for no more than 50 years can be assessed to income tax. The definition is in *ICTA 1988, s 24(1)(3)* and the charge is made by *ICTA 1988, s 34*, albeit only at basic rate (even where the premium is received by trustees of an accumulation or discretionary trust).

In a case where a capital sum is received on selling or developing land, there can be an assessment to income tax under Case VI of Schedule D. The charging section is *ICTA 1988, s 776*. Section 776(2)(ii) attacks arrangements or schemes which enable gains to be realised by an indirect method. The section is aimed at traders in property who regularly managed to avoid the appearance of trading in the years before the introduction of capital gains tax. There being no tax on capital gains, if they could avoid income tax, they escaped tax altogether. The leading case for trustees is *Page v Lowther, CA [1983] STC 799*. In that case, trustees owned 2.6 acres in Kensington. They granted a building lease to a developer who was to clear the site and erect 28 houses, 33 flats, garages etc. As these were sold, a proportion of the proceeds was payable to the trustees. In this way the trustees received over £1 million. This transaction was not trading, nor were the trustees in the habit of trading. They were simply realising a valuable property in the most rewarding manner. They were caught by the section. Note that, because the proceeds of sale are trust capital, the income tax charge (even in a discretionary or accumulation trust) can only be at 22% (23% for 1999/2000): this may, subject to taper relief in future, produce a better net result than a chargeable gain taxed at 34%. That is, there could be circumstances when taxpayer trustees want to pray in aid the anti-avoidance section 776!

Miscellaneous

6.48 In the past, trustees would submit the trust instrument to the Inland Revenue where a file had to be opened for a new settlement. The Revenue would respond with a note of their view as to the way in which the settlement would be taxed. Unfortunately, this practice has now been abandoned (see Inland Revenue Press Release of 19 December 1990 in Appendix A).

6.49 As a matter of practice, the Inland Revenue select one trustee and direct assessments to him. This follows on from their old practice of assessing the precedent trustee. Usually they choose the first-named in the trust instrument. This has statutory backing now. [*FA 1989, s 151*]. The trustee selected will be one of the 'relevant trustees' (see 5.18 above).

6.50 On 20 January 1997 the Inland Revenue issued a Press Release to ensure that where there is a bare trust, the trustees know that they should not complete a self-assessment return. They should give details of

6.51 *Income Tax*

the income to the beneficiary for him to report. More recently we have been told that bare trustees can self-assess. Then their figures are incorporated in their principal's return. They must only self-assess income, however; capital gains must be reported by the principal.

6.51 The manner in which expenses affect the calculation of the income of beneficiaries has already been explained. Income paid to the beneficiaries will be marshalled in the way which gives them the greatest benefit, i.e. the first sums which reach them are from basic rate tax which could be repaid, then lower rate repayable tax, non-repayable basic rate and, finally, non-repayable lower rate. Beneficiaries will want their tax vouchers early in the tax year because many of them will not want to self-assess. They will wish to file their returns on or before 30 September and let the Revenue compute their tax liability.

Chapter 7

Capital Gains Tax

Occasions of charge

7.1 The charge to CGT is based on disposals and deemed disposals by persons resident or ordinarily resident in the UK in any part of the tax year in which the disposal or deemed disposal takes place. [*TCGA 1992, s 2(1)*]. Extra-statutory Concession D2 (amended following *FA 1998*), can provide relief from the strict statutory rule where the disposal is made during the tax year in which, but before, a person becomes a new UK resident or in which, but after, a person ceases to be UK resident: see further 19.3 below. See Chapter 19 generally for residence and ordinary residence.

7.2 The normal dealings of trustees will produce disposals with gains taxable in the normal way.

Termination of a life interest

7.3 The termination of a life interest is a deemed disposal if it results from a death or if the consequence is that a beneficiary becomes absolutely entitled against the trustees. Therefore, if there is no death and the property continues settled, there is no occasion of charge. Termination can also occur when an original life tenant buys out the remainderman and so becomes absolutely entitled to the settled property. In such a case there is a charge on the trustees under *section 71(1)* and market value will be substituted for the consideration which would, in any case, have gone to the remainderman. The remainderman is not chargeable. There is no charge under *section 76(2)*. A similar situation emerges if the remainderman buys out the life tenant. The identification of assets subject to an interest in possession is explained in SPD10 as amended (see Appendix A).

7.4 Termination on death is in principle a no gain/no loss situation. Normally the base values of those assets which supported the life interest are changed to the market value at the date of death. If the life interest is in part of a fund, then this provision applies to an appropriate part. Where the property reverts to the settlor, there is no chargeable gain but the deemed disposal is at a value such as to ensure neither a gain nor a loss arises to the trustees (i.e. not at market value). [*TCGA 1992, ss 71–73*].

7.5 Capital Gains Tax

Example

Two sisters, Ann and Kate, are life tenants of a single block of shares with a base value of £50,000. Ann dies when the market value is £100,000. The trustees' base value alters as follows.

	£
Old base value of one half (Kate's share)	25,000
Base value of one half on death of Ann	50,000
Revised base value of holding	£75,000

What happens is that the base value of each individual holding alters because the proportion attributable to the life interest of the deceased life tenant is updated. [*TCGA 1992, s 72(1)*].

There are interests in possession which are not life interests within the definition in *TCGA 1992, s 72*. For instance a beneficiary might have an interest in the income which terminates on his reaching a particular age. The death of such a beneficiary has been brought into line with the death of a beneficiary having a life interest by *FA 1996, 39 Sch 5* which amends *TCGA 1992, ss 72* and *73*. Before this amendment the same situation was achieved by ESC D43 published in February 1993. Of course if the trustees had losses they would not have invoked the concession. However, legislation is generally preferable to a concession.

Sometimes the trust instrument requires assets to be appropriated to a capital beneficiary on the death of one of two life tenants. Therefore, until the appropriation is made it is not known what is the 'corresponding part' mentioned in *TCGA 1992, s 72(1)(a)*. In such a case the base value of each individual holding is not altered as in the Ann and Kate illustration above. Instead it is the base value of the appropriated assets which alters. So, for instance, if trustees had holdings of equal value in two companies and the life tenant of one half of the settlement died, given a power of appropriation, they could appropriate one holding. Only that holding's base value would change. See Inland Revenue Manual CG 37530–37532.

7.5 Where trust assets were received subject to hold-over relief, the held over gain is brought into charge on the death of the life tenant. [*TCGA 1992, s 74*]. If possible, the trustees will hold over this amount a second time under either *section 260* or *section 165*: it is only where a surviving spouse inherits non-business assets that a further hold-over claim will not be possible. Note that if the deceased was UK domiciled for inheritance tax purposes but the survivor was not, there will be a chargeable transfer enabling a *section 260* election. [*IHTA 1984, s 18(2)*]. The base value will then be the value at death reduced by the amount held over. If hold-over is not possible, the trustees may still benefit from:

(i) re-basing. Effectively this means that there is no charge under *section 74* if the gain was held over prior to 1 April 1982; or

(ii) the half-gain rule (see 7.23 below).

Capital Gains Tax **7.8**

The clawback on death is a reasonable precaution so far as the Revenue are concerned. Their worry would be the use of elderly people of little means as life tenants purely so as to wash out a capital gain.

See Inland Revenue Manual CG 33553 for the hold-over of a clawed-back gain.

Absolute entitlement

7.6 When a person becomes absolutely entitled to settled property as against the trustees (other than on the death of a life tenant: *TCGA 1992, s 73(1)(a)*, there is a charge to CGT on the deemed disposal. This will normally be the case where a life interest comes to an end without there being another life tenant. It will also take place where a contingent interest vests. For instance, an accumulation and maintenance settlement may provide for a child to take his share of capital on reaching the age of 25, although in such a case it is to be hoped that hold-over would still be available (see 7.15(c), 7.17 below). The charge is calculated as if the disposal had been at market value at the date when the beneficiary became absolutely entitled. [*TCGA 1992, s 71(1)*]. (See also 7.3 above).

Where two or more beneficiaries become absolutely entitled to settled property at the same moment, this can affect the valuation. For instance, there might be unquoted shares comprising 60% of a company's capital and they might be split between two beneficiaries. The valuation required is of 60%. See Inland Revenue Manual CG 37370.

A recent case related to the date when beneficiaries became absolutely entitled as against the trustee. There had been a class gift so that settled property was held for such of the settlor's children as might attain the age of 21. Therefore, the answer to the question when the class closed (i.e. when no further children could be added) would determine when the children became absolutely entitled. The settlor was paralysed from the chest down as a result of an accident in 1964. He died in 1990. The Inland Revenue took the view that the settlor's incapacity was not relevant in determining the beneficial interests in the settlement. Therefore the children did not become absolutely entitled until 1990. The court found in favour of the Inland Revenue *(Figg v Clarke, Ch D 1996, [1997] STC 247)*.

7.7 The trustees often continue to hold an asset of this sort pending transfer and then they do so as bare trustees. The subsequent transfer to the beneficiary is a non-event for CGT. Similarly, a transfer directed by the beneficiary is treated as a transfer by him. [*TCGA 1992, s 60*].

7.8 Sometimes, the trustees will be able to hold over a gain when a beneficiary becomes beneficially entitled (see 7.10 *et seq.* below). If this is impossible, then they may be able to use the relief available on disposing of an asset on which the settlor claimed hold-over relief (see

7.8 Capital Gains Tax

7.23 below). Where hold-over is available to the trustees, they must be protected against the recapture of the relief should the beneficiary become non-resident within the six years following the year of his acquisition (see 5.13 above). It is possible for some of the assets to be left with the trustees as security. The trustees then hold those assets as bare trustees. [*TCGA 1992, s 60(2)*].

The rule that the moment when a person becomes absolutely entitled is the occasion of a deemed disposal is intended, amongst other things, to ensure that all beneficiaries are treated equally. The actual date of transfer by the trustees is then irrelevant.

There are cases on the subject of what is meant by becoming absolutely entitled as against the trustees and the reader may find help in: *Hoare Trustees v Gardner, Ch D [1978] STC 89; Roome and Denne v Edwards, HL [1981] STC 96; Bond v Pickford, CA [1983] STC 517* and *Swires v Renton, Ch D [1991] STC 490*. In *Crowe v Appleby, Ch D [1975] STC 502* freehold property was held by trustees of a Will in equal undivided shares. While one of the shares had vested absolutely, the remaining shares were held in trust for the children of the deceased for their lifetimes. When one of the children died so that her share vested absolutely in her children, the Court of Appeal held that the children had not become absolutely entitled against the trustees, since there were still shares in the property held in trust. Note that absolute entitlement includes a case where a person would be so entitled but for being under the age of 18 or otherwise under a disability. [*TCGA 1992, s 71(3)*]. The definition of 'absolutely entitled' in *TCGA 1992, s 60(2)* shows that the right to the assets should only be subject to expenses, taxes and other outgoings. A power of appointment is not, of itself, a right to the assets. It may become one when exercised.

In *CIR v Matthew's Exors CS, [1984] STC 386* trustees allocated an area of land with development potential equally among the twelve charities which were the beneficiaries. They then entered into a contract for the sale of the land as agents for the beneficiaries. They told the charities later. It was held that the allocation of the land was of no effect and that the land was not held on trust for the beneficiaries absolutely as against the trustees.

See also Inland Revenue Statement of Practice SP7/84, reproduced in Appendix A, for the Revenue view as to when the exercise of a power of appointment or advancement falls within the deemed disposal rules of *TCGA 1992, s 71*.

Where a beneficiary becomes absolutely entitled to settled property on or before 15 June 1999 and there are unusable losses, they are transferred to him if they have arisen on:

(*a*) the assets to which he has become entitled or
(*b*) the assets in which his share of the settlement was previously invested. [*TCGA 1992, s 71(2)*]. See Inland Revenue Manual CG 37200–37201.

Capital Gains Tax **7.9**

This general rule was changed by *FA 1999, s 75* with effect from 16 June 1999, following perceived abuse 'on a very significant scale' (according to Inland Revenue Press Release, 16 June 1999) of the rule in *section 71(2)*. Now, upon a beneficiary becoming entitled absolutely to an asset standing at a loss, which cannot be offset by the trustees against past trust gains, the loss is available to the beneficiary only for offset against a subsequent gain arising to him on disposing of that asset or, if the asset is land, on disposing of that asset or any asset derived from it. There is therefore now no longer the ability to offset trust losses generally under *section 71(2)* against other capital gains which may arise to the beneficiary in that or a future tax year.

The severe restriction by *FA 1999* of the rule under *section 71(2)*, whereby losses within a trust can be inherited by a beneficiary upon receiving an advance of capital, encouraged the development of an arrangement to use the trustees' losses. A person would transfer under hold-over relief to a trust business assets with a large inherent gain, having acquired the right to become a beneficiary. The trustees would then realise the assets triggering the gain which they would offset against their own losses. There would subsequently be an advance of capital out of the trust to the transferor as a beneficiary. Now, under new *TCGA 1992, s 79A* (inserted by *FA 2000 s 93*) there is a restriction of the set-off of trustees' losses against capital gains arising on the disposal by trustees of assets transferred to them, in circumstances where gains arising on that transfer have been deferred under a hold-over claim. The restriction applies where the transferor of the asset or any connected person has purchased an interest in the trust or entered into any arrangement to purchase such an interest. The new rule applies for trust gains arising on or after 21 March 2000.

Deeds of variation

7.9 Deeds of variation are effective for capital gains tax where, within two years of an individual's death, dispositions of his property effected by will or intestacy are varied or a benefit is disclaimed. There has to be a written deed of variation and an election to the Board (generally within six months of the date of the deed). The variation is then treated as if it had been made by the deceased in his will. This is limited, see paragraph 4.16 above [*TCGA 1992, s 62(6)(7)*].

There remains a sword of Damocles hanging over deeds of variation for inheritance tax (as witness the abortive attempt to repeal *IHTA 1984, s 142* in the Finance Bill 1989 and the expressed intentions of repeal of the November 1994 Labour Party document 'Tackling Tax Abuse – Tackling Unemployment'). There have been no visible signs of disquiet about these deeds for capital gains tax, no doubt because the relief is so limited and does not apply for wider capital gains tax purposes.

It would seem obvious that these deeds should be used to roll gains away to exempt or low rate taxpayers.

7.9 Capital Gains Tax

However, an attempt to re-route a gift to take advantage for capital gains tax purposes of the deceased's non-resident status failed in *Marshall v Kerr HL [1994] STC 638*.

The deceased testator died in 1977 resident and domiciled in Jersey. His daughter, Mrs Kerr, was resident and domiciled in England. In 1978 she settled the half of the estate to which she was entitled by a deed of variation. As the law was understood at the time, this caused the testator to be deemed to be the settlor so that the result was a Jersey settlement by a Jersey settlor. This view was challenged. In June 1994 the House of Lords found Mrs Kerr to be the settlor for the purposes of *FA 1981, s 80* (now *TCGA 1992, s 87*) so that the settlement turned out to be one made by a UK resident, etc. Two tacit but unjustified assumptions had been made by the courts below: first, that Mrs Kerr could settle the assets concerned (whereas during the administration she had only the right to have the estate duly administered); secondly, that the assets were those which the testator was deemed to dispose of on his death (while the executors might themselves acquire and dispose of assets during the administration). This analysis, however impeccable as legal theory, runs counter to the approach generally taken to deeming provisions, which is to follow them through to their inevitable consequences and corollaries. *Marshall v Kerr* may therefore affect the interpretation of other deeming provisions in the tax statutes. Interestingly, it was in the High Court that, to the authors at least, the most straightforward reason was given as to why the taxpayers had to fail. *TCGA 1992, s 62(6)(b)* states expressly that where a valid election is made and notice is duly given: 'this section shall apply as if the variation had been effected by the deceased'. In other words, *section 62* leaves untouched the rest of the capital gains tax regime which in the case of settlements depend on who was the settlor, (*section 77* in the case of a UK resident settlement and *sections 86* and *87* for a non-resident settlement). In the case of a UK resident settlement this means that, if the original beneficiary varies his or her entitlement into a trust under which he or his spouse can benefit, the gains of the trustees will be assessed on the original beneficiary settlor. By contrast, the deeming provisions for inheritance tax purposes in *IHTA 1984 s 142(1)* state that: 'this Act shall apply as if the variation had been effected by the deceased'. That means, of course, that in considering the application of the reservation of benefit provisions in *FA 1986, s 102* and *Sch 20*, the disposition is treated as having been made by the testator and not by the beneficiary.

Where property is held by the personal representatives on discretionary trusts, they may appoint assets to a beneficiary within two years of the death. *IHTA 1984, s 144* prevents that being an occasion of charge for inheritance tax. There is no equivalent provision for capital gains tax so that, the beneficiary having become absolutely entitled as against the estate [*TCGA 1992, s 71*] there is an occasion of charge. However, there is a distinction between the case where, on the one hand, the personal representatives assent the asset or assets concerned to the trustees who then make the appointment and, on the other, there is an appointment by

Capital Gains Tax **7.11**

the trustees before the assets have been assented to them. Only in the former case is there a capital gains tax disposal. In the latter, the trustees being entitled at that point only to the chose in action which every beneficiary under a Will acquires at date of death, the effect of the appointment is simply to declare the trustees as bare trustees for the beneficiary. When the assent takes place there is no disposal and the acquisition date and cost of the beneficiary is read back to the date of death in the normal way under *TCGA 1992, s 62(4)*.

Hold-over relief

7.10 The changes to hold-over relief in *FA 1989*, effective for disposals after 13 March 1989, have a profound effect upon trustees.

7.11 So far as business property is concerned, hold-over relief continues. The settlor can settle this type of property and hold over the gain. If retirement relief is available, this is deducted before calculating the gain to be held over. [*TCGA 1992, s 165(4)(6), 7 Sch*]. Business property is defined in similar terms to property which qualifies for retirement relief, so that the terms will be familiar:

(i) an asset or an interest in an asset used in a trade etc. carried on by the transferor or his personal company etc.;

(ii) shares etc. in an unlisted trading company etc.;

(iii) shares etc. in a listed company etc. which is the transferor's personal company etc.

[*TCGA 1992, s 165(2)*].

As from 9 November 1999, it is no longer possible to hold over a gain on shares or securities which are transferred to a company. This change is effected by *FA 2000, s 90* amending *TCGA 1992, s 165(3)*.

Business assets intended to be used by a life tenant would not normally be settled. This is because roll-over relief [*TCGA 1992, s 152*] would not be available upon their replacement. That relief requires the assets and the trade to be in the same proprietorship.

The word 'etc.' is added to the word 'trade' to signify that professions, vocations, woodlands and agriculture are included, and to 'personal company' and 'unlisted trading company' to indicate that group structures are acceptable. It is added to 'shares' to signify that securities also qualify. 'Listed' includes the AIM. (Note this is not the same treatment for IHT, see 14.6). A personal company is one where not less than 5% of the votes are exercisable by the individual.

Agriculture is defined by reference to the inheritance tax definition (see *TCGA 1992, 7 Sch (1)(a)*). It is only the definition which is borrowed in this way and provisions such as those which prescribe a minimum period

63

7.12 *Capital Gains Tax*

of ownership in order to qualify for the inheritance tax relief are not borrowed for the hold-over relief.

[*TCGA 1992, s 165, 7 Sch*].

As family trusts are not commonly concerned with listed companies whether on the AIM or not, the question as to whether the company is a personal company or not will rarely have to be answered except in the unusual case where assets used in a 'personal company' are transferred. The upshot is that the settlement of shares in a family company will usually be possible with the benefit of hold-over relief.

7.12 So far as transfers by trustees are concerned, a similar result is achieved by *TCGA 1992, 7 Sch 2*. The shareholding test is that the trustees have 25% of the votes if the company is listed (including the AIM). There is no minimum holding requirement if the company is not quoted.

7.13 Where a company is only partially a trading company, partial hold-over is possible on a transfer of shares (see *TCGA 1992, 7 Sch 7*). This is a repeat of the restriction on retirement relief. One looks at the chargeable assets of the company at the time of the disposal of the shares. The fraction which qualifies for hold-over is:

$$\frac{\text{Company's chargeable business assets}}{\text{Company's chargeable assets}}$$

7.14 Where other (i.e. non-business) assets are transferred *in specie* there can still be hold-over where the gift is of a work of art or other heritage asset which is:

(*a*) the subject of a private treaty sale to an approved museum or other body; or

(*b*) accepted by the Inland Revenue in lieu of tax; or

(*c*) the subject of a conditionally exempt transfer for inheritance tax purposes (including a gift to a maintenance fund for an historic building).

[*TCGA 1992, s 258*].

7.15 More important in the context of family trusts is the fact that assets may also be transferred in and out of trusts subject to hold-over in the following cases:

(*a*) the disposal is also a chargeable transfer for inheritance tax purposes or would be if not covered by the annual £3,000 exemption. Potentially exempt transfers which fail by reason of the donor's premature death do not qualify for this hold-over relief;

(*b*) the disposal is a deemed chargeable transfer by reason of the property leaving a discretionary settlement. The words of the provision are not totally clear but the debates on the Finance Bill 1989 and correspondence with the Inland Revenue confirm the intention. When a discretionary legacy in a will is closed out within the two-year period (i.e. so as to use *IHTA 1984, s 144*) this is not a deemed chargeable transfer and this form of hold-over relief is not available in such a case. There can be technical arguments where the personal representatives are also trustees of the will. The personal representatives cannot exercise the discretions which will come to them as trustees until they are trustees. A well drafted will will now allow the trustees to make an appointment before residue has been ascertained (or even before application has been made for probate). The likelihood is that the appointment will be exercised shortly after the death, before there has been time for a chargeable gain arising on assets vesting absolutely, so that in a case where there is a surviving spouse the appointment and the Inland Revenue Account can be submitted at the same time, obviating the need to pay over inheritance tax and then reclaim it subsequently.

The CIOT and the Inland Revenue have corresponded on this subject (see *Taxation Practitioner* of September 1995). The official view is that discretionary trustees can exercise their power of appointment at any time but that there is no capital gains tax effect if this occurs before there is an assent to the trustees (see 7.10 above).

(c) the disposal is by the trustees of an accumulation and maintenance trust when a beneficiary attains the age of 25 (or other lower specified age) (but see 7.17 below).

Transfers of relevant business property and agricultural property (as defined for inheritance tax) can attract 100% business relief. Where the transfer would be a chargeable transfer in the ordinary way it is still regarded as a chargeable transfer (but no tax is payable). This means that hold-over under *section 260* is available. There will be cases where this gives a better position than that under *TCGA 1992, s 165*. This is because there can be non-business chargeable assets which restrict *section 165* but not *section 260*. Where both sections could apply *section 260* has precedence. [*TCGA 1992, s 165(3)(d)*].

Trustees of discretionary settlements must have regard to the fact that once the discretion has gone, so has the power to hold over gains under *TCGA 1992, s 260*. This must be taken into account when considering an appointment of capital to a sub-trust. [*TCGA 1992, s 260(2)(a)(d)*].

FA 2000, s 92 has counteracted the so-called 'flip-flop' scheme, with effect from 21 March 2000. This scheme was intended to circumvent the settlor-interested trust rules under *TCGA 1992, s 77* by means of two trusts, the first of which would borrow cash commercially against the security of an asset (typically shares in a private company) which was to be sold at a substantial gain. Some 75% of the funds would be transferred by the trustees to the second trust which would be settlor-interested. The settlor and spouse would then be excluded from benefit

7.16 *Capital Gains Tax*

under the first trust, so that when the sale was made the gain would not be assessed on the settlor and any tax on the trustees (which used to be at 23%, but now 34%) would be paid out of the proceeds of sale, which would also enable repayment of the bank loan. Now, if there is a transfer by trustees of funds to another person at a time when the trustees are in debt and any borrowed money is not used wholly for normal trust purposes, there will be a disposal and reacquisition of the settled property at that time *(TCGA 1992, s 76B* and *Sch 4B)*. The increase in the rate of capital gains tax to 34% effected by *FA 1998* made these schemes less attractive for UK trusts; however, they have continued to be used with offshore trusts, which are also made ineffective by *FA 2000*.

7.16 Because we now have two types of hold-over relief for disposals to and from trustees (i.e. *section 165* for business assets and *section 260* for any chargeable transfer) discretionary settlements are now more interesting to estate planners. The nil rate band settlement has been with us for some time and, if annual exemptions for inheritance tax are available, this can be a settlement of £237,000 or £240,000. However, business or agricultural property with 100% BPR or APR is even more interesting.

Because trustees can themselves make disposals with hold-over, a conduit effect can occur, assets being put into a discretionary settlement and, later, being passed to beneficiaries. This point is, of course, subject to general anti-avoidance principles.

7.17 There can be problems in connection with hold-over and accumulation and maintenance settlements. Hold-over of the gain on a non-business asset is not available if the beneficiary already has a life interest. This is because the disposal has to be one which 'by virtue of *subsection (4)* of *section 71* of *IHTA 1984* does not constitute an occasion on which inheritance tax is chargeable under that section'. [*TCGA 1992, s 260(2)(d)*]. When a beneficiary becomes a life tenant by reason of attaining 18 years there is neither disposal nor chargeable transfer. If he then becomes entitled to the capital at age 25 that is a disposal but not one which is within *IHTA 1984, s 71(4)*. Apart from this anomaly there is yet another problem for trustees of accumulation and maintenance settlements whose beneficiaries become entitled to their share without hold-over being available. That is because it is extremely likely that the original transfer to the settlement did qualify for hold-over. Therefore there will be tax on the gain accruing during the trusteeship and also on the original hold-over. The half-gain rule (see 7.23 below) may apply. In such a case the life tenant who is not yet 25 might be encouraged to resettle his interest. This would be done by a settlement in which the trustees joined and which ensured that the interest in possession did not emerge until the age of 25. A rather unfortunate case is that of *Begg-McBrearty v Stilwell (Trustee of the G E Coke Settlement) [1996] STC 413*. A discretionary settlement was made in February 1959, when the age of majority was 21. The trustees made an appointment in favour of an infant beneficiary in 1975, contingent upon her attaining 21. When the age of majority was reduced to 18, in 1969, documents already in existence were to be read under the old rule, so the trustees thought that, having a 1959 settlement, *Trustee Act 1925, s 31* would not give a life interest at age 18. However, the court took the view that the appointment of 1975, being post-1969 did give a life interest at the earlier age. Therefore, in this case, hold-over would not have been possible. As a matter of interest, the position in Scotland may be different. Following this case Statement of Practice E8 (age of majority) was withdrawn.

7.18 The usual rules for making a hold-over election prevail, now on Helpsheet IR 295. Note the need to specify whether the claim is made under section 165 or under section 260.

7.19 There are anti-avoidance provisions to deny hold-over relief to transfers to non-residents [*TCGA 1992, ss 166, 261*] and foreign-controlled companies. [*TCGA 1992, s 167*].

7.20 In addition, any previously held over gains will crystallise if donees migrate from the UK or cease to be liable to UK tax as a result of becoming dual resident for the purposes of a double tax treaty, in either case within six years after the end of the year of assessment in which the transfer under hold-over took place. See 5.13 and 5.14 above and 21.10 and 21.11 below. [*TCGA 1992, ss 80, 83, 168, 288(1)*].

7.21 In certain cases where a disposal does bear capital gains tax because it is not eligible for hold-over, the tax may be paid by equal instalments over ten years. There is no interest exemption, i.e. interest accrues on the unpaid tax and the interest to date must be added to each instalment. The instalment cases are where the asset is:

(*a*) land (or an interest in land);

(*b*) a controlling shareholding;

(*c*) other shares not listed nor dealt in on the AIM.

[*TCGA 1992, s 281*].

7.22 The avowed intention of the restrictions on hold-over explained above was to ensure that gifts were not, in effect, exempted from both capital taxes by being PETs and disposals sheltered by hold-overs at the same time. Unfortunately, a form of double taxation now arises. It is possible to make a gift which is not subject to hold-over and so capital gains tax is paid; the donor does not pay inheritance tax at the time (perhaps it is a potentially exempt transfer), but because of the donor's premature death (within seven years) the donee does have to pay that tax. The capital gains tax will reduce the donor's estate and to that extent there will be no double counting. However, the total tax which is related to the one gift can be substantial. Perhaps this will encourage the making of gifts where the donee pays the capital gains tax. This has the effect of reducing the amount of the chargeable transfer for inheritance tax (see *IHTA 1984, s 165*).

7.23   Capital Gains Tax

Disposal following earlier hold-over (the half-gain rule)

7.23   Where trustees have received an asset subject to a hold-over by the settlor a special relief may be available. To qualify:

(a)   the trustees must have acquired the asset after 31 March 1982,

(b)   the settlor must have acquired the asset before 31 March 1982,

(c)   the settlor must have given the asset to the trustees before 6 April 1988, subject to a hold-over, and

(d)   the trustees' disposal must be after 5 April 1988.

The relief is a restriction of the deduction from the base value by reason of the hold-over. The deduction is reduced to one half. The relief must be claimed within two years of the end of the fiscal year of disposal. Extensions can be requested.

[*TCGA 1992, 4 Sch 1, 2, 9*].

Example

On 1 March 1982, a settlor acquired shares for £50,000. These were settled on 31 March 1988 when they were worth £500,000.

The gain held over was:

	£	£
Market value		500,000
Base value	50,000	
Indexation (31%)	15,500	
		65,500
		£434,500

The trustees sold the shares for £1,000,000 on 31 March 2000. The chargeable gain was:

	£	£
Proceeds		1,000,000
Acquisition 31 March 1988	500,000	
Less 50% of gain held over	217,250	
	282,750	
Indexation (54.5%)	154,099	436,849
		563,151
Annual exemption		3,550
Chargeable		£559,601

Until 18 March 1991, it was possible for the half gain rule to apply to disposals subsequent to that which was the first disposal after the

holdover. This may have been a drafting error in *FA 1988*. At any rate this was stopped by *FA 1991, s 101*.

Retirement relief

7.24 An interest in possession settlement can benefit from capital gains tax retirement relief where a beneficiary uses trust assets in a business. [*TCGA 1992, s 164*]. Bearing in mind the uses to which accumulation and maintenance settlements are put, this will happen from time to time, although rarely. A more likely use of retirement relief in connection with trusts is that a settlor might settle assets at a time when he could claim the relief, which, despite the phase-out introduced by *FA 1998*, remains quite generous for the next year or two.

Main residence relief

7.25 The familiar main residence relief for individuals is extended by *TCGA 1992, s 225* to trustees. Provided that during all or part of the trustees' period of ownership, the dwelling-house is occupied as his only or main residence by a person entitled to do so under the terms of the settlement, the provisions of *ss 222 to 224* are applied to the trustees' gain. If there is any question of a main residence election being made under *s 222(5)(a)*, it must be the subject of a joint notice by the trustees and the beneficiary. The interesting thing about *s 225* is that there is no *pro rata* test. That means that, whether in a life interest or (see 7.26 below) a discretionary trust, there is a number of beneficiaries, occupation by just one of them can secure the relief for the whole gain accruing on disposal of the dwelling house.

7.26 The case of *Sansom and Another v Peay*, Ch D [1976] STC 494 established that section 225 relief is available in a case where trustees permit a beneficiary to live in a house belonging to a discretionary settlement. In this case the power to permit beneficiaries to live in a dwelling held within the settlement was 'for such period and generally upon such terms as the trustees in their discretion think fit'. The trustees bought a house and permitted beneficiaries to occupy it as their principal place of residence. The question was raised as to whether they occupied the house as of right or only at the trustees' discretion. The judgment showed that there had been a valid exercise of a power and that the beneficiaries were entitled to occupy the house as of right until permission was withdrawn. Accordingly, the main residence exemption was available to the trustees on selling the house at a gain. [*TCGA 1992, ss 222, 225*]. If it is intended that the beneficiaries shall have a permanent home, then this can cause inheritance tax problems by creating an interest in possession. This subject is further discussed in Inland Revenue Statement of Practice SP10/79 (see Appendix A and also 15.6 below).

7.27 *Capital Gains Tax*

Reinvestment relief

7.27 This relief was introduced by *FA 1993* but, in its original form, seemed unattractive. It is and was a roll-over relief. In its first form, which lasted from 16 March 1993 to 29 November 1993, trustees could qualify if there was an interest in possession in their trust. *FA 1994*, by wholesale repeal and amendment of *TCGA 1992, ss 164A–164N*, introduced a new version which was useful. This relief was repealed from 6 April 1998.

Enterprise Investment Scheme ('EIS')

7.28 The old reinvestment relief provisions which gave relief to some trustees have been carried over into the new EIS deferral regime. [*TCGA 1992, 5B Sch 17*]. In broad terms, the gain on the disposal of any chargeable asset can be deferred by reinvestment. This requires a subscription for shares in a qualifying trading company within twelve months before or three years after the disposal. In the case of a discretionary trust, all the beneficiaries must be individuals. With an interest in possession trust, relief is given if any of the beneficiaries are individuals. If there are non-individual beneficiaries, then (as under reinvestment relief) *pro rata* relief is obtained according to the proportion of the individual interests in possession borne to all the interests in possession. While individuals include charities, interests in possession do not include interest for a fixed term.

Since it is the trustees who realise the gain, it is they who must make the qualifying EIS investment. There might be thought to be a problem with a settlor-interested trust since, while it will be the trustees who have made the disposal, the tax is assessed on the settlor, either under *s 77* in a UK resident trust or *s 86* in a non-UK resident trust. However, in the UK resident case, the Revenue accept that the scheme of *TCGA 1992, 5B Sch 17* is that a qualifying reinvestment by the trustees effectively franks their gain, so that (if in full) there is no residual trust gain to be assessed on the settlor under *s 77*. The same, however, does not apply in the non-resident trust case, where the pre-relieved gains are assessed on the settlor under *s 86*, assuming of course that for the year of assessment in question, he is UK resident and domiciled and has an interest in the settlement. There could conceivably be cases where the non-resident trust is not subject to *s 86* but the trustees are still liable to capital gains tax on the gain, for example because it arises from the disposal of chargeable assets used in a trade carried on in the UK under *TCGA 1992, s 10*. In such a case, an EIS investment would be open to the non-resident trustees.

Base values

7.29 In dealing with will trusts and trusts arising from intestacies, the acquisition value of the assets for the executors is probate value. *TCGA 1992, s 274* lays down that where the value of an asset in the deceased's

Capital Gains Tax **7.29**

estate has been ascertained for CTT or IHT, that is the market value at the date of death. The word 'ascertained' is important. If there is no tax due, it is quite possible for the Capital Taxes Office to file the papers without agreeing anything. In such a case the value has not been ascertained. There will be an increase in the number of cases where there has been no negotiation with Shares Valuation Division now that business property relief can be 100%. That must alter the basis on which the acquisition value of shares held by the trustees of the will is calculated. The relevant provision is *TCGA 1992, s 62(1)*. That section lays down market value as the acquisition value and it is *section 274* which says that a negotiated probate value is to be taken as the market value. Once we are back on market value without the benefit of *section 274*, then *section 272* applies and, for instance, the related property provisions are irrelevant. There will be a considerable difference between market value under *section 272* and a negotiated probate value in the majority of cases. The Inland Revenue Tax Bulletin of April 1995 made the official view quite clear. When the market has fallen in the year following death it is quite likely that the executors have taken advantage of the relief for the sale of shares etc. from the deceased's estate contained in *IHTA 1984, ss 178–189*. That relief permits the substitution of gross proceeds of sale for the original probate value. Cancellation and suspension of a quotation can be treated as sales where the death is on or after 16 March 1992. [*IHTA 1984, ss 186A, 186B*]. The resulting revised probate value becomes the ascertained value for *TCGA 1992, s 274*. A similar relief operates on the sale of land at less than probate value during the four years following the death. [*IHTA 1984, ss 190–198*]. A small CGT loss must always result. This is because the revised base value is the gross proceeds of sale. The disposal for CGT is the net proceeds of sale. The loss is therefore the difference, i.e. the dealing costs. A recent case related to a sale of land where notice to complete was served but completion did not take place and the intended purchaser forfeited his deposit. Within a matter of months a sale to a different purchaser was successfully carried out. The first sale could not be treated as a sale for the purposes of the relief under *section 191* (*Jones & another (Balls' Administrators) v CIR, Ch D [1997] STC 358*).

The costs of valuation are incidental to a disposal and so are an allowable expense. [*TCGA 1992, s 38(2)(b)*]. The Inland Revenue regard only the costs of making a valuation as being within the *section*. The costs of negotiating a value with the District Valuer or Shares Valuation Division will therefore be disallowed. In a recent valuation case this was confirmed (*Administrators of the estate of Caton (dec'd) v Couch CA [1997] STC 970*). Incidental costs of trustees could include the cost of varying a settlement so as to produce a termination and fees in respect of discharges (but not insurance premiums and not bank trust company's withdrawal fees except as covered by an agreement with the clearing banks). See Inland Revenue Manual CG 33521–33522.

One further point on base values in will trusts etc. flows from *CIR v Richards' Executors, HL 1971, 46 TC 626*. This showed that personal

7.30 *Capital Gains Tax*

representatives could add the costs of obtaining probate to the probate value in calculating their base value for CGT. A scale has been published in Inland Revenue Statement of Practice SP8/94 (revising the earlier SP7/81) following meetings between the Board of Inland Revenue and professional bodies so that a reasonable figure can be added to the probate value without the necessity of agreeing the actual costs incurred. SP8/94 is reproduced in Appendix D.

TCGA 1992 s 38(1)(b) is the authority for the addition to the base value of expenditure on enhancement of value and on establishing title etc. That subsection refers to expenditure by the owner and is strictly interpreted by the Inland Revenue. Therefore, for instance although the executors may claim the probate costs (as in the *Richards* case) they would not be available to a legatee.

A topical valuation point relates to building societies and other mutual bodies which float on The Stock Exchange. Once such a body has announced its intention to abandon mutuality, its members have the expectation of a windfall gain. This affects the value of their holdings for inheritance tax. The CTO have their own tables of valuation which were published in June 1998.

7.30 A further point on base values is that the trustees and the settlor are 'connected persons'. This extends to persons connected with the settlor. Sometimes a family company can be connected with the trustees. [*TCGA 1992, s 286*]. There are two practical consequences as follows.

(*a*) Transactions (including the settlement of capital) between the settlor and the trustees are deemed to be at market value. [*TCGA 1992, ss 17, 18(1)(2)*].

(*b*) Any loss incurred by the settlor on transferring assets to the trustees can only be used against a chargeable gain arising from some other transaction with the same trustees. [*TCGA 1992, s 18(3)*].

7.31 Where an asset has been settled and the gain held over, there can be a charge to inheritance tax. This may be because of the premature death of the settlor of a potentially exempt transfer. It can be because the gift to the trustees is a chargeable transfer. Whatever the reason and whether the inheritance tax is paid by the settlor or by the trustees, it is effectively treated as part of the base value by the trustees. Note that:

(*a*) CTT was treated in the same manner;

(*b*) the inheritance tax is discounted if it would otherwise result in a CGT loss on disposal. The result will be a no gain/no loss situation;

(*c*) the gift by the settlor must have been made after 5 April 1980;

(*d*) if the inheritance tax was paid on the making of the settlement and the settlor dies within seven years, an additional assessment will be made on the trustees. This also attracts the relief;

(*e*) although the inheritance tax is an allowable deduction, it does not attract CGT indexation relief.

[*FA 1980, s 79,* now *TCGA 1992, s 67*].

FA 1980, s 79 was repealed by *FA 1989, s 124* in relation to disposals on or after 14 March 1989, but these provisions are kept in being in respect of assets settled before that date. [*Section 67*]. Further, *section 165(10)* continues the relief for settlements made on or after 14 March 1989 where hold-over is claimed under the new provisions. An identical relief is incorporated in *TCGA 1992, s 260(7)(8)*. Where a donor settles shares where there is no capital gain at the time of the gift, could he simply go through the motions of making a claim under *TCGA 1992, s 165,* so that if the trustees have to pay any inheritance tax it can be added to the base value of the shares? It is thought that this question must be answered negatively.

Example

A settlor settles a business asset worth £50,000. He elects for hold-over relief and the base value to the trustees becomes £20,000. The settlement is potentially exempt but the settlor dies a year later. The clawback under *IHTA 1984, s 113A* retrospectively denies business property relief and the trustees pay the IHT. His nil rate band for IHT had been used on chargeable lifetime transfers. The trustees sell the asset for £60,000, producing a chargeable gain (before indexation and taper relief) as follows:

	£	£
Sale proceeds		60,000
Original market value	50,000	
Gain held over	(30,000)	
	20,000	
IHT at 40% on £50,000	20,000	
	£40,000	(40,000)
Chargeable gain		£20,000

Rates of tax and exemptions

7.32 The rate of CGT for all trustees is 34% for 1998/99 onwards. In earlier years there was a 23% rate for trusts with an interest in possession and a 34% rate for discretionary and accumulation settlements. Undoubtedly there had been settlements made to ensure that the 23% rate applied to some considerable gain which, had it been made by an individual, would have borne tax at 40%. However, there will be hard cases. One of the classic formulae for wills has been a gift to 'my wife with remainder over to our children in equal shares'. These people are now saddled with a 34% rate even though their personal rates might not be so high. What is worse, they are still caught if the testator died before the new legislation was enacted.

7.33 *Capital Gains Tax*

Trustees are entitled to an exemption equal to half that of an individual, i.e. £3,600 (= ½ of £7,200) for 2000/01. Where there is a group of settlements made by the same settlor, the annual exemption for each is the amount obtained by dividing half the individual's exemption (i.e. the £3,600) by the number of settlements, but with a minimum of one-tenth of the individual's exemption for each of them (i.e. £720 for 2000/01). When counting the number of settlements the taxpayer should include the trusts of a death benefit of a personal pension scheme within *ICTA 1988, s 631*, but not of an old-style retirement annuity. He should also include a settlor-interested trust and a trust of a term life policy taken out for inheritance tax protection. Looking at *TCGA 1992, 1 Sch 2(8)* this is not obvious and the point is not well known. Thus, by making 20 settlements, a settlor could increase the total annual exemptions available to his family by £14,400. The professional costs would be substantial. This sharing of exemptions does not apply to settlements made before 7 June 1978. Those settlements each have a £3,600 exemption. [*TCGA 1992, 1 Sch (2)*]. A disabled person's trust has the full £7,200. [*TCGA 1992, 1 Sch (1)*]. The annual exemptions should be index-linked. [*TCGA 1992, s 3(3)*]. This index-linking can be prevented by Parliament and has been so prevented. When not prevented the index-linking takes place in the September of the preceding fiscal year.

An anomaly can arise when an estate is in course of administration and will, in due time, become a trust. The personal representatives have an annual exempt amount equal to that of an individual. This is restricted to the year of death and the next two years of assessment. [*TCGA 1992, s 3(7)*]. If the administration continues beyond that period then, until a trust is set up, there is no annual exemption at all.

7.33 If there are separate funds within one trust, this does not mean that there are two taxpayers. There may well be two files with HM Inspector because there are, say, two funds, one for a discretionary, the other for a life tenant's fund. He will often start by making two assessments but this is wrong. One trust is one taxpayer for capital gains tax. There can be fiduciary problems where there are separate funds. Should the trustees take a loss in one fund and set it against a gain in another without compensation, for instance?

Interaction of accrued income scheme etc. and capital gains tax

7.34 Gilt-edged securities and qualifying corporate bonds (see *FA 1984, s 64*) are exempt from capital gains tax but within the accrued income scheme. Other securities (but not shares) (see *ICTA 1988, s 710*) are within both capital gains tax and the accrued income scheme. The position for these is covered by *TCGA 1992, s 119*. This is aimed at producing a clean price for capital gains tax by deducting accrued interest from, or adding the rebate amount to, the consideration for the disposal.

There are numerous special cases covered by the legislation, but these are rare. For instance, a convertible security may be converted into equity so that the accrued income scheme creates an assessment to income tax, but there is no disposal for capital gains tax. For items of this sort, the reader is referred to the legislation.

See 6.5 *et seq.* above for the income tax effects of the accrued income scheme.

7.35 Where the disposal of an investment in an offshore roll-up fund is made and income tax is assessed under *ICTA 1988, s 761*, there are no capital gains tax consequences so far as the gain is deemed to be income. [*TCGA 1992, s 37*].

Appointments and distributions

7.36 Care is needed where discretionary trustees make an appointment. If the result is a sub-trust, there is no occasion of charge. However, if the appointed capital leaves the settlement, there is an occasion of charge (even though it may be possible to hold over the gain). The distinction between the two types of appointment has received judicial scrutiny and the present position is explained in Inland Revenue Statement of Practice SP7/84 (see Appendix A). This distinction still gives trouble. See *Swires v Renton, Ch D [1991] STC 490*.

7.37 In a protective trust, the principal beneficiary's interest can be forfeited by his seeking to anticipate income, to borrow against his interest and so on. The termination of the life interest in such a case is ignored for capital gains tax.

Demergers

7.38 Demergers are a relatively new phenomenon using *ICTA 1988, ss 213, 218*. The first were, probably, BAT Industries PLC and the demergers of Argos PLC and Arjo Wiggins Appleton PLC and, secondly the Racal/Vodafone demerger. Then came ICI and Zeneca. There is a line of trust cases in which the courts held that, for anything of value to come from a company as capital it must be capital under company law (e.g. a liquidation, a reduction of capital). Anything else must be income. Very probably there is an income connection in that companies do put profits to reserve and it is accumulations of past profits which provide the capital for growth or for a distribution which looks like capital to the recipient. The purchaser of shares looks upon the company's reserves as being capital and they will be reflected, in a way, in the price paid for the shares. From his viewpoint any distribution which is not a dividend must be capital.

When demergers were invented, it was commonly thought that the demerged shares were income and belonged to the life tenant. This was unreal when over 40% of the value might be in the demerged shares.

7.39 Capital Gains Tax

However, the ICI/Zeneca demerger was unique in that ICI PLC transferred the Zeneca business to Zeneca PLC in exchange for that company issuing its shares to the holders of shares in ICI PLC. This has become known as an indirect demerger, in contrast to a direct demerger where the principal company distributes shares in a subsidiary to its shareholders. The indirect demerger of Zeneca PLC was considered in *Sinclair v Lee & Another, Ch D [1993] 3 All ER 926*. The court was able to distinguish indirect demergers and to hold that the shares in Zeneca PLC would be capital. In the judgment it was said that if the earlier decisions 'would produce a result manifestly inconsistent with the presumed intention of the testator or settlor, the court should not be required to apply them slavishly. In origin they were guidelines . . .'.

Trustees have to decide how to account for the demerged shares. In a direct demerger will they hand the demerged shares over to the life tenant? If they do, there is no question of a charge under *TCGA 1992, s 71* because they are owned by the life tenant *ab initio* and they never form part of the trust capital. There has been no disposal by the trustees. There is no suggestion that the life tenant should be assessed to income tax on the value of the shares. If on a direct demerger the life tenant is entitled to the shares his base value is the market value at the date of the demerger. [*TCGA 1992, s 17*]. If, on an indirect demerger the life tenant receives the demerged shares then, again, there is no disposal by the trustees and the life tenant has a nil acquisition value. [*s 17(2)*]. This must be exceptional perhaps because the law of the trust is not that of England or because there is a clause permitting the trustees to ignore case law in allocating special distributions, etc. The base value of the shares in the old company is undisturbed.

If the trustees retain the shares then it will be with the acquiescence, at the least, of the life tenant and that must amount to a settlement by him. That will not affect the income tax position. If the settlement resulted in a gain exceeding the life tenant's £7,200 exemption, etc. then that would trigger a charge on the life tenant. That probably means that in small cases the trustees will retain the demerged shares without there being any immediate tax consequences. They would have to be sure that there was general agreement among the family of course. The Inland Revenue view is fully explained in the October 1994 edition of their Tax Bulletin (issue 13, page 162).

Connected persons

7.39 The 'connected person' rules [*TCGA 1992, s 18*] apply to settlements. A trustee is connected with the settlor, any person connected with the settlor and with a connected body corporate. [*TCGA 1992, s 286(3)*]. The most common area of difficulty is with losses. A loss on a disposal to a connected person can be set off only against a gain made on a disposal to the same person. In the February 1993 issue 6, page 56, of the Inland Revenue's Tax Bulletin it was made clear that:

Capital Gains Tax **7.43**

(*a*) the settlor and the trustees are connected at the moment when the settlement comes into existence.

(*b*) once the settlor is dead the connection is broken.

(*c*) the transfer of losses to beneficiaries under *section 71(2)* is not inhibited by *section 18(3)*.

7.40 The transfer of losses under *section 71(2)* comes about because the value of an asset to which a beneficiary has become absolutely entitled has fallen during the period from the date of acquisition by the trustees to the deemed date of disposal legislated by *section 71(1)*. The resultant loss is transferred to the beneficiary. Loss claims now have to be calculated by the taxpayer and a claim made. [*TCGA 1992, s 16(2A)*]. Provided the advance to the beneficiary pre-dated 16 June 1999, the loss can be used by the beneficiary immediately, perhaps on a gain in no way related to assets acquired from the trust. For the position since 16 June 1999, see 7.8 above.

Miscellaneous

7.41 *FA 1995* made some administrative changes which really relate to the introduction of self-assessment. *Section 107A* inserted by *FA 1995, s 103* introduces 'relevant trustees' to CGT from 6 April 1996. These are the same relevant trustees as appear in income tax legislation, namely those who are trustees in the year of assessment when the chargeable event takes place and those who subsequently become trustees. Anything done by one relevant trustee is treated as being done by them all and any or all of them can be pursued. There is a modest protection for penalties accruing prior to appointment. *FA 1995, s 114* makes it possible to assess any trustee on behalf of all the trustees from 6 April 1996. It does this by amending *TCGA 1992, s 65(1)*. Another amendment which is made in preparation for self-assessment is in *FA 1995, s 113* which makes it necessary for a capital gains loss to be calculated and claimed. The losses of 1996/97 and subsequent years will be relieved in priority to old losses brought forward. This is a change in approach because in the past the Inland Revenue have been unwilling to agree losses until they were likely to be used. However, once self-assessment is in position, it is easier for them if the losses are calculated and reported by the taxpayer.

7.42 From 1 April 1996 the word 'quoted' in relation to investments is not to be used. 'Listed' is the modern word. [*FA 1996, s 199* and *38 Sch*].

7.43 Trustees often have holdings in unquoted companies which are really the only reason for the settlement and so date back some time. Rebasing to 31 March 1982 is still part of capital gains tax and can cause doubts if the trustees dispose of part of an old holding and want to rebase the value of the shares disposed of. The worry is whether the whole holding should be rebased or just the number of shares disposed of. The

7.44 *Capital Gains Tax*

Inland Revenue CGT manual makes it clear that the whole holding is to be revalued (50901, 50904, 50905).

7.44 Occasionally, a family pools its assets in order that they can be managed as one unit. This will be to do with holdings in a company or landed estates. The trusts which are used as the vehicle for the pooling tend to be bare trusts for tax purposes. The most recent case was *Jenkins v Brown, Ch D [1989] STC 577*. There is a published concession (ESC D26) relating to exchanges of interests in land where individuals have property in joint ownership and wish to separate their affairs. Relief from *ad valorem* stamp duty is unfortunately no longer given to such exchanges.

7.45 Many family trusts retain the assets which were the original gift. This is because it is more intelligent for the holder of shares in a family company or of a landed estate to settle shares or land rather than cash or realisable securities. In such cases, hold-over will probably have been claimed (before the changes made by the *FA 1989*). This means that, unless re-basing to 31 March 1982 is possible, indexation, on a subsequent disposal, will be on an unnaturally low figure.

7.46 Even if the settlor has a beneficial interest in the settlement, his disposal when he creates the settlement or transfers assets into it causes a capital gains tax charge. [*TCGA 1992, s 70*].

7.47 The disposal by a beneficiary of his interest under the settlement does not trigger a chargeable gain (*TCGA 1992, s 76(1)*). This provision would, for example, protect the gift of a reversionary interest for inheritance tax mitigation purposes. The protection is given to an original beneficiary or anyone else who did not acquire his interest for a consideration in money or money's worth (other than consideration consisting of another interest under the settlement). Since 6 March 1998, this rule applies only if the settlement has never been resident outside the UK (*TCGA 1992 s 76(1A)*). *FA 2000, s 91* has provided a further limitation to this principle from 21 March 2000 by inserting a new *s 76A* and *Sch 4A*. The new provisions create a charge to capital gains tax in certain circumstances where a beneficiary sells his interest in the trust on or after 21 March 2000. The type of trusts caught are those which are settlor-interested or where any of the trust property is derived from a trust which was a settlor-interested trust at any time in the previous two tax years. If the rules apply, the assets underlying the interest are treated as though they are disposed of and immediately re-acquired by the trustees at market value.

Variation of trusts

7.48 There are times when it would suit everybody concerned to vary a trust. Some variations are made to correct drafting or typing mistakes, others to vary the entitlement of beneficiaries. Also, there are the

Capital Gains Tax **7.48**

variations when some new administrative power is needed, perhaps to delegate investment matters to an investment manager or to put investments in the names of nominees (perhaps a stockbroker's nominee company). In general anything directed at beneficiaries' rights will require an application under the *Variation of Trusts Act 1958* and may prove to be expensive. Administrative matters can be dealt with, probably at far less expense, by the use of *Trustee Act 1925, s 57*. Very occasionally the variation may be under *Settled Land Act 1925, s 64*. The ability to vary a trust can be important in that the taxpayer is still the same even though there may have been some redirection of wealth. The variation is not a disposal and is not the occasion of a capital gains tax charge, whereas resettlement must involve the trustees in capital gains tax and inheritance tax. Variations which have greater tax consequences are disclaimers, surrenders and assignments. Any of these will be of interest to HM Inspector of Taxes (see TM 2235, 2251).

Chapter 8

Inheritance Tax—Definitions

8.1 There are a number of definitions which are fundamental to an understanding of the inheritance tax legislation. These are examined below.

8.2 'Settlement' means any disposition of property, however effected, where the property is held:

(*a*)   in trust for persons in succession; or

(*b*)   for any person subject to a contingency; or

(*c*)   on trust to accumulate income; or

(*d*)   on trust with power to make payments at the discretion of the trustees with or without power to accumulate surplus income; or

(*e*)   to fund an annuity or other periodical payment.

A lease of property for life or for lives is also treated as a settlement where made for less than full consideration.

[*IHTA 1984, s 43*].

It is possible for trustees to receive gifts from someone other than the original settlor. The most common is probably where a man and his wife both make transfers to the same trust. This possibility is covered by *IHTA 1984, s 44(2)* which applies to discretionary settlements. As a consequence, each transferor is treated as a separate settlor and his or her gifts as separate settlements. There will then be problems of identification.

8.3   'Interest in possession' means the interest of a person who has the immediate entitlement (subject to expenses or other similar outgoings) to any income produced by the settled property as it arises. The fact that this interest could be revoked or defeated in any way is not important. Most practitioners will treat this as meaning a life interest or an annuity. Interest in possession is not defined in the legislation but the meaning has been tested in *Pearson and Others v CIR, HL [1980] STC 318*. Appendix A contains the text of a statement issued by the Inland Revenue on 12 February 1976 and now published as Appendix A in the booklet IHT 16 Settled Property. This gives the official view as to the meaning of 'interest in possession'. Reference has already been made to the case of *Sansom and Another v Peay, Ch D [1976] STC 494* (see 7.34 above) and Inland Revenue Statement of Practice SP10/79 (Appendix A). These show that an interest in possession in the family home can be

Inheritance Tax—Definitions   **8.5**

created by the trustees of a discretionary settlement who allow exclusive occupation of the property by a beneficiary. It would not follow that the lending of any asset or the existence of a standing order for the payment of income to a beneficiary would have the same effect. The latter point was looked at in *Swales v CIR, Ch D [1984] STC 413.*

8.4 'Qualifying interest in possession' has been explained (see 2.20 above). It is theoretically possible for an interest in possession to be held by a company which is not a reversionary or insurance company. This is not a qualifying interest in possession and the property is treated as being held on discretionary trusts (see Hansard, Standing Committee A debates, col 662, 15 June 1982). The practitioner will, in most cases, meet only two forms of qualifying interest in possession, namely a life interest or an annuity.

8.5 'Excluded property' has a special meaning so far as the trustees of settlements are concerned.

(*a*)   Where the settlor was domiciled outside the UK when the settlement was made, foreign property in the settlement is excluded property. When the settlement was made on or after 10 December 1974, the extended meaning of domicile set out in *IHTA 1984, s 267* is used (see 19.10 and 22.10 below).

(*b*)   A large number of government securities have been issued free of tax while in foreign ownership. [*IHTA 1984, s 6(2)*]. These are now known as FOTRA securities (i.e. free of tax to residents abroad). [*FA 1996, s 154*]. Before 6 April 1996 the tax exemption depended upon domicile and ordinary residence. Now it depends upon compliance with conditions under which the securities are issued [*IHTA 1984, s 6(2)* and *s 48(4)* as amended by *FA 1996, 28 Sch 7, 8*] (i.e. the conditions set out in the prospectus). From 6 April 1998 all gilt-edged securities issued previously are FOTRA securities. This may mean that, where held by or for non-domiciliaries, they are excluded property. The change from being ordinary assets to excluded property is not an occasion of charge. So far as the trustees of a discretionary settlement are concerned, they are excluded property provided that the objects of the discretion are within the conditions. If held by the trustees of an interest in possession or an accumulation and maintenance settlement, they are excluded property to the extent that there is a qualifying interest in possession (see 2.20 above) in them and the beneficiary is within the conditions. They can also be excluded property if all possible beneficiaries are within the conditions. The test of domicile is that of the general law and not the special one in *IHTA 1984, s 267*. Schemes are sometimes based on FOTRA securities. It is known that the Treasury is unwilling to see anything happen which could be regarded as going back on the promises made when the securities were issued. However, if there is the slightest weakness in any scheme based on FOTRA securities, it will fail in its purpose (see, for instance, *Montague Trust v CIR, Ch D [1989] STC 477*).

8.6 *Inheritance Tax—Definitions*

(c) Reversionary interests under settlements are also usually excluded property. See 9.5, 9.6 and 22.6 below for further discussion on this point.

Excluded property is property excluded from the charge to inheritance tax. See also 22.2, 22.3 and 22.7 to 22.9 below for further discussion of excluded property. See 7.9 above for a note on the variation of a will to introduce a non-domiciliary as settlor of an offshore trust, effective for inheritance tax but not for capital gains tax purposes.

[*IHTA 1984, s 48, FA 1998, s 161*].

8.6 'Relevant property' can be taken by the practitioner to mean property contained in a family settlement and subject to the discretionary regime. A detailed explanation is given in 2.20 above.

8.7 'Payment' includes a transfer of assets other than money. 'Quarter' means a period of three months. [*IHTA 1984, s 63*].

8.8 'Gift with reservation' means any gift made by an individual on or after 18 March 1986 where the donee has not assumed possession and enjoyment at or before the beginning of the 'relevant period' or where throughout the 'relevant period' the donee does not enjoy the gift to the entire exclusion or virtually the entire exclusion of the donor and of any benefit to him by contract or otherwise. [*FA 1986, s 102*]. The 'relevant period' is the seven year period ending with the donor's death or, if shorter, the period commencing with the gift and ending with the death. The Inland Revenue Tax Bulletin, issue 9 (November 1993) devoted over a page to an explanation of their view of 'virtual exclusion', largely in relation to a gift of the family home.

This produces three tests:

(i) the donee must take possession and must have the enjoyment of his gift;

(ii) the donor must be excluded (or virtually so) from the asset which he has given away;

(iii) the donor's exclusion must extend to any arrangement whereby he might benefit from the asset or from the gift.

8.9 'Potentially exempt transfer' is a transfer of value made by an individual on or after 18 March 1986 which is a gift to an individual or to the trustees of an accumulation and maintenance settlement or to a disabled trust and is not an exempt transfer. A gift to an accumulation and maintenance settlement or to a disabled trust must become settled property.

For transfers on or after 17 March 1987, the deemed ownership where there is an interest in possession settlement is treated as if it were true ownership. Thus, a gift in which there is a life interest is a potentially exempt transfer. So is a gift where the income beneficiary transfers his

Inheritance Tax—Definitions **8.9**

rights to someone else. A termination of an interest in possession can produce a potentially exempt transfer (see 9.10 below).

If the donor outlives the gift by seven years, the transfer becomes exempt. If he dies during the seven years, it is chargeable. If death occurs within three years of the gift, the full rate of tax is paid. Taper relief is given in the fourth, fifth, sixth and seventh years. The relief is against tax and does not alter the amount of the transfer which has become chargeable by reason of the premature death. It follows that taper relief achieves nothing if the transfer is within the nil rate band.

There are numerous 'lookalikes' which are not potentially exempt, e.g.

(*a*) a policy on the settlor's own life is settled on accumulation and maintenance trusts. The payment of the premium does not create settled property and the gift does not qualify. [*IHTA 1984, s 3A(3)*]. A payment of cash to the trustees to permit payment of the premium does qualify;

(*b*) grandfather pays school fees to his grandson's school. This is not a gift to an individual etc. and does not qualify. If the money is given to the father and he pays the fees, there is then a PET;

(*c*) the transfer of woodlands where there has been an estate duty deferment cannot be a PET. However, business property relief should be available.

[*IHTA 1984, s 3A; FA 1986, 19 Sch 1; FA 1986, 19 Sch 46; F(No 2)A 1987, s 96*].

Chapter 9

Inheritance Tax—Interest in Possession Settlements

9.1 Property subject to an interest in possession is taxed almost as if it belonged to the income beneficiary. This is made clear in *IHTA 1984, s 49(1)* which says that a person beneficially entitled to an interest in possession shall be treated as beneficially entitled to the property in which the interest subsists. However, the *section 49(1)* rule does carry traps. One such is in the context of agricultural property relief. Trustees of an interest in possession settlement may own an interest in agricultural property and belong to a family farming partnership, perhaps as limited partners. However, on the death of the life tenant, advantage cannot be taken of the two-year occupation rule in *IHTA 1984, s 117(a)* unless the life tenant also occupies in his own capacity, for example as a general partner, albeit with a minimal share in the partnership. Otherwise, the seven-year ownership test must be satisfied under *section 117(b)*.

9.2 The chargeable event is the termination of the interest in possession. Tax is then charged as if the income beneficiary had made a transfer of value equal to the value of the property in which his interest subsisted. [*IHTA 1984, s 52(1)*]. In many cases such a transfer of value will not attract tax, e.g.

(*a*) the capital has been advanced to the income beneficiary;

(*b*) the termination is a PET which becomes exempt because the life tenant survives for at least seven years;

(*c*) the termination is prevented from becoming a chargeable transfer because of an exemption, perhaps because it goes to the income beneficiary's spouse;

(*d*) the settled property was within the old surviving spouse exemption which is preserved by *IHTA 1984, 6 Sch 2*. For that exemption to apply, the settled property must have been subject to estate duty on the death of the first spouse (i.e. the first spouse died before 13 November 1974) and the second spouse must have had a life interest. There must have been no right for the surviving spouse to draw on the capital. The protection of this rule is obtained if there would have been a liability to estate duty on the first death but for either the threshold or the relief for agricultural or business property.

9.3 The charge is not the same as if the property truly belonged to the income beneficiary because it is restricted to '... the value of the property in which his interest subsisted.' A transfer by the beneficiary from his free estate would be calculated as the fall in value of his estate.

Originally it was thought that *section 49(1)* had an effect for valuation purposes in that the holding of an income beneficiary was plainly part of his estate but shares settled on him were deemed to be his as well. Therefore if there were 20 shares settled and 60 owned outright, the valuation of the 20 shares was thought to be 20/80ths of the value of 80 shares. However, in March 1990 a new view was communicated to the professional bodies by the Inland Revenue (see Appendix A, 21 March 1990).

This now requires the settled property to be valued in isolation (subject, however, in appropriate cases to the application of the *Ramsay* principle or the associated operations provisions of *IHTA 1984, s 268*).

Examples

Shares in a company are valued at £1,000 each in parcels of 200 and £5,000 each in parcels of 800. The total issued capital is 1,000 shares.

Example 1

The income beneficiary has an interest in possession in 200 shares and has 600 shares in his own name. His interest in possession terminates. There is a transfer of value of £200,000 (subject to BPR @ 100%).

Example 2

The income beneficiary has an interest in possession in 800 shares. His interest terminates in 200 shares. There is a transfer of value of £1,000,000 (subject to BPR @ 100%).

Example 3

The income beneficiary has an interest in possession in 200 shares. His wife owns 600 shares. The interest in possession terminates. There is a transfer of value of £200,000 (subject to BPR @ 100%).

Example 4

The income beneficiary has an interest in possession in 200 shares. He owns 600 shares himself. He dies. There is a transfer of value of £4,000,000 (subject to BPR @ 100%). This is because there is a single transfer of value. Note the BPR effect of the words 'either by themselves or together with other such shares owned by the transferor' and 'together with any shares which are related property'. [*IHTA 1984, ss 105(1)(b), (1A)*].

9.4 *Inheritance Tax—Interest in Possession Settlements*

9.4 Where the interest in possession extends to only a part of an undivided fund, the 'property in which his interest subsisted' [*IHTA 1984, s 52(1)*] is his fraction of the whole fund. [*IHTA 1984, s 50(1)*]. There are provisions [*IHTA 1984, s 50(3)*] to prevent trustees from pretending that all the high-yielding investments support one beneficiary's interest whilst the low-yielding ones benefit another where tax is chargeable by reference to the value of part of a property producing a specified amount (e.g. an annuity) or by reference to the value of the remainder.

9.5 Because the income beneficiary is deemed to own the property impressed with his interest, it is not possible to deem anybody else to be a proprietor and therefore the reversionary interest is generally excluded property. [*IHTA 1984, s 48(1)*].

9.6 The beneficiary with a vested interest in reversion has a property right which is capable of transfer. Therefore, even if the transaction takes place only days before the death of the life tenant, he can give away or re-settle his reversion. There will be no tax because it is excluded property. This is a most useful planning technique.

Potentially exempt transfers

9.7 The making of an interest in possession settlement is almost certainly a PET. There can still be problems if the draftsman ignores the anti-avoidance legislation, e.g.

(*a*) the settlor might benefit (a gift with reservation of benefit);

(*b*) the settlement is initially for life or some short period and on termination of the interest in possession, the capital is held on discretionary trusts.

There was a period when the device in (*b*) above was used with the settlor's spouse as the life tenant and the short period was one month. The idea was to use the spouse exemption to exempt the making of the settlement and then to use the spouse's nil rate band etc., if this was tax efficient, to cover the transfer to discretionary trusts. This scheme would have been adapted when PET treatment was extended to interest in possession settlements in 1987, and therefore *IHTA 1984, ss 54A, 54B* were introduced to block the possible loophole.

9.8 The manner in which *IHTA 1984, ss 54A, 54B* work is to relate back to the settlor any transfer which is caught by the following circumstances:

(*a*) the settlor has made a settlement of property after 16 March 1987,

(*b*) there is an interest in possession and the making of the settlement was a PET,

(*c*) the interest in possession terminates during the first seven years of the settlement and there is then a deemed chargeable transfer either

Inheritance Tax—Interest in Possession Settlements **9.11**

because the income beneficiary has died or the settlement has become discretionary, and

(*d*) the settlor is alive at the time.

In other words someone with a cumulative total of chargeable transfers has made a discretionary settlement etc. in such a way as (were it not for the anti-avoidance rule) to use someone else's nil rate band.

The resultant chargeable transfer is, broadly, treated as having been made by the settlor. There is protection for cases where within six months of the interest in possession coming to an end, the settled property is transferred to an individual or to an accumulation and maintenance trust.

9.9 The fact that the settlement is potentially exempt means that the trustees should know the risks inherent in this. They will be aware that the premature death of the settlor will cause a liability. To guess at the liability, they need to know the settlor's cumulative total and have details of his earlier PETs.

9.10 The termination of an interest in possession, other than on death, will generally be a PET. This was not so until the enactment of *F(No 2)A 1987, s 96* which amended *IHTA 1984, s 3A(2)(6)* and introduced *section 3A(7)*. To be potentially exempt, the termination must produce a transfer to an individual, to another interest in possession settlement, to an accumulation and maintenance trust or to a disabled trust. The termination may not be a gift. For instance an interest in possession may be given to a widow during widowhood. Her re-marriage brings her interest to an end. If the result is a transfer of the sort described there is a PET. There are other beneficial consequences:

(*a*) because there is no gift there cannot be a gift with reservation of a benefit (see 8.8 above);

(*b*) the erstwhile life tenant is not a settlor for the purposes of *ICTA 1988, s 660B* (settlements on own infant children); and

(*c*) the erstwhile life tenant is not a settlor for the purposes of *TCGA 1992, s 77* (see 4.12 above) or *TCGA 1992, s 86* (see 21.13 below) (CGT and settlor with an interest in a settlement).

On the inter vivos termination of an interest in possession, just as on a beneficial gift, there are available the annual £3,000 exemption and the marriage exemption. However, both these depend upon the giving of notice by the beneficiary to the trustees as to the availability of the exemption and the extent to which it is available (*IHTA 1984, s 57*). The notice must be given within six months of the event on Form 222.

Valuation

9.11 As has been indicated in the examples in 9.3 above, the valuation rules tend to ignore *IHTA 1984, s 49(1)* when *section 52(1)*

9.12   Inheritance Tax—Interest in Possession Settlements

(lifetime termination of interest in possession) is in point. That is to say that, although the income beneficiary is deemed to own the capital supporting his interest, when there is a termination of that interest, the assets held in trust are valued without reference to those in his free estate. However, the converse is not the case. If there is a transfer of value of assets in his free estate they can be valued as if the income beneficiary owned the settled property as well. In either case the valuation reliefs (i.e. business property relief and agricultural property relief) are operated as if the income beneficiary owned both (see examples in 9.3 above). The 'related property' rules are unchanged so that, for example, shares settled on one's spouse for life could be aggregated with those given to a charity, for valuation purposes. Once again because of the new approach to *section 52(1)*, this would not be so if the settled shares had to be valued. In this connection it is interesting to see (Inland Revenue Tax Bulletin 27 February 1997) that the official view is that excluded property can still be related property.

Administration

9.12   Although the income beneficiary is, in so many ways, the deemed owner of the settled property, it is the duty of the trustees to notify liability (on Inland Revenue Account form IHT 100) and pay tax.

Chapter 10

Inheritance Tax—Accumulation and Maintenance Settlements

The potentially exempt transfer

10.1 Any lifetime gift to an accumulation and maintenance settlement is a PET. [*IHTA 1984, s 3A(1)(c)*]. This is not because such settlements are favoured *per se*. It is simply because the idea behind PETs was to free outright gifts to individuals from inheritance tax and it was desired that gifts to infants should be on a par with those to adults. Rather than introduce some new class of donee, it was decided to permit potentially exempt transfers to accumulation and maintenance settlements as a convenient method of freeing gifts to or for the benefit of infants.

The words in *section 3A(1)(c)* require a gift to be made. Therefore, there can still be chargeable transfers where value is transferred to the settlement without there being a gift. For instance, the settlor may pay fees in connection with gifts to the settlement or he might pay the acceptance fee of a bank trust company so that the funds settled are not reduced by fees. To illustrate the point further, there could be transactions with a company whose shares had been settled; those transactions might be transfers of value but they would not be a gift to the trustees and so would not be PETs. Another illustration is given in 8.9(*a*) above.

Qualifying conditions

10.2 The conditions which have to be met for a trust to be an accumulation and maintenance settlement are explained in 2.15 to 2.18 above. *IHTA 1984, s 71*, the relevant statutory provision, is reproduced in full in Appendix F.

10.3 There will still be a few settlements which satisfied the old legislation before the 25-year test and one generation tests were enacted in 1976. Transitional provisions protect them. [*IHTA 1984, s 71(6)*].

Exemption from charge on making a qualifying settlement

10.4 The initial transfer of assets to the trustees will be a PET by the settlor. Should the settlor fail to survive the seven-year period (see 8.9 above), the transfer will be chargeable. The trustees will be responsible for the tax and primarily liable (and indeed this may have been made clear by the trust deed). They must deliver an account [*IHTA 1984, s 216(1)(bb)*] and pay the tax out of the settled funds. This subject is further explained in 14.2 below.

10.5 Inheritance Tax—Accumulation and Maintenance Settlements

10.5 Once the seventh anniversary of an accumulation and maintenance settlement has passed without the settlor dying, the settlement can run for a very long time without there being any further charge to IHT. There is no ten-year charge because the settled property is not relevant property (see 2.20 above). Nor is there a charge when property becomes subject to an interest in possession because a beneficiary has attained the specified age. Nor is there a charge on the death of a beneficiary before attaining a specified age (see 10.15 below). [*IHTA 1984, s 71(4)*]. Therefore, subject to two peculiarities explained in 10.6 and 10.7 below, the next occasion of charge after a beneficiary has attained the specified age would be when he makes a chargeable transfer from the capital he has received from the settlement or when his interest in possession terminates and the termination is a chargeable transfer. Death is the most obvious termination which is an occasion of charge. Another is a resettlement on discretionary trusts. Most other terminations will themselves be PETs because surrender or assignment in favour of an individual or for the benefit of children are the likeliest occasions of termination.

10.6 Before 17 March 1987 there could have been an occasion of charge where there was a class gift and the class increased after a beneficiary had achieved an interest in possession. This was because the birth of the new beneficiary would reduce the share of the beneficiary who had an interest in possession. *Pro tanto* there was a termination. Now, these terminations would be PETs.

The use of accumulation and maintenance settlements

10.7 In designing such a settlement, care has to be taken because of the rule against accumulations. Normally the power to accumulate will cease after 21 years although other periods are possible. Therefore it is not possible to start a settlement for twins aged 1, and provide that income may be accumulated until their 24th birthday and that then the children shall take an interest in possession. In such a case the children must achieve the interest in possession at age 22 at the latest.

10.8 The draftsman of an accumulation and maintenance settlement will be careful to exclude powers which could divert income to something which is not an accumulation, maintenance, education or benefit. One common administrative power is to pay insurance premiums out of income and it is clear that this must be excluded.

10.9 Because a class gift is possible, the setting up of an accumulation and maintenance settlement can be the means of making a gift to unborn children. Therefore, they are very suitable for families where further children are expected. It is even possible to use a child who is not intended to benefit as the basis of such a settlement.

Example

Brother John is 35 and unmarried. Sister Kate is 30 and has one child aged one. Mother is still alive, aged 75 and with a poor expectation of life. She has no wealth of her own but she is the life tenant of father's

Inheritance Tax—Accumulation and Maintenance Settlements **10.11**

estate. Father died at a time when estate duty was payable and therefore mother's death will not cause any inheritance tax on the estate. [*IHTA 1984, 6 Sch 2*]. On her death, father's estate goes to brother John and sister Kate in equal shares. Brother John is engaged to be married and plans to start a family fairly soon after marriage. His reversionary interest in his father's estate is excluded property (see *IHTA 1984, s 48(1)*). Fearful of mother's death and having adequate capital of his own, he settles his reversion for such of the grandchildren of his father as attain the age of 25, if more than one in equal shares. The settlement deed provides that, at any time before a child has achieved an interest in possession, that child's share may be varied in such a manner that the shares are not equal. Upon commencement of the settlement there is only one beneficiary, namely the child of sister Kate. Mother dies, father's estate is divided into two, one half for sister Kate and the other for brother John's settlement. Brother John marries, has a family of three children and the trustees vary the shares in the settlement before any of sister Kate's children has attained 25, so that only the children of brother John can benefit. As events have turned out, brother John was able to make a gift to his children some years before the first of them was born.

10.10 It is possible for a class gift to run into difficulties through a temporary deficiency of members.

Example

In the example in 10.9 above, brother John's settlement for such of the grandchildren of his father as attain the age of 25 was duly set up. A fortnight afterwards, sister Kate's only child is killed in a road accident. There is now no beneficiary. A year later, brother John's first child is born. In such a case *IHTA 1984, s 71(7)* comes to the trustees' aid by providing that the persons who are going to attain the age of 25 can include unborn children provided there is or has been a living beneficiary. Therefore sister Kate's child has given the settlement the start which was necessary to get inside *section 71*.

10.11 Accumulation and maintenance settlements are useful where there is an asset which is important to the family and should be managed as one unit. An influential holding of shares is of this sort. Rather than split it amongst one's children, it might be better to settle it on them on accumulation and maintenance trusts so that they achieve only a life interest. This enables the trustees, of whom the settlor might be one, to manage the shareholding. Something similar can be done with a landed estate where good management requires the estate to be kept intact. If the capital remains settled then this rules out the possibility of a CGT charge under *TCGA 1992, s 71* (the charge upon a person becoming absolutely entitled to settled property).

Example

The Duke of Bermondsey is 30, has one child and hopes to have another three. He settles all his properties in three important London streets

10.12 *Inheritance Tax—Accumulation and Maintenance Settlements*

(£200 million worth) on 'such of my children as attain the age of 25, if more than one in equal shares'. The children are to attain an interest in possession at age 25 with reversion to their children. This is a PET and seven years and three children later, the whole estate can be free of capital taxes for, perhaps 60 years and need never be divided up. The Duke or his land agent may be a trustee and can manage the estate without much reference to the children.

10.12 Accumulation and maintenance settlements can be a useful vehicle for holding shares in a family company of which the parents wish to retain control.

Unlisted shares in a trading company qualify for 100% BPR. Therefore the older generation may well feel that there is no tax problem if they retain the shares. If kept until death they attract BPR and there is no CGT to pay. If the shares are given away it would seem likely that holdover relief would be available [*TCGA 1992, s 165*] so that a gift seems to offer the poorer position for CGT. There is a slight mismatch between the two taxes in that, for CGT, shares listed on the AIM are treated as listed whilst for BPR purposes they are unlisted. Before the taxpayer is allowed to make up his mind to do nothing he should check the CGT position:

(*a*) retirement relief remains available to those aged 50 or more if still active in business. Under the phase-out gains of £150,000 in 2000/01 can attract 100% relief and the next £450,000 of gains 50% relief (as reduced by gains already relieved for that taxpayer). [*TCGA 1992, s 163*].

(*b*) re-basing at 31 March 1982 plus nearly 100% indexation since then can not only minimise a gain, it can sometimes cause a loss. Unfortunately this loss will be useless. It will be an 'indexation' loss.

(*c*) taper relief introduced by *FA 1998* has not yet had much time to build up. That said, the improvements to the business assets rate of taper by *FA 2000* may have a dramatic effect in certain circumstances. For the period 6 April 1998 to 5 April 2000, to attract the business assets rate of taper relief on shares in a trading company, trustees had to hold at least 25% (or, within a life interest trust, at least 5% if the life tenant was a full-time working officer or employee). There was also the additional 'bonus year' given to shareholdings held at 17 March 1998, although, following 6 April 2000, this disappears except for non-business assets. From 6 April 2000, any holding of shares in a qualifying trading company will attract the higher business rate of taper. Not only that, but the full benefit of business assets taper is now obtained after only four (rather than, as previously, ten) complete years ownership. However, there is the trap presented in a case where an asset, e.g. a shareholding, attracts the business assets rate from 6 April 2000, but only the non-business rate before then, e.g. a trustee holding of 20% in a discretionary or (where the life tenant is not a full-time working officer

Inheritance Tax—Accumulation and Maintenance Settlements **10.12**

or employee) life interest case. The effect of the apportionment provisions ensures that some part of the gain will attract only the non-business rate of taper, except in a case where the disposal of the shares is made on or after 6 April 2010. The planning point presented by this conundrum is, as with preservation of the retirement relief thresholds before the phase-out started on 6 April 1999, to trigger a disposal of shares by the individual shareholder to a life interest trust, so as to start a new period of ownership. In this way after four years ownership by the trustees the maximum benefit of business assets taper is obtained, the gain on transfer into the trust having been held over under *TCGA 1992, s 165* (albeit losing any accrued taper to that point). While a good idea in principle, this is not a step that should be taken lightly, as there are circumstances in which a taxpayer could be worse off thereby, e.g. if the trustees have to sell the shares soon after the date of settlement: if within twelve months, there would be no taper relief at all.

The fiscal argument for making an accumulation and maintenance settlement is, simply, that some future Chancellor might find the present rate of BPR and APR too generous and they would then be restricted. It is known that some MPs are unhappy about transfers of shares, etc. where both capital taxes are avoided.

The non-fiscal argument is to do with the control of the shares. The benefits from the shares go to the children but, if they are settled for life, they never own the shares. That might please the older generation.

The question of trusteeship is important in relation to remuneration. As a general rule and in the absence of any special clause in the trust instrument, if the settlor needs the votes of the settled shares to secure his remuneration, it must belong to the trust (see e.g. *re Gee, Wood and Others v Staples and Others Ch D, [1948] 1 All ER 498*). Incidentally the question whether the directorship causes there to be a gift with reservation is usually covered by *IHTA 1984, s 90* which permits reasonable remuneration or by the fact that reasonable remuneration does not seem to excite the Capital Taxes Office.

The Inland Revenue have said that a gift of shares by a shareholder-director can be a gift with reservation of benefit where the directorship continues. However, if the remuneration package is that which an outsider would have had, the point is not raised. If the remuneration is really excessive, then the gift is caught.

Remuneration received by trustees is always a difficult area. There is the general rule that trustees may not profit from their trusteeship, which gave rise to the *Gee, Wood* case already mentioned. Modern trust deeds are generously worded so as to allow remuneration. However cases do turn up where the remuneration is clearly unearned. In *re Keeler's Settled Trusts, Ch D, [1981] 1 All ER 888* there was a charging clause and power to appoint trustees to be directors but no clause authorising those people

10.13 *Inheritance Tax—Accumulation and Maintenance Settlements*

to retain fees. The court allowed remuneration appropriate to their efforts. Anything else had to be handed over to the trust. This included all the emoluments of the settlor's wife.

10.13 Accumulation and maintenance settlements may be set up by wills or by intestacy. They can also be set up by a deed of variation of the will of a deceased person so as to take advantage of *IHTA 1984, s 142(1)*. Reference has already been made to the income tax pitfalls where a beneficiary varies the will in favour of his infant children and then uses income for their benefit (see 4.7 above).

10.14 If the PET which starts the settlement does turn into a chargeable transfer then the charge is on the value at the date of the transfer. The rates of tax will be those applicable at the date of death if lower than those at the date of gift. The consequences if the value of the asset given should grow and the rates of tax fall are obvious. Occasionally there will be cases where the value falls between the date of transfer and date of death. In such a case the lower value can be used only where and to the extent that the value at the date of transfer exceeded the nil rate band threshold. [*IHTA 1984, s 131*].

The charge to tax on failure

10.15 In the unlikely event of an accumulation and maintenance settlement failing there will be a charge to inheritance tax. The likeliest occasion of charge seems to be where a settlement with no common grandparent subsists for more than 25 years. There can be no charge:

(a) on a beneficiary becoming entitled to the settled property or to an interest in possession in it by reaching the age of 25 or any earlier qualifying age specified in the trust instrument; nor

(b) on the death of a beneficiary before reaching the qualifying age. It would seem that, even if all the beneficiaries died, and as a consequence the settlement ceased to be within *IHTA 1984, s 71, section 71(4)* would prevent a charge to inheritance tax.

[*IHTA 1984, s 71(4)*].

Where there is a charge, the rate of tax increases quarter by quarter for the period during which the settlement has existed, as follows:

	Maximum %
0.25% for the first 40 quarters	10
0.20% for the next 40 quarters	8
0.15% for the next 40 quarters	6
0.10% for the next 40 quarters	4
0.05% for the next 40 quarters	2
Maximum charge after 50 years	30%

Inheritance Tax—Accumulation and Maintenance Settlements **10.16**

The first quarter which is caught, where the settlement dates back so far, is that commencing on 13 March 1975. For a quarter to be caught, it must be a complete quarter ended before the occasion of charge. [*IHTA 1984, ss 70(6)(8), 71(3)(5)*].

It is hard to see how an accumulation and maintenance settlement could be involved for so many quarters, but this table is a standard table applied to a number of sheltered types of settlement when their shelter fails.

Example

There is only one beneficiary of an accumulation and maintenance settlement. Accumulation and maintenance can continue until he is aged 25. At the age of 22, he assigns all his interest in the settlement to his girlfriend, then aged 26.

The settled property is worth £60,000 at the date of the assignment and the settlement has been in existence for 15 years and a day. There will be a charge of £8,400 calculated as follows:

	%
0.25% per quarter for 40 quarters	10
0.20% per quarter for 20 quarters	4
	14%
14% of £60,000	£8,400

Note that, had the beneficiary waited until age 25, when he would have obtained either an interest in possession or an absolute interest in the capital, or if the trustees had exercised powers in the settlement to accelerate the interest in possession before the assignment, the gift would have been a PET.

10.16 Accumulation and maintenance settlements which, correctly designed, may shelter capital from capital taxes as we know them for anything up to 80 years (depending upon the longevity of the beneficiaries) are understandably popular. For 1997/98, 277 ten year charges were made on £245m of assets (and for 1996/97 300 charges on £167m). This total is gross before deducting liabilities and exemptions. It will be on the low side because there are always late returns which can run to the odd £100m. If that represented one tenth of the wealth contained in discretionary settlements their popularity is demonstrated. There seem to be no recent figures for accumulation and maintenance settlements. A nil rate band discretionary settlement pays no inheritance tax and, even if good investment makes the capital grow, the marginal rate of 6% (= 30% of ½ of 40%) is trifling. The ten year charge on a one million pound discretionary settlement with no qualifying business or agricultural property is £45,960 (assuming full use of the nil rate band). That amount subject to a death charge would cost £306,400. Therefore the death charge is 6⅔ times

10.17 *Inheritance Tax—Accumulation and Maintenance Settlements*

the ten year charge and that is a powerful if oversimplified illustration of the benefits which can be had from discretionary settlements. The problem with accumulation and maintenance settlements is that once the beneficiaries have reached 25, etc. the capital is susceptible to the death charge unless it is invested in business or agricultural property. Obviously one would hope that no death charge would occur for several decades but the risk is there. A discretionary settlement can do anything which an accumulation and maintenance settlement can do. However, because tax has to be paid on making discretionary settlements outside the nil rate band and an accumulation and maintenance settlement is a PET, the latter are more popular.

10.17 Because an accumulation and maintenance settlement is not relevant property [*IHTA 1984, s 58(1)(b)*], an appointment on accumulation and maintenance trusts by the trustees of a discretionary settlement is an occasion of charge (see 12.2 below). [*IHTA 1984, s 65(1)(a)*]. However, the rate of tax will be found by going back to the beginning of the ten-year period. If the discretionary settlement starts within the nil rate band (other than on account of BPR or APR: see 12.9 and 12.12 below), it does not matter what the capital value is after 9½ years, it can be appointed on accumulation and maintenance trusts at a nil rate. The trustees should probably do some sort of a stock taking after seven and a half years. They could then consider reinvestment in business property with the two-year ownership test in mind. Then, of course, after nine and a half years they should consider appointments.

Chapter 11

Inheritance Tax—Discretionary Settlements

The ten-year charge

11.1 The ten-year charge is the principal charge to inheritance tax for discretionary settlements. The charge at other times is based on the ten-year charge but is scaled down to allow for the fact that ten years will not have elapsed. This is the proportionate charge (described in Chapter 12).

11.2 The rules for inheritance tax on discretionary settlements created before 27 March 1974 were slightly different and these are explained in Chapter 13.

11.3 Many practitioners are put off by the complexity of the sections dealing with discretionary settlements. Most of the legislation is about things which should not happen in practice, such as settlements which are only partly discretionary, or where there are related settlements, added property and so on. The sections which apply to a simple case are themselves simple. The rates of tax are low. Most modern discretionary settlements are modest in size to begin with. The capital remains undisturbed. They suffer tax every ten years. The tax is calculated at 30% of half the death rate of tax and most settlements have their nil rate band intact. Much of what follows is a warning of what happens if a settlement is not so simple.

The ten-year anniversary

11.4 In order to discover when the ten-year charge is due, the ten-year anniversary must be known. It is any tenth anniversary of the date of commencement of the settlement. [*IHTA 1984, s 61(1)*]. The commencement of a settlement is the date when property is first settled. [*IHTA 1984, s 60*]. It is not uncommon to form a settlement with a nominal trust fund of £10 or £100 and to add property later. It is the settling of the initial capital which is the commencement of the settlement and it is this date which will determine the ten-year anniversary. The way in which the legislation allows for added property is by an adjustment which affects the rate of tax rather than by an attempt to tax it as if it were a separate settlement. The adjustments for added property are explained in 11.23 below.

11.5 *Inheritance Tax—Discretionary Settlements*

No date before 1 April 1983 could have been a ten-year anniversary. In certain cases, where a chargeable event occurred during the year to 31 March 1984 as a result of court proceedings, the first ten-year anniversary could be deferred until 1 April 1984. This does not affect the dates of later anniversaries. [*IHTA 1984, s 61(3)(4)*].

11.5 *IHTA 1984, s 80* could have caused a difficulty in deciding the proper ten-year anniversary. Section 80 deals with the case where a modern settlement (i.e. one made after 26 March 1974) has become discretionary on the termination of an interest in possession to which the settlor or his spouse, widow or widower is entitled. This could happen where a man died leaving his estate to his widow for life with remainder over on discretionary trusts for other members of his family. In such a case, *section 80* treats the entry into the discretionary regime as if it were a separate settlement made by the deceased life tenant. Despite this provision, the ten-year anniversaries of the settlement will be determined by reference to the original date of commencement and not to the date on which the interest in possession ceased. [*IHTA 1984, s 61(2)*].

11.6 Property can be left on discretionary trusts by a will. In that case, the settlor's death is the commencement of the settlement and the ten-year anniversaries are determined accordingly. [*IHTA 1984, s 83*]. One does not have to consider the administration period, since death is the commencement. Where a discretionary settlement is established by a post-death deed of variation for which the election is made under *IHTA 1984, s 142(2)*, it is the date of death which constitutes commencement of the settlement (and not the date of the deed). For income tax the position is different. For the period during which the estate administration is in progress, there is no settlement for income tax. The settlement commences when the administration period comes to an end.

The amount which is chargeable

11.7 The amount which will bear the ten-year charge is the value of all relevant property (see 2.20 above) contained in the settlement immediately before the anniversary. [*IHTA 1984, s 64*]. The words 'immediately before' are taken to require the valuation of shares by reference to prices on the day before the anniversary. As the relevant property is all the settled property in which there is no qualifying interest in possession, it was originally thought that undistributed income was caught. The Inland Revenue now take the view that accumulations are caught but not undistributed income (Inland Revenue Statement of Practice SP8/86, see Appendix A below).

Accumulations are brought in as part of the capital at the ten-year anniversary. Therefore, they affect the rate and the amount which is chargeable. The problems arising from their not having been part of the settled property throughout the period are discussed at 11.17 below.

Expenses of valuation for the ten-year charge may not be deducted because they will not have become a liability at the anniversary. The valuation principles which apply are those of *IHTA 1984, s 160* (market value) and *section 162* (liabilities). Where trustees hold property which is expensive to value, such as a landed estate or a holding of shares in a private company, they might commission a valuation shortly before the ten-year anniversary and update it at the anniversary. Alternatively, they might make progress payments against bills rendered before the ten-year anniversary. Anything which lessens the total of the relevant property may be good planning although, given that the tax rate is so low, such planning seems not worth the trouble.

If settled property has increased in value, there may seem to be an anomaly in that the potential liability to capital gains tax cannot be deducted. If there is no expectation of a sale this seems fair. However if the sale of a holding, say two years after a ten-year anniversary, causes a substantial payment of CGT, the settled capital might well be less than that assessed to the ten-year charge. No relief is available in these circumstances.

Given re-basing to 31 March 1982, indexation allowance and taper relief (which will start to apply to some non-business assets for disposals on or after 6 April 2000), this point should not be so important in a normal portfolio. As the ten-year charge will not collect tax on shares, etc. attracting 100% BPR or APR holdings in family trading companies should not be at risk. However, it must be possible for shares in other family companies to rise in value and be ripe for flotation, etc. just two or three years after a ten-year anniversary.

11.8 BPR and APR are available to discretionary settlements. [*IHTA 1984, ss 103(1), 115(1)*]. These are valuation reliefs and, therefore, only affect the amount which is brought into charge. They have no direct effect on the rate of tax. They do, however, affect it indirectly. This gives a clear incentive to the trustees of discretionary settlements to invest in assets carrying the 100% reliefs. A discretionary settlement is charged on the lifetime scale (i.e. half the rates in *IHTA 1984, 1 Sch*). The highest rate (currently the only rate once out of the nil rate band) is 40%. The ten-year charge is 30% of the half rate. Therefore the highest rate for a ten-year charge can never exceed 6% (40 × ½ × 30%). If the property carries a 100% relief, there is no tax.

11.9 The normal valuation principles of *IHTA 1984, Pt VI* apply. These include a provision directing that a liability secured on a property reduces the value of that property. [*IHTA 1984, s 162(4)*]. Therefore, to mortgage agricultural or business property when there are other assets available as security must be bad planning. The contrary position is possible, namely that trustees borrow on the security of assets with no relief, in order to invest in assets attracting the relief. *Section 162(4)* would then cause the debt to be deducted from the assets on which it is secured. As a consequence, a settlement which is half invested in assets bearing no relief and half in relevant business property which is financed by debt secured on the first half, could be treated as wholly invested in relevant business property when it came to charging inheritance tax.

11.10 *Inheritance Tax—Discretionary Settlements*

Example

	£
As viewed for IHT	
Government securities	100
Less: borrowing secured thereon	100
	Nil
Relevant business property purchased with above borrowing, attracting BPR	£100
As viewed for other purposes	
Government securities	100
Relevant business property	100
	200
Less: borrowing	100
Net capital	£100

It is not possible to prevent some reduction in the value of the business where there are liabilities incurred for the purposes of the business. These have to be deducted. [*IHTA 1984, s 110(b)*].

Settled heritage property which is the subject of conditional exemption is excluded from the ten-year charge, but it is not possible for trustees to lessen the charge on other property by purchasing such property, as the cost of the property is added to the deemed cumulative total when calculating the next ten-year charge on other property in the settlement. [*IHTA 1984, s 79(8)(9)*].

The calculation of the tax

11.10 Having discovered the amount on which tax is chargeable, it is necessary to discover the rate of tax. This will be 30% of the effective rate (see 11.15 below) applicable to a lifetime charge (which is of course half the death rates). The effective rate is determined by reference to a deemed chargeable transfer and a deemed cumulative total. There were different rules for settlements created before 27 March 1974 and those created on or after that date. The rules for pre-27 March 1974 settlements are dealt with in Chapter 13. The cumulative total of a settlement made after 26 March 1974 includes the settlor's cumulative total of chargeable transfers for the seven years ending with the making of the settlement. There are special rules where property is added (see 11.23 below). The rules for these settlements are explained below, taking the simplest and likeliest situations first and the more complicated ones later. [*IHTA 1984, s 66*].

The ten-year charge (simple case)

The deemed chargeable transfer

11.11 The simplest case is a discretionary settlement with no related settlements, no non-relevant property, no added property and no accumulations of income. In such a case there will be only one component in the deemed chargeable transfer, namely the value immediately before the ten-year anniversary of the relevant property contained in the settlement. This will be everything within the settlement except for any undistributed income.

The deemed cumulative total

11.12 The cumulative total which will determine the starting point on the rate scale is found by adding:

(*a*) the cumulative total of the settlor in the period of seven years prior to the making of the settlement (i.e. excluding all transactions on the day when the settlement commenced). Before 18 March 1986, the settlor's cumulative total during the previous ten years was used, but that is irrelevant to any current calculation. [*IHTA 1984, s 66(5)(6)*]; and

(*b*) the amounts assessed to the proportionate charge (see Chapter 12) during the ten-year period prior to the ten-year anniversary.

11.13 Note that whatever the anniversary, the settlor's cumulative total which is used is always the same because it is always the seven years ending with the making of the settlement which counts. This may be viewed as an anomaly because the individual can shake off his old seven-year cumulation with the passage of time, but the trustees never can. If there is such a thing as a reasonable anomaly, this must be one. A moment's thought as to the likely number of tax saving discretionary settlements which would spring up were they permitted their second, third etc. ten-year charges without any deemed cumulative total will explain this. Note too that all transfers on the day of the settlement are ignored in discovering the cumulative total. However, these transfers will be brought in as related settlements if they are transfers into settlement (see 11.18 below).

11.14 In calculating the deemed cumulative total, distribution payments used to be included. Before 9 March 1982, there was no proportionate charge. The removal of capital from discretionary settlements was still taxed but the charge was on 'distribution payments'. [*IHTA 1984, s 66(6)*].

The effective rate

11.15 Having calculated the deemed chargeable transfer and the deemed cumulative total, the lifetime scale (i.e. the half rate [*IHTA 1984, s 7(2)*] is used to discover the tax appropriate to the deemed chargeable transfer. The tax divided by the deemed chargeable transfer and expressed as a percentage gives the effective (i.e. average) rate. [*IHTA 1984, s 66(1)*].

The rate of ten-year charge

11.16 The rate of tax actually charged is 30% of the effective rate (see 11.15 above). This is applied to the value of the relevant property immediately before the ten-year anniversary to discover the tax payable. [*IHTA 1984, ss 64, 66(1)*].

11.17 *Inheritance Tax—Discretionary Settlements*

Example

Mr Smith, having been generous, used all his exemptions up to and including 1999/2000 and, by the end of that year, had a cumulative total of £234,000 of chargeable transfers over seven years. On 30 April 2000, he gave away £3,000 to use up his annual exemption and the next day he settled £75,000 on discretionary trusts. He paid inheritance tax of £18,750 (on the grossed up amount of the gift). He lived for more than seven years. His trustees invested the £75,000 and distributed income regularly. By 1 May 2010, their investments were worth £234,000. Strangely, the inheritance tax rates etc. in 2010/11 are the same as in 2000/01. The ten-year charge is therefore as follows.

	£
Deemed chargeable transfer (i.e. the value of the relevant property immediately before 1 May 2010)	234,000
Deemed cumulative total (i.e. the settlor's chargeable transfers before commencement)	234,000
Total to determine rate	£468,000
Inheritance tax on lifetime scale (half rate)	£46,800

Effective rate = $\dfrac{46,800}{234,000}$ = 20%

Rate of ten-year charge = 30% of 20% = 6%
Ten-year charge (6% of £234,000) (= 30% of £46,800)   £14,040

Note that in such a simple example, the calculation of the effective rate is an unnecessary step; the tax has to be 30% of the charge which would have been due on the lifetime scale.

The ten-year charge where there are accumulations

11.17 Undistributed income is excluded from the calculations but accumulations are part of the total of relevant property. [*IHTA 1984, s 64*]. Therefore, they affect the rate. However, they are not taxed at the same rate as other relevant property because they have not been comprised in the settlement for the whole ten years. That part of the relevant property at the ten-year anniversary which represents accumulations must be taxed at a proportion of the rate, calculated on a time basis. [*IHTA 1984, s 66(2)*].

The rate on each accumulation is reduced by one fortieth for each successive quarter before that accumulation became relevant property. In other words if an accumulation took place 2½ years (i.e. 10 quarters) after the last ten-year anniversary it will be taxed at 30/40ths of the rate suffered by ordinary relevant property. If there are many investments, sales, payments of expenses, reinvestments and so on, it is impossible to point to any particular asset held at the ten-year anniversary and say that that is an accumulation made on a particular date. The Capital Taxes Office have an actuarial formula which can cope with this sort of problem. It assumes even growth over the ten years. Fortunately, most settlements only contain a few holdings, so that the origin of capital at the ten-year anniversary can be traced back. This leads to the question of when undistributed income becomes an accumulation. Sometimes, the investment of the income demonstrates accumulation. In many cases it will be related to the date when the trustees consider the accounts for the year.

There are reported cases dealing with this subject, e.g. *re Gulbenkian's Settlement Trusts (No 2), Stephens and Another v Maun and Others Ch D, [1969] 2 All ER 1173*. That case related to two settlements made in 1929 and 1938 by Calouste Sarkis Gulbenkian. He died domiciled in Portugal in 1955 but the proper law of the settlements was that of England. The trustees doubted their powers and made no decision as to income. There was a possibility of the settlements being void for uncertainty. The point was resolved in the House of Lords in 1968. The income not distributed dated back to 1957 when the doubts first arose. It was found to have been reasonable for the trustees to have left matters undecided for so long, and their power to accumulate the income of past years could still be exercised.

Whatever basis the taxpayer uses for the calculation will be accepted by the Capital Taxes Office provided it seems reasonable. The amounts of tax at stake can never amount to much and the Capital Taxes Office can therefore take a relaxed view.

The ten-year charge where there are related settlements

11.18 The first complication which can affect the calculation of the ten-year charge, but which will not often be seen in practice, is the related settlement. Settlements are related if the settlor is the same and they commence on the same day. There is an exception for charitable settlements (but not temporary ones). [*IHTA 1984, s 62*]. There is no exception for anything else, so that if a discretionary settlement and an accumulation and maintenance settlement were made on the same day, the discretionary settlement would have a related settlement. In a lifetime situation, a related settlement could be an avoidance device because the deemed cumulative total does not include transfers made on the day on which the settlement commences. Therefore, were the related settlement not brought into account, there might be occasions when a settlor could have a number of small settlements all made on the same day with the intention of producing a lower rate. Ten settlements each with £10,000, all sharing the same deemed cumulative total, would obviously be better than one with £100,000, were it not for the aggregation of related settlements. If the property will grow enormously in value, several settlements on the same day may be acceptable, as the related settlement is brought into the calculation at its value at commencement. Nevertheless, a better result will normally be achieved by a series of small settlements on separate days. Some advisers have recommended a series of trivial discretionary settlements each on a separate day to be followed up by a substantial gift on one day. The result is a series of settlements each with a different commencement date, not being related settlements. There would, of course, be tax on the substantial gift. That said, however the Capital Taxes

11.19 *Inheritance Tax—Discretionary Settlements*

Office are known to challenge both a series of settlements and small settlements made on the same day (if further capital is phased in over a period), even in cases where there are only three or four settlements, on the basis of the associated operations rules. [*IHTA 1984, s 268*]. There has not as yet been a case in the courts on the point.

The most likely occasion when related settlements will be met is following a death. A fairly common formula is for a legacy equal to the nil rate band to be settled by the will on discretionary terms and for the residue to be settled on the widow for life. The widow's fund would not be a related settlement when calculating a ten-year charge on the nil rate band settlement because of the exception provided by *IHTA 1984, s 80*. If, after the widow's death, the residuary estate remained settled for the benefit of the children of the marriage, then it would still not 'relate' to the nil rate band legacy as the section deems the children's interest to have been settled by their mother (and, accordingly, could be related to a discretionary settlement made under the widow's will). However, if the will did not benefit the surviving spouse, the section has no relevance. Therefore, if the will set up a nil rate band discretionary settlement and a residuary settlement for children, the residuary settlement would be 'related' to the other. If, by contrast, the testator had on the day on which he made his will established a £10 'pilot' settlement and then under his will directed the transfer of the nil-rate band amount to the lifetime settlement, there would not be a related settlement problem arising out of the residuary settlement for his children. This is because, under *IHTA 1984, s 62*, the discretionary settlement would be treated as having been made on the date of the pilot settlement.

11.19 The attack on related settlements is to be found in *IHTA 1984, s 66(4)(c)*. The deemed chargeable transfer mentioned in 11.11 above is increased by the value of the related settlement at the time it was set up. Note that this value is not itself charged to tax, unless it is chargeable in its own right (i.e. the related settlement is itself discretionary); it is brought into account in order to fix the rate applicable to the main settlement.

As has been said, the value of the related settlement which has to be brought in to the deemed chargeable transfer is the value of the property comprised in it at the time it was set up. Once ascertained, this figure will recur on every ten-year anniversary. Changes in the related settlement once it has been set up have no consequence. It can have been distributed but the figure will still recur as part of the deemed chargeable transfer.

The ten-year charge where there is relevant and non-relevant property

11.20 The next complication which can affect the calculation is an adjustment which is necessary if there are assets within the settlement which have never been within the discretionary regime (i.e. non-relevant property). This is something of a parallel to the idea of related settlements and, in the same way, the deemed chargeable transfer is increased by the value of the non-relevant property immediately after the

Inheritance Tax—Discretionary Settlements 11.20

capital was settled. [*IHTA 1984, s 66(4)(b)*]. It is considered necessary to bring in these assets because of the possibility of syphoning value between parts of the same settlement. The likeliest situation for this to emerge is a settlement where some members of a family are given fixed interests (i.e. life interests) and there is some fund within the settlement where others are to benefit from a discretionary power. This must be something of a rarity. In such a case the value of the assets which have never been relevant property (i.e. never within the discretionary regime) is brought in to the deemed chargeable transfer to fix the rate, but is not itself charged to tax. These assets are not part of the cumulative total because the cumulative total does not include transactions effected on the day on which the discretionary settlement commenced.

A variation of the above is that property could have changed in character having been non-relevant for part of the ten-year period whilst being relevant immediately before the ten-year anniversary. This is dealt with by an adjustment to the rate and not to the deemed chargeable transfer. For instance, the trustees of a discretionary settlement might purchase a house for the beneficiary and thereby (applying Statement of Practice SP 10/79) create an interest in possession. In due course, the beneficiary leaves and the property reverts to being relevant property. The rate applicable to such property is reduced by one-fortieth for each successive complete quarter before it became or last became relevant property. [*IHTA 1984, s 66(2)*]. See 11.17 above, and see also 11.29 below for an additional example of the alteration to the deemed cumulative total which is necessary when, within the ten-year period, relevant property became non-relevant and relevant again before the ten-year anniversary.

Example 1

Mr Robinson's case is identical to that of Mr Smith in the example in 11.16 above except that his settlement was discretionary as to one half and there was a life interest of the other half. The ten-year charge is calculated as follows.

	£
Deemed chargeable transfer	
Value of relevant property immediately before 1 May 2010	117,000
Value of non-relevant property on 1 May 2000 (*not* 2010)	37,500
	154,500
Deemed cumulative total	234,000
Total to determine rate	£388,500
Inheritance tax on lifetime scale (half rate)	£30,900

11.21 Inheritance Tax—Discretionary Settlements

Effective rate = $\frac{30,900}{154,500}$ = 20%

Rate of ten-year charge = 30% of 20% = 6%
Ten-year charge (6% of £117,000)   £7,050

Example 2

Mr Jones' case was identical to that of Mr Robinson in Example 1 above except that the life interest lasted only two years. Therefore, as with Mr Robinson, Mr Jones' seven year cumulative total of chargeable transfers by 1 May 2000 was £234,000. On 1 May 2000, he also settled £75,000 as to one half on discretionary trusts and one half subject to a life interest. The life interest ceases on 1 May 2002. On 1 May 2010, the settled funds are worth £234,000. The ten-year charge is calculated thus:

	£
Deemed chargeable transfer	
Value of relevant property immediately before 1 May 2010	234,000
Deemed cumulative total	234,000
Total to determine rate	£468,000
Inheritance tax on lifetime scale (half rate)	£46,800

Effective rate = $\frac{46,800}{234,000}$ = 20%

Rate of ten-year charge = 30% of 20% = 6%
(i.e. as in the example in 11.16 above)
Ten-year charge:
  6% on one half (£117,000)   7,050
  32/40ths of 6% on other half   5,640
                                                                £12,690

(This example is deliberately constructed so that the alteration to the deemed cumulative total mentioned in 11.29 below is unnecessary.)

11.21 The opposite case, where the capital is all discretionary at the commencement but is appointed away from the discretionary regime before the ten-year anniversary and remains outside, is taxed by a proportionate charge (see Chapter 12).

11.22 It is not unknown for settlements to have a life tenant and for discretionary trusts to emerge on the death of the life tenant. This could most easily happen in a settlement made by a will. If the settlement is an *inter vivos* settlement then the question of avoidance arises since the insertion of *IHTA 1984, ss 54A, 54B* by *F(No 2)A 1987, 7 Sch 1* (see

Inheritance Tax—Discretionary Settlements 11.23

9.7, 9.8 above). Those provisions are aimed at the use of PETs as a cheap method of creating discretionary settlements. Once interest in possession settlements became PETs, the way was open to settle capital on someone who had not yet used his nil rate band and after a short period arrange for the termination of his interest. If the result of the termination was that the capital was held on discretionary trusts, the result was a discretionary settlement sheltered by the former life tenant's nil rate band. This device became impossible on 17 March 1987 when *sections 54A* and *54B* became effective. It can still be used on a longer term where the termination is not to take place within the next seven years nor at a time when the settlor is still alive, but the creation of such a settlement seems unlikely. There will be older settlements where there is a discretionary trust upon the termination of an interest in possession. The most common may be those where the income beneficiary is the settlor, his spouse, widow or widower. If the settlor is a beneficiary, then the settlement was probably made before the attack on gifts with reservation (i.e. before 18 March 1986). Nowadays, a settlement where there is provision for a widow, or one made by will where the surviving spouse has the income and discretionary trusts emerge on her death, are still a feature. In such a case, the property subject to the interest in possession is not brought into the calculation of the ten-year charge because the property is treated as not yet comprised in the settlement. When it does become relevant property it is treated as a separate settlement made by the deceased life tenant (see also 11.5 above). [*IHTA 1984, s 80*].

The ten-year charge where property is added to the settlement

11.23 Settlors should not add to an existing settlement except, perhaps, by an exempt transfer (i.e. within the annual £3,000 or the normal expenditure out of income exemptions). This is because, where a chargeable transfer by the settlor increases the settled capital, the deemed cumulative total of the trustees is recalculated. [*IHTA 1984, s 67(1)(3)*]. The settlor's cumulative total before the commencement is replaced, if this is greater, by his cumulative total before the addition. The chargeable transfer could be a transfer of fresh capital or it could be a deemed disposition increasing the value rather than the amount of property within the settlement. One situation which arises in practice and must be mentioned is where a life policy is settled on discretionary trusts and premiums continue to be paid by the settlor. The premiums are added property unless the settlor does not make a chargeable transfer when he pays them (e.g. as falling within the normal expenditure out of income exemption).

To prevent minor or accidental transfers from being caught, certain transfers are ignored. These are such transfers as are not primarily intended to increase the value of the settled property and do not, in fact, increase the value by more than 5%. [*IHTA 1984, s 67(2)*]. In the Parliamentary debates on this provision, the example given was of a family company having financial problems which caused the family to

11.24 *Inheritance Tax—Discretionary Settlements*

introduce cash. If the shares were held in a discretionary settlement, the value of the trust property would be increased. The increase would be unintentional and, were it within the 5% limit, would not be within the added property provisions (see Standing Committee A debates on the Finance Bill 1982, col 689, 15 June 1982). The waiver of dividends is another possibility.

11.24 If the added property provisions do apply, the deemed cumulative total is likely to be increased.

Assuming that the settlor has only made two chargeable transfers to the settlement, namely the first to set it up and a second to trigger the added property provisions, the steps are as follows.

(*a*) Note the original deemed cumulative total (i.e. the settlor's total in the seven years prior to the making of the settlement).

(*b*) Note the settlor's deemed cumulative total for the seven years prior to the second transfer. From this total, deduct, to the extent that they are included in the total, the chargeable transfers:

(i) made on the day when property was 'added' to the settlement, and

(ii) which created the settlement and any related settlements.

(*c*) Work out the deemed cumulative total on a normal basis, i.e. the original total plus the total of amounts subject to the proportionate charge.

(*d*) Compare this with the settlor's current cumulative total as adjusted in (*b*) above.

(*e*) The higher figure is the current deemed cumulative total of the trustees. [*IHTA 1984, s 67*].

11.25 There are further rules for more complex cases (e.g. where there have been more chargeable transfers to the settlement). However, these should never arise in practice because once the consequences of adding property have been digested, the settlor is never likely to add further property. It is, in any event, usual for the solicitor to draft a separate trust deed for each significant gift which is to be settled. It is rare to see property being added, apart from occasions when a nominal £100 is settled in order to set things going and the real gift is made a week or two later.

11.26 The manner in which added property is dealt with has to be extraordinarily complicated. The alternative would have been even worse. It would have been necessary to treat each chargeable transfer to the trustees as a new settlement.

Note that the tax consequences of added property are much worse if the addition of property to the settlement follows a significant increase in the settlor's cumulative total of transfers, so that the order of his gifts will matter. The deduction of the first property settled is necessary to the second calculation of the deemed cumulative total (11.24(b) above) because that property would otherwise be counted into the total twice. It would have formed part of the second deemed cumulative total as well as being part of the relevant property brought into the deemed chargeable transfer.

11.27 If there is an existing discretionary settlement and, on the settlor's death, his will or intestacy causes property to be added to it, that property is treated as property added on the date of the death. [*IHTA 1984, s 83*]. This is a sensible provision because the general law would cause the property to vest in the settlement trustees only when appropriated or assented to by the personal representatives. The effect of the section is to ignore the administration period.

11.28 Reference has been made earlier in this chapter (see 11.5 and 11.22 above) to the possibility of the discretionary property being added to after 26 March 1974 by the termination of an interest in possession held by the settlor or his spouse. This is treated as a separate settlement [*IHTA 1984, s 80*] and the added property rules do not apply. There can be a rather specialised problem for the settlement which reserves a life interest to a non-domiciled settlor or spouse and is held thereafter on discretionary terms. This would normally contain excluded property. However, there will be inheritance tax upon the discretionary trust coming into operation unless the former life tenant is still not domiciled in the UK at that date *and* that property remains situated outside the UK. [*IHTA 1984, ss 48(3), 80, 82*].

The ten-year charge where property changes character within the settlement

11.29 The reduction of rates where relevant property is not relevant for the full ten years has already been explained (see 11.20 above). Because the values caught by the proportionate charges are added in to the deemed cumulative total (see 11.12 above), there could be double counting. This would happen if property had remained within the settlement but had been subject to a proportionate charge in the ten years prior to the anniversary concerned. For example, a life interest might have arisen in respect of part of the property for part of the ten-year period. This would have precipitated a proportionate charge and yet the property, being still within the settlement at the ten-year anniversary and having become relevant property again, would form part of the deemed chargeable transfer. In order to overcome this, the deemed cumulative total is reduced by the lesser of two figures, the first being the amount charged to the proportionate charge and the second being the value included for that property in the deemed chargeable transfer (i.e. the value immediately before the ten-year anniversary of the property which had been, for a while, subject to a life interest). [*IHTA 1984, s 67(6)(7)*].

11.30 *Inheritance Tax—Discretionary Settlements*

Example

		£
1 May 1990	A discretionary settlement is made–initial capital	100,000
1 May 1992	A block of property is appointed to A for life with reversion to the main trusts of the settlement. It is valued at	50,000
1 May 1996	A dies and the property reverts	
1 May 2000	The settled property is valued as follows:	
	The block of property	120,000
	Other assets	75,000
	Total	£195,000

In calculating the ten-year charge, the deemed chargeable transfer is:

Per valuation	£195,000

and the deemed cumulative total is:

	£
Settlor's seven-year cumulations [*IHTA 1984, s 66(5)(a)*] (say)	10,000
Amounts charged to proportionate charge [*IHTA 1984, s 66(5)(b)*]	50,000
Adjustment per *IHTA 1984, s 67(6)*—the lesser of £50,000 and £120,000	(50,000)
Deemed cumulative total	£10,000

This is not one of those cases where a proportionate charge under *section 65* and a distribution payment under the old *FA 1975* legislation are equivalent. Only an amount charged under *section 65* can be compared with the valuation on the ten-year anniversary.

The ten-year charge where property becomes relevant property on death

11.30 Property can be held on discretionary trusts by reason of a settled legacy. The property so settled is treated as being comprised in the resultant will trust upon the death of the testator. [*IHTA 1984, s 83*]. A death causes a deemed transfer of value of the deceased person's estate immediately before his death. [*IHTA 1984, s 4(1)*]. The deceased is the settlor of the settled legacy and his cumulative total of chargeable lifetime transfers (including any PETs which become chargeable as a result of death within seven years) becomes the deemed cumulative total of the

Inheritance Tax—Discretionary Settlements **11.31**

trustees. The solicitor who drafts a will cannot guess at the chargeable transfers which his client might make in the seven years prior to death. Therefore, he should warn his client that his gifts within those seven years can substantially alter the tax position of his trustees.

The solicitor should also consider the effect of any other settled legacies (noting the definition of 'settlement' in *IHTA 1984, s 43(2)*), because the general rule is that they are related settlements, having the same settlor and being made on the same day. A legacy settled on a surviving spouse will not be a related settlement. This is the effect of *IHTA 1984, s 80*. Section 80(2) causes the surviving spouse to be within the ambit of the provision. Section 80(1) deals with the case where the settlor, his spouse and (by virtue of *subsection (2)*) his surviving spouse are beneficially entitled to an interest in possession from the commencement of the settlement. Section 80(1) then directs that the settled property shall 'be treated as not having become comprised in the settlement on that occasion'. Therefore, the widow's settled legacy cannot be related to another legacy for which the will declares discretionary trusts. This *section* has already been addressed in 11.5, 11.18 and 11.22 above.

Anti-avoidance measures

Property moving between settlements

11.31 Were there no check on property moving between settlements it would be possible to move property from one rate scale to another or from one ten-year anniversary to another. Non-relevant property within a discretionary settlement is brought into the calculation of the rate. Therefore the Inland Revenue need no protection if the movement is within the settlement (e.g. an appointment to a sub-trust). Property is not likely to be transferred to another settlement if capital gains tax is a possibility (see e.g. *Hart v Briscoe and Others, Ch D [1978] STC 89*). However, cash could be transferred.

Although the modest tax rates mean that there is really little at stake, it is clear that the Inland Revenue need protection against property moving between settlements. Therefore, in any case where tax has to be calculated on a discretionary settlement, *IHTA 1984, s 81* comes into play and the property which has moved is deemed to remain within the first settlement. There have been slightly different details in previous legislation but it has been there since *FA 1975, 5 Sch* was enacted.

Example

Grandfather left his estate to grandmother for life with remainder over to their three adult grandchildren. The grandchildren expected to inherit £702,000 after tax (i.e. £234,000 each). They re-settled their interests on discretionary trusts, hoping to have three nil rate band settlements in due course.

11.32 *Inheritance Tax—Discretionary Settlements*

Section 81 would require the £702,000 to be treated as one settlement and not three. Had the grandchildren waited for grandmother's death and settled their inheritance, then the section would have been irrelevant.

Excluded property

11.32 *IHTA 1984, s 82* is directed at the possibility of avoidance by the use of excluded property in connection with non-domiciliaries. There are two situations where it applies:

(a) where *IHTA 1984, s 80* applies. That provision applies where the settlor or his spouse had an interest in possession, that interest ceased and the capital is then held on fresh trusts. The provision deems the new settlement to have been made by the last person to have had an interest in possession; and

(b) where *IHTA 1984, s 81* applies and property is deemed not to have moved from one settlement to another.

Using excluded property such as FOTRA securities where dealing with non-residents or non-domiciliaries, such a person might have settled capital on himself or his wife with remainder over on discretionary trusts with the intention that *section 80* would give him a discretionary settlement based on excluded property, in due course. *Section 82* prevents this unless:

(i) the original settlor complied with the conditions (see 8.5(b) above) when the settlement was made; and

(ii) the deemed settlor under *section 80* complied with the conditions when his interest came to an end.

In the case covered by *section 81*, the excluded property only remains excluded if the settlors of both the transferor and the transferee settlements complied with the conditions at the time they made their settlements.

11.33 Where all the potential beneficiaries of a discretionary settlement comply with the conditions (see 8.5(b) above), FOTRA securities held by the trustees are excluded property. [*IHTA 1984, s 48(4)(b)*]. If any such securities are transferred between settlements, it is necessary to consider the domicile and residence of the potential beneficiaries of both settlements, because they must all qualify if the transfer is to be of excluded property. [*IHTA 1984, s 48(5)*].

Practical difficulties

Identification

11.34 There are occasions when property has to be identified. Apart from the reduction in the rate of tax which follows where property has not been relevant property for ten years, there is a requirement to identify property for other purposes, as with added property, gifts from different settlors, property coming in on the termination of an interest in possession and so on. The ten-year charge (or a proportionate charge) may be paid either from capital or from accumulated income. Accumulated income, if still represented by relevant property at the next ten-year anniversary, requires a special calculation (see 11.17 above). Therefore it is going to be necessary to know which property was used to make payments, whether to beneficiaries or for expenses. There are no special rules to show how one traces property back to its origins. The only advice which can be given is that record keeping should be impeccable and the trust accounts should be suitably explanatory. There is a rule in *IHTA 1984, s 44(2)* which deals with the case where more than one person contributes to a settlement. In such case, part III of the *IHTA 1984* (dealing with settled property) is to have effect as if the settled property were comprised in separate settlements, each made by one individual settlor, provided that 'the circumstances so require'. Specifically, however, the provisions of *section 48(4)–(6)* are outside the ambit of this rule, dealing respectively with FOTRA securities and movements between settlements between 19 April 1978 and 10 December 1981.

Potentially exempt transfers

11.35 Brief mention has been made (see 9.9 above) of the problems caused by the settlor's premature death. The trustees of a discretionary settlement may be at the greatest disadvantage as they will almost certainly have assets not easily converted into cash and, because the trustees are more likely to be professionals rather than those close to the settlor, they may well not know about the settlor's earlier gifts. The failed PET becomes a chargeable transfer. Taper relief applies where death occurs more than three but less than seven years after the gift. There is a difficulty with the attribution of the annual exemption in a case where a PET and a chargeable transfer are made in the same year. The Capital Taxes Office interpret the interaction of *IHTA 1984, s 3A* and *s 19(3A)* as requiring the exemption to be allocated to the first transfer in the tax year, even if it is a PET which subsequently becomes exempt. The moral is, in a case where a person wishes to make both a discretionary and an accumulation and maintenance settlement, to make the discretionary settlement first, to secure the annual exemption both for the current year and any balance available from the preceding year. The further reason is, of course, that this order of events guards against the possibility of the settlor's death occurring within seven years after the PET, thereby making it chargeable and causing it to fall within his cumulative total for calculating the proportionate and the ten-year anniversary charge.

The problems of the trustees of a discretionary settlement where the settlor dies prematurely can be illustrated as follows.

Example

The settlor made the following gifts.

Each year on 6 April, £3,000 to use his annual exemption.
10 March 1995, to his son, £50,000

11.35 *Inheritance Tax—Discretionary Settlements*

10 May 1996, to his daughter, £125,000
10 June 1997, to trustees of a discretionary settlement, £250,000
He had no history of chargeable transfers before 10 March 1995. He died on 10 April 2000.

The original inheritance tax calculations were:

10 March 1995
A PET of £50,000. Ignored *pro tem*, as assumed to be exempt.

10 May 1996
A PET of £125,000. Ignored *pro tem*, as assumed to be exempt.

10 June 1997
A transfer of value of £250,000, with a nil cumulative total, in 1997/98 when the nil rate band was £215,000.

	£
Chargeable transfer (grossed-up)	258,750
Cumulative total	nil
	£258,750
Tax paid by settlor (£258,750 − 215,000 = £43,750 × 20%)	£8,750

The death changes the calculations:

10 March 1995—no charge (within nil rate band).

10 May 1996
The transfer of value of £125,000 is the amount of the chargeable transfer if there is no grossing-up. The fact that the nil-rate band in 1996/97 was £154,000 is irrelevant because the failed PET is charged at the rates of 2000/01 (the year of death).

	£
Chargeable transfer	125,000
Cumulative total	50,000
	175,000
Tax paid by daughter	Nil

10 June 1997
The chargeable transfer is not changed. However there is now a cumulative total of £175,000.

	£
Chargeable transfer	258,750
Cumulative total	175,000
	433,750
Tax at death rate (£433,750 − 234,000 = £199,750 × 40%)	79,900
Less: paid in 1997/98	8,750
Payable by trustees	71,150

11.36 If there has been a PET before the setting-up of a discretionary trust then it is possible, in theory at least, for the trustees to calculate their maximum risk. *IHTA 1984, 2 Sch 1A* lays down that the rates of tax are those of the year of death if less than those in the year of transfer. Thus the worst which can happen is a charge at the rates used in the year of the transfer.

Gifts with reservation

11.37 There can be inheritance tax problems when the discretionary settlement can benefit the settlor. This will usually be due to a drafting error in the trust deed, because the result is a gift with reservation of benefit. [*FA 1986, s 102*]. It will also be a chargeable transfer. There is nothing to prevent a gift to trustees from being both. Therefore, the death of the settlor, before any remedial action is taken, results in the settled capital being assessed as if it were part of his estate. There are provisions covering the resultant double taxation. [*Inheritance Tax (Double Charges Relief) Regulations, SI 1987, No 1130*]. If the defect is noticed and the possibility of benefit to the settlor is removed there is a danger period of seven years because the remedial action is a deemed PET. [*FA 1986, s 102(4)*]. There are valuation problems with this deemed PET because *section 102(4)* provides that it is deemed to be made by a disposition and there must then be a question as to what is disposed of.

11.38 There may be planning possibilities in this area (especially with a view to securing the capital gains tax holdover under *TCGA 1992, s 260*) through setting up a discretionary trust which is also a gift with reservation. If there is a reserved benefit then the value of the chargeable transfer will be minimal. The benefit is then released and the resultant deemed PET will not be charged if the settlor lives a further seven years. Plainly any such planning requires expert legal guidance. It is quite easy and quite wrong to think that a discretionary settlement in which the settlor retains a benefit is much the same as having the settlor own the settled capital. However, the settlement is still discretionary, there is still a ten year charge and an extra charge upon the death of the settlor.

Chapter 12

Discretionary Settlements—The Proportionate Charge

Introduction

12.1 The proportionate charge is the charge made when property leaves the discretionary settlement regime at times other than a ten-year anniversary. In character it is a topping-up charge, a proportionate part of a ten-year charge, rather than a true exit charge. The proportion depends upon the number of quarters that settled property has been within the discretionary regime, each ten-year period being divided into forty periods, each of three months. Therefore, if a discretionary settlement were wound up at the end of its fourth year, the proportionate charge would be 16/40ths of a ten-year charge. Plainly there are other differences from the ten-year charge, particularly in the field of valuation, as the proportionate charge is based on the 'loss to donor' principle. However, the proportionate charge is completely derived from the ten-year charge. Some authors refer to it as an exit charge. The Inland Revenue, in their booklet IHT 16 'Inheritance tax: Settled property' use the term 'proportionate charge'.

The general rules are explained below. There were modifications for settlements which commenced before 27 March 1974. These are explained in Chapter 13.

The occasions of charge

12.2 There are two possible occasions of charge.

(a) When settled property ceases to be relevant property. [*IHTA 1984, s 65(1)(a)*].

(b) When there is a fall in value of relevant property as a result of a disposition made by the trustees, and the property remains relevant property. [*IHTA 1984, s 65(1)(b)*].

See 2.20 above for the meaning of relevant property.

The property which ceases to be relevant property may do so by leaving the settlement (e.g. when the trustees vote a capital sum to an object of the discretion). Alternatively, the property may still remain within the

Discretionary Settlements—The Proportionate Charge **12.5**

settlement. A conventional discretionary settlement gives powers of appointment in the widest terms so that the trustees could perhaps declare charitable trusts of part of the capital, appoint part as an accumulation and maintenance sub-trust, declare a life interest of part or appoint to any other of the trusts mentioned in 2.20 above. Any such appointment causes property to cease to be relevant property whilst remaining within the settlement. In some cases, there may be no proportionate charge, for example on a charitable appointment (see 12.8 below).

12.3 The disposition in 12.2(*b*) above which causes relevant property to fall in value is intended to bring discretionary settlements into line with individuals who are taxed on the 'loss to donor' principle. [*IHTA 1984, s 3(1)*]. As with transfers of value by individuals the disposition is not caught if it is on arm's length terms and not intended to confer a gratuitous benefit. There is also protection for the grant of tenancies of agricultural property at a full rent. [*IHTA 1984, s 65(6)*]. It is hard to imagine a transaction which causes the capital to fall in value and which is not intended to confer a gratuitous benefit. When the trustees are dealing with the objects of the discretion, they must have a gratuitous intent. Their transactions with others should not be such as to be gifts. Therefore, the practical meaning of this provision is that syphoning is caught (e.g. a change of rights in shares so that the trust shares fall in value and a beneficiary's shares appreciate). The case *Macpherson and Another v CIR, HL [1988] STC 362*, shows that there may be further point in this section. This concerned a change in arrangements for the custody, insurance etc. of a collection of paintings which was settled property. Originally the collection was left at an individual's house. He paid the trustees £100 p.a. for the enjoyment he derived from the pictures and the arrangement could be brought to an end on three months notice. He also undertook the custody, care and insurance of the pictures. A subsequent agreement gave him the pictures for a term of years and at a reduced fee, and this reduced the value of the collection to the trustees. It was held that the subsequent agreement, together with an associated transaction, did confer a gratuitous benefit.

12.4 Again, moving towards parity with treatment of the individual (see *IHTA 1984, s 3(3)*), the deliberate omission to exercise a right is a disposition by the trustees. The usual example is the failure to take up a rights issue in a family company. The deemed disposition is taken to be made at the latest time when the trustees could have exercised the right. [*IHTA 1984, s 65(9)*].

Exemptions from the proportionate charge

12.5 Property ceases to be relevant property upon becoming excluded property. Without specific legislation to this effect, there could have been a charge merely when trustees changed investments. Therefore, *IHTA 1984, s 65(8)* ensures that there shall not be a charge when the trustees of a settlement made by a person not domiciled in the UK when the

12.6 *Discretionary Settlements—The Proportionate Charge*

settlement was made invest in the tax-sheltered government securities mentioned in *IHTA 1984, s 6(2)* i.e. FOTRA securities. Similarly, *IHTA 1984, s 65(7)* covers the position where such trustees move capital from the UK. In deciding where the settlor was domiciled, if the capital was settled before 10 December 1974, or if the capital becomes invested in exempt gilts, the normal tests for domicile apply. If the capital was settled on or after that date, or if property leaves the UK, then the deemed tests of domicile in *IHTA 1984, s 267* will be used (see 22.10 below).

12.6 Payments which do not represent gratuitous transfers of capital are not caught. Thus the payment of costs, expenses or income does not trigger a proportionate charge. In case the costs or expenses relate both to relevant and non-relevant property the exemption applies only to the amounts fairly attributable to relevant property. Dispositions which are payments of income are ignored if the payment is income of the recipient for income tax purposes or would be were he a resident of the UK. [*IHTA 1984, s 65(5)*].

12.7 There is an exemption if the occasion of charge happens in the first quarter of existence of a settlement or within the quarter following a ten-year anniversary. [*IHTA 1984, s 65(4)*]. Where property is settled on discretionary terms by will, there is an effective two year exemption which enables property to be appointed out without incurring any additional charge to inheritance tax, with the appointment being treated as made by the testator at the time of his death. [*IHTA 1984, s 144*].

The appointment should not be made within three months of the death (*Frankland v CIR CA, [1997] STC 1450, Harding & another (executor of Loveday dec'd) v CIR, [1997] STC (SCD) 321*).

The reason for this is that *section 144* is a relieving section and, for reasons mentioned in the previous paragraph, there would have been no proportionate charge on capital leaving the discretionary regime within the first three months of the existence of the settlement.

12.8 Other exemptions cover property which becomes held on certain trusts which are themselves sheltered from the tax, namely:

(*a*)   employee trusts [*IHTA 1984, s 75*];

(*b*)   maintenance funds for historic buildings [*IHTA 1984, 4 Sch 16*];

(*c*)   permanent charities [*IHTA 1984, s 76(1)(a)*];

(*d*)   political parties qualifying for exemption under *IHTA 1984, s 24* [*IHTA 1984, s 76(1)(b)*]; and

(*e*)   national heritage bodies as in *IHTA 1984, 3 Sch* [*IHTA 1984, s 76(1)(c)*].

Until 17 March 1998 there was also an exemption for non-profit-making bodies approved by the Treasury and holding heritage property. For practical purposes the general exemption for charities will serve just as well.

There is a restriction on the exemption for the last three types of beneficiary (i.e. those mentioned in *IHTA 1984, s 76(1)*). If the value of the property going to them is one figure in the hands of the discretionary settlement's trustees and a lower amount in the hands of the body which is the beneficiary, then it is the lesser amount which is exempt. In making this comparison, the value of the property to the trustees making the transfer is not reduced by agricultural or business property relief, and it is not grossed up. [*IHTA 1984, s 76(3)(4)*]. The logic behind this can be seen where there is a controlling interest in a company, say 51%, and the trustees planned to give 2% to a charity before appointing 49% to an individual. In practice the strict letter of the law is not enforced (see Inland Revenue Statement of Practice E13 in Appendix A). Further anti-avoidance legislation prevents the exemption applying where the disposition is defeasible, the asset can be deflected to some other person and where interests under the discretionary settlement have been purchased by certain exempt bodies. [*IHTA 1984, s 76(5)–(8)*].

The amount chargeable

12.9 The amount subject to the proportionate charge is the fall in value of the relevant property, and if the tax is paid out of the remaining relevant property, the amount is grossed up. [*IHTA 1984, s 65(2)*]. The rate of tax on proportionate charges before the first ten-year anniversary is explained in *IHTA 1984, s 68*. Section 68(1) sets the rate by reference to 'the value transferred' by a deemed chargeable transfer, the amount of which is 'equal to ... the value, immediately after the settlement commenced, of the property then comprised in it'. [*Section 68(5)(a)*]. There are provisions to bring in related settlements etc. There is no reduction of these values by reason of BPR/APR, because the reference in *section 68(5)(a)* is to the gross unrelieved value of the property. (The value chargeable, however, may attract BPR or APR even before the first ten-year anniversary.) The rate is not calculated by reference to the amount charged to tax but by reference to an artificial deemed chargeable transfer and a valuation relief can operate only by reducing an amount which is to be taxed.

Bearing in mind the nature of discretionary settlements there should not be too many cases where relevant business property or agricultural property is removed before the first ten-year anniversary. The likeliest is where an asset has appreciated very considerably and, shortly before the ten years has elapsed, some restructuring is desired. For instance if a nil rate discretionary settlement contained shares in a family company, the gross value of which was within the nil rate on settlement, it is possible that after nine years those shares are worth, say, £750,000. That, in itself, might be a reason to create a sub-trust on accumulation and maintenance trusts. Because it started as a nil rate settlement, the appointment to the sub-trust can be made at a nil rate and the absence of BPR is of no consequence. It is only where the shares do not qualify for 100% relief that tax planning may point to an appointment shortly before the ten-year anniversary.

12.10 *Discretionary Settlements—The Proportionate Charge*

The legislation for the ten-year charge is worded differently and the two valuation reliefs are available against the charge on the relevant property at the ten-year anniversary. The rate calculation requires the trustees to bring in non-relevant property which has remained non-relevant and the value of related settlements when they commenced [*IHTA 1984, s 66(4)(b)(c)*] and no valuation reliefs can be deducted from these two components of the deemed chargeable transfer. The valuation reliefs cannot reduce the value of something not being charged to tax.

The rate of charge

12.10 The rules which were applied to a settlement made before 27 March 1974 are explained in Chapter 13.

12.11 A proportionate charge requires there to be ascertained a deemed chargeable transfer and a deemed cumulative total. The deemed chargeable transfer has nothing to do with the amount which is chargeable. This is because the scheme of the proportionate charge is to use the rate which was charged on the last ten-year anniversary. Therefore, the deemed chargeable transfer is that which was calculated for the last ten-year charge or a substitute for it where no ten-year charge has been made so far. The rate of tax can be varied retrospectively if the settlor dies within seven years of making the settlement and there are prior potentially exempt transfers. Those transfers are made chargeable by the death and alter the charge on making the discretionary settlement. If the result is a higher rate of tax, subsequent proportionate charges due before the settlor's death will be reworked and the trustees will have to reclaim the extra tax from the recipient of the capital which they released. This subject was discussed in 11.35 above.

Proportionate charge before first ten-year anniversary

The deemed chargeable transfer

12.12 The deemed chargeable transfer before the first ten-year anniversary comprises:

(*a*) the value of the settled property on commencement;

(*b*) the value of any related settlement (see 11.18 above) upon its commencement;

(*c*) the value of added property at the time of its addition, where added before the event giving rise to the proportionate charge.

[*IHTA 1984, s 68(5)*].

Thus no new valuation of the settled property is necessary, save to discover the chargeable amount by reference to the fall in value of the relevant property (see 12.3 above). The usual scheme for payment of tax over ten years is available either where instalment assets are subject to

Discretionary Settlements—The Proportionate Charge **12.14**

the charge (see 14.14 below), which might be interest-free so long as each instalment is paid on time, or more generally if the beneficiary pays the tax (see 14.16 below).

BPR or APR may, depending upon the circumstances (i.e. if the trustees themselves qualify), apply to reduce the value chargeable by either 100% or 50%.

The deemed cumulative total

12.13 The deemed cumulative total is the cumulative total of the settlor in the seven years ending on the day the settlement commenced but excluding transfers made on that day. [*IHTA 1984, s 68(4)(b)*].

Rate of charge

12.14 Once the deemed chargeable transfer and deemed cumulative total have been ascertained, the current lifetime rates (i.e. the half rates) are used to discover the effective rate (i.e. the average rate on the deemed chargeable transfer). Next, 30% of the effective rate is calculated. So far, the calculation is similar to that of a ten-year charge. However, this is a proportionate charge and the proportion is calculated by reference to complete quarters ended before the occasion of charge. There are forty quarters in ten years. Therefore, the 30% of the effective rate is reduced in proportion to the number of complete successive quarters which have elapsed since the commencement of the settlement. The quarter within which the occasion of charge occurs is ignored. This fraction of the 30% of the effective rate is then applied to the amount which is chargeable (see 12.9 above). [*IHTA 1984, s 68(1)(2)*].

Example 1—with a substantial cumulative total (not at all usual).

Mr Black settled £150,000 on discretionary trusts on 1 May 1994. At that time he had used his annual exemptions and had a cumulative total of chargeable transfers of £200,000. There were no related settlements. He paid tax on the lifetime transfer of £150,000. No further property was added. By 10 May 2000, when the trustees made their first disposition, the capital had trebled and the £150,000 had become £450,000. They appointed £150,000 on accumulation and maintenance trusts on 10 May 2000.

The proportionate charge is calculated as follows:

	£
Deemed chargeable transfer (i.e. the original settlement of capital *s 68(5)*)	150,000
Deemed cumulative total (i.e. settlor's total down to 30.4.94 *s 68(4)(b)*)	200,000
Total to determine rate	£350,000

12.14 Discretionary Settlements—The Proportionate Charge

		£
Inheritance tax, lifetime rate	234,000 @ nil	
	116,000 @ 20%	23,200
	350,000	£23,200

Effective rate $\quad\dfrac{23,200}{150,000} = 15.47\%$

30% of effective rate $\quad\quad\quad\quad = 4.64\%$

There are 24 complete quarters between 1 May 1993 and 10 May 1999. The charge is:

24/40ths of 4.64% of £150,000 = £4,176

The point of this example is to show how the calculation depends on figures dating back to 1994.

Example 2—with no cumulative total (much more usual).

Everything is as in Example 1 but Mr Black made no chargeable transfers before 1 May 1994. The figures then become:

	£
Deemed chargeable transfer	150,000
Deemed cumulative total	–
Total to determine rate	£150,000

The rate is nil.

Example 3

Immediately following the appointment of 10 May 2000 in Example 1 the trustees appointed the remaining £300,000 to Miss Black for life. The effective rate, etc. is as in Example 1 so that the tax on the appointment to Miss Black is:

24/40ths of 4.64% of £300,000 = £8,352

Because the rate of tax is effectively always an historic one, i.e. either the rate at the commencement of the settlement or at the commencement of the ten-year period, it is essential that, several months before any ten-year anniversary, the trustees consider their position. If the assets have grown fast, then some appointment etc. is clearly indicated, as in the example above where £450,000 with a deemed cumulative total of £200,000 could be moved at the rate appropriate to £150,000 with a deemed cumulative total of £200,000. This has been touched upon in 12.9 above. Any such planning must allow for capital gains tax. For the moment, the rate of CGT is 34%. However, hold-over relief is available only in a limited number of cases. These include those where trustees make a deemed

Discretionary Settlements—The Proportionate Charge **12.16**

chargeable transfer (i.e. from a discretionary trust). Therefore, to move property out of the discretionary regime may sometimes prevent any *future* use of holdover relief (except where business assets are concerned which would attract relief under *TCGA 1992, s 165*).

12.15 The proportionate charge on a discretionary settlement before its first ten-year anniversary is not too clouded by problems arising from added property as that is included in the deemed chargeable transfer (see 12.12(*c*) above). Nevertheless, because the number of quarters used in the first proportionate charge depends on the date of commencement of the settlement, there could be an anomaly if the property charged were property which had only recently been added. Similarly, property could have changed its character and only been relevant property for part of the period. If such property is to be taxed, then the quarters before it became relevant property or before it was added are ignored. [*IHTA 1984, s 68(3)*]. One would hope that this problem would be rare in practice because it is normally inadvisable to add to an existing settlement.

Proportionate charge between ten-year anniversaries

12.16 In a simple case, the rate between ten-year anniversaries is the rate charged on the last ten-year anniversary, scaled down by reference to the number of quarters which have elapsed since then. [*IHTA 1984, s 69(1)(4)*].

Example

Mr Lemon's discretionary settlement is made on 25 May 2000 and the first ten year charge is assessed on 25 May 2010. The legislation, rates of tax, etc. have not changed, there is no added property and, indeed, nothing to make matters complicated.

On 25 May 2010 the settled property is valued at	£500,000
On 25 May 2000 Mr Lemon's cumulative total was	£300,000

	£
The ten year charge is:	
Deemed chargeable transfer	500,000
Deemed cumulative total	300,000
Total for rate	£800,000
234,000 @ nil	–
566,000 @ 20%	113,200
Tax on lifetime scale	£113,200

Of this £113,200, only £100,000 is referable to the settled property of £500,000.

Effective rate = $\dfrac{100,000}{500,000}$ = 20.0%

12.17 *Discretionary Settlements—The Proportionate Charge*

Rate of ten year charge = 30% of 20.0% = 6.0%
Ten year charge = 6.0% of £500,000 = £30,000

On 26 August 2010 (i.e. just after one complete quarter has passed) the value of the investments is £600,000 (i.e. a 20% increase since the 10-year anniversary) and half is appointed to Miss Lemon for life. The proportionate charge is:

1/40th of 6.0% of £300,000 = £450

The tax is paid from the capital impressed with the life interest so that grossing-up is unnecessary.

12.17 The rate of the ten-year charge may have been reduced because there was added property, or because property was not relevant property for the whole period etc. These reductions are ignored in calculating a subsequent proportionate charge. [*IHTA 1984, s 69(1)*].

12.18 Where the table of rates is less at the date of the proportionate charge than it was at the date of the preceding ten-year charge, then the effective rate is re-worked on the new scale. [*IHTA 1984, 2 Sch 3*].

Example

Mr Lemon's trustees in the example in 12.16 above incur a proportionate charge on 26 April 2011. In that year's Budget, the nil rate band remains unchanged but the lifetime charge is reduced by one-third. The rate of the ten-year charge had been 6.0%.

There have still been only three complete quarters so that the rate of the proportionate charge is:

2/3rds of 3/40ths of 6.0% = 0.3%.

12.19 Complications arise where property has been added since the last ten-year anniversary or property which was then non-relevant property has since become relevant property (e.g. as a result of a life interest coming to an end, property has reverted to the discretionary regime). In such a case, the rate of the last ten-year charge is adjusted to what it would have been had the new property or newly relevant property been included in the ten-year charge. The value used where property has been added is the value immediately after it was added to the settlement. If the capital was within the settlement at the ten-year anniversary but was then non-relevant property, it is valued at the date when it became relevant property. This fits the philosophy of the proportionate charge in that the only valuations which are required at the time of the charge are those for the property which ceases to be relevant property.

[*IHTA 1984, s 69(2)(3)*].

Chapter 13

Discretionary Settlements Made Before 27 March 1974

13.1 Settlements made before 27 March 1974 were treated differently until they had been taxed on a ten-year anniversary. After that, the treatment is not dissimilar from that of settlements made after 26 March 1974. There could have been no ten-year anniversary until after 31 March 1983 (see 11.4 above). All pre-27 March 1974 settlements will now have had a ten-year anniversary. Readers who have to check the calculation of a charge made before the first ten-year anniversary are referred to earlier editions of this work.

The transitional charge

13.2 The principal charge was still the ten year charge and there was still a deemed chargeable transfer and a deemed cumulative total. The deemed chargeable transfer was the value of the relevant property at the time of the anniversary. The deemed cumulative total was the total subject to proportionate charges and their predecessor charges during the previous ten years. The usual adjustments were made where property was added or had not been relevant property for the whole of the period. The rate of tax was calculated in the same way as for other settlements, namely the tax due on a lifetime charge was calculated, averaged to give the effective rate. The tax was then 30% of the effective rate.

The proportionate charge

13.3 This would have been prior to the first ten year anniversary. The main difference was the rate of tax, which was 30% of the lifetime rates with no reduction for quarter years. Therefore these settlements were generally left undisturbed until after the first ten-year anniversary.

Chapter 14

Inheritance Tax—Administrative Matters

14.1 Most of the administrative provisions which relate to inheritance tax and settlements are to be found in *IHTA 1984, Pt VIII (ss 215–261)*. In many of the paragraphs of those provisions references to chargeable transfers appear. *IHTA 1984, s 2(3)* ensures that references to chargeable transfers can be construed as references to occasions of charge on discretionary settlements, whether they be ten-year charges or proportionate charges.

Determination of tax chargeable

14.2 The first administrative step will be the rendering of an account by the trustees of the settlement: the form for a transfer of value is IHT 100 and that for a chargeable event (within discretionary trusts) is IHT 101. This is their responsibility. *[IHTA 1984, s 216(1)(b)(c)]*. An account is the equivalent in inheritance tax terms of a return for other taxes. The account can be held over for quite some time because the last day for it to be delivered to the Capital Taxes Office is twelve months after the end of the month in which the occasion of charge took place. Alternatively, if the period of three months beginning with the date on which the trustees become liable for tax takes them to a later date, then that is the final date for delivery. There can be different dates where heritage property is concerned. *[IHTA 1984, s 216(6)]*.

The tax will often be due for payment before the last date for delivery of the account, as follows.

Chargeable Event   *Tax Due*
(a) After 5 April and before   30 April next year.
    1 October
(b) The rest of the fiscal year   Six months after the end of the
                               month when the event occurred.

[IHTA 1984, s 226].

The trustees of any family settlement must find some way of being informed of the settlor's death should that occur within seven years of the gift(s) into settlement. If their settlement is an accumulation and maintenance settlement, then, if it was set up after 17 March 1986 it will have been a PET. The same is true of an interest in possession settlement made after 16 March 1987. The death of the settlor within seven years removes these from the potentially exempt to the chargeable category [*IHTA 1984, s 3A(4)*] and they will not have been reported. [*IHTA 1984, s 3A(5)*]. The trustees will be expected to pay the tax but the personal representatives of the deceased settlor can also be liable if the tax remains unpaid. [*IHTA 1984, ss 199(2), 204(5)–(8)*].

As a matter of prudence, trustees who receive transfers of value (whether PETs or immediately chargeable transfers) should enquire as to the settlor's history of transfers. The need to know about chargeable transfers is obvious. However, the settlor's PETs can turn into chargeable transfers and this upsets the arithmetic of subsequent transfers which were chargeable during his lifetime. If the gift is of shares in a private company, the trustees might ask for recent published accounts and generally assemble a file so that, in the event of the settlor's premature death, they have the material from which a valuation can be made. This assumes that no valuation reliefs are available at 100%. The trustees of a discretionary settlement or of a settlement made prior to 18 March 1986 will not have received PETs, but the passage of the seven years will now have freed them from any possibility of a charge under *IHTA 1984, s 7(4)*. Where a PET to trustees has become chargeable an account is required from the trustees. [*IHTA 1984, s 216(1)(bb)(bc)*]. The time limit for delivery of these accounts is twelve months after the month of death but the due date for tax is six months after the end of the month of death. [*IHTA 1984, ss 216(6), 226(3)(3A)(3B)*].

Early in 1991 the Inland Revenue wrote to the Law Society to give some reassurance to personal representatives liable for inheritance tax under *section 199(2)* on lifetime transfers made by their deceased during the seven years prior to his death. Personal representatives should not usually be pursued where they have distributed the estate before a chargeable lifetime transfer comes to light, having:

(*a*) made the fullest enquiries that are reasonably practicable to discover lifetime transfers; and

(*b*) made full disclosure of everything known to them; and

(*c*) obtained a certificate of discharge.

Although not directly referring to the liabilities of trustees this letter must give some comfort.

14.3 Tax paid late is subject to interest and the interest is not deductible for income tax purposes, so that it can be expensive to delay filing the account, even though the account may not be due. [*IHTA 1984, s 233*]. Where there is certain to be a valuation argument (e.g. about land or shares in a family company), it will be difficult to avoid paying interest unless one overpays. Trustees would not normally

14.4 *Inheritance Tax—Administrative Matters*

overpay. However, there is provision for them to receive interest on tax overpaid. *[IHTA 1984, s 235]*. There is an anomaly in that repayment is necessary to produce the interest. If there were instalment assets then it is possible for a generous deposit and a leisurely agreement of the tax to produce a repayment equal to the excess of the deposit over the tax due on non-instalment assets and, say, the first two instalments on the instalment assets. The Revenue will not allow interest on that proportion of the deposit used to discharge the instalments, because it is never repaid. It is also possible to buy certificates of tax deposit (see 14.20 below) and this may enable trustees to reconcile their duty to preserve the settled capital and enhance its income to the possibility of paying over too much by way of a provisional payment of inheritance tax. The certificates can pay tax but not interest on tax. Interest on certificates will offset the interest on the tax.

The rate of interest is changed from time to time. The rate now current (5% at 31 August 2000) is calculated pursuant to *SI 1989, No 1297 (The Taxes (Interest Rate) Regulations 1989)* which came into force in August 1989. This provides for rates to change on the sixth day of each month if bank lending rates have changed. Changes in interest rates on tax paid late or overpaid continue to be notified by Inland Revenue press release and details can also be obtained from the Inland Revenue Press Office, North West Wing, Bush House, Aldwych, London, WC2B 4PP.

14.4 The Capital Taxes Office can call for information about settlements simply by giving written notice. *[IHTA 1984, s 219(1)]*. The notice need not be to the trustees; it may go to any person, e.g. the bank, a stockbroker etc. The consent of a Special Commissioner has since 25 July 1990 been required for a notice under *section 219*. *[IHTA 1984, s 219(1A)]*. A response is required within thirty days. Barristers and solicitors can claim professional privilege but, even so, a solicitor may have to disclose his client's name and address and other items. *[IHTA 1984, s 219(3)(4)]*. If a UK domiciled settlor either appoints non-resident trustees or gives a professional person concerned with the making of a settlement cause to think that non-resident trustees will be appointed, then, whether requested or not, that professional person (but not a barrister) is bound to report the matter unless someone else has already done so. *[IHTA 1984, s 218]*. For these purposes, the trustees are non-resident if the general administration of the settlement is not ordinarily carried on in the UK and if the majority of the trustees are for the time being resident outside the UK. *[IHTA 1984, s 218(3)]*. This statutory reporting requirement should be taken seriously by professional firms: they should circulate their tax partners on the subject once every year. This practice may be something worthy of more general adoption.

14.5 The Board has power to make a determination. This is the parallel of an assessment in income tax legislation and must be appealed within thirty days if the taxpayer is to keep the position open. Late appeals are possible if there is reasonable excuse. Appeals are to the

Inheritance Tax—Administrative Matters **14.6**

Special Commissioners and it is they who deal with arguments about the valuation of shares. Reports of cases dealt with by the Special Commissioners are published and already there have been reports on valuation cases. Arguments about the value of land in the UK have to go to the Lands Tribunal. It is possible for appeals to go direct to the High Court (generally by agreement). If the appeal is made to the Special Commissioners or to the High Court and the dispute relates to land values, it will be referred to the appropriate Lands Tribunal. [*FA 1993, s 200*]. Determinations are relatively rare. In most cases the Account will be completed so that a determination is unnecessary and all that the Board have to do to collect the tax will be to assess it on forms 301 and 302 (for individuals) or 303 and 304 (for trustees). [*IHTA 1984, ss 221–223*].

Reliefs

14.6 Business property relief was so altered in 1992 and in 1996 that it bears explanation. Firstly, there has to be a transfer of value or a deemed transfer. The termination of an interest in possession is a deemed transfer. [*IHTA 1984, s 52*]. So is a ten year charge or a proportionate charge. [*IHTA 1984, s 103(1)*]. Exceptionally a proportionate charge before the first ten year charge is not so treated (see 12.9 above). Secondly, some or all of the value transferred has to be attributable to 'relevant business property'. It is not necessary for that property to be transferred. All that is required is for part of the value of the transfer, etc. to be the value of 'relevant business property'. Therefore trustees will normally be given business property relief if they hold the right category of asset. As from 6 April 1996 the commonest forms of relevant business property fall into two categories.

First category:

(*a*) a business;

(*b*) an interest in a business (the interest of a proprietor so that e.g. loan account balances do not qualify: see *Beckman v IRC [2000] STC (SCD) 59*);

(*c*) unlisted shares in a trading company or group holding company.

Second category:

(*d*) fixed assets (premises, plant) used for the business of a company controlled by the transferor or by his partnership or of the business carried on by a life tenant (or other interest in possession).

The first category of relevant business property ((*a*) (*b*) or (*c*)) generates 100% relief, whilst the other category gives 50% relief. The relief is given by a reduction in the value for tax purposes. Misunderstandings have been reported regarding groups of companies. The simplest group is a parent company and its subsidiaries. However, there can be sub-

14.6 Inheritance Tax—Administrative Matters

subsidiaries and, for a time it was thought possible for the sub-subsidiaries to be outside the relief. This is not the case: it does not matter how many tiers of holding company there are to get the protection of *IHTA 1984, s 105(4)(b)*.

The relief is intended to benefit trades and professions so that there are clauses designed to exclude property not really likely to be used for trade, etc. and to exclude recently acquired property and property in the course of sale or winding up. There are 'see through' provisions in *IHTA 1984, ss 107* and *108* which protect the relief for company reconstructions, inheritance and so on.

There are two definitions of unlisted shares for inheritance tax. 'Unlisted' is now used instead of 'unquoted'. [*FA 1996, s 199* and *38 Sch*]. *IHTA 1984, s 272* is the definition section. It defines 'quoted' as meaning 'listed on a recognised stock exchange or dealt in on the USM'. However, for the business property relief a different definition is used. This is in *s 105(1ZA)* which says that 'quoted' means listed on a recognised stock exchange. The AIM was introduced on 19 June 1995. The Inland Revenue Press Release of 20 February 1995 gave advance notice that, for the purpose of business property relief, AIM investments would be treated as unlisted. It is curious that *section 272* has not been expressly amended accordingly.

BES shares are unlisted, although these will not normally appear in settlements and there are not many left.

The rules before 10 March 1992 were different. There are occasions when it is necessary to test a transfer for business property relief twice. For instance, a PET may have been made before 10 March 1992 and, within the seven years but after 10 March 1992, the donor may die. Whenever there is an occasion of charge on or after 10 March 1992 the new rules are used and for the purpose of that charge are deemed to have applied at the time of the original transfer. Another similar case is where there is additional tax because of a chargeable transfer made within the seven years prior to death. The legislation is contained in *F(No 2)A 1992, 15 Sch 8, 9*. The words used are not entirely clear but the Revenue have confirmed that, in practice, the new rules apply for any computation occasioned by an event on or after 10 March 1992.

The tests for the business of a company are not quite the same as those for an unincorporated business. *Section 105(3)* excludes business assets, whether incorporated or not, where the business consists wholly or mainly of

(*a*) dealing in securities, stocks or shares, land or buildings; or

(*b*) making or holding investments.

This has been tested by taxpayers with caravan parks and properties which, despite taking up much of their time in management, constituted mainly a Schedule A business for income tax purposes. Following two Special Commissioners' cases in 1995 and a further two in 1997, 1999 saw four such cases. Of these, most significant were the two caravan cases, *Furness v IRC [1999] STC (SCD) 232* and *Weston v IRC [2000] STC (SCD) 30*, and *Farmer v IRC [1999] STC (SCD) 321*. *Furness* and *Weston* were both caravan park cases which were won by the taxpayer and by the Revenue respectively. *Farmer,* won by the taxpayer, concerned the letting by a farmer of property in the centre of the farm surplus to agricultural requirements. What emerges from these cases is that, in applying the *section 105(3)* rule, there is no single test. Rather, the matter must be regarded 'in the round', with regard not just to the profitability and turnover of the trading and investment sides of the business respectively, but also to the overall context of the business, the capital employed and the time spent in the various sides of the business by the proprietors and the employees.

If at the date of the chargeable transfer the company has sold its business for cash, the Capital Taxes Office are likely to contend that the company has become an investment company, precluding relief under *section 105(3)*. There has been a case involving a company which had just sold its nightclub and was looking for another went the other way. At the time of death of the principal shareholder (22 months after the sale) the company's main asset was cash on short-term deposit. The activities of the company showed that it was not in the business of making investments because it was looking for a replacement nightclub and maintained an administrative office. Therefore, business property relief was available (*Brown, Ralph Louis (Exor of) v CIR, Sp C 83 [1996] STC (SCD) 277*). Had Mr Brown owned the nightclub himself and had he sold it shortly before death there would have been no business and no business property relief.

Relief is denied to the extent that the assets of the business constitute 'excepted assets' defined in *IHTA 1984, s 112* as (broadly) not required for the business. Cash surplus to reasonable business requirements will typically be an excepted asset. In *Barclays Bank Trust Co Ltd v CIR, Sp C 158 [1998] STC (SCD) 125* £300,000 out of £450,000 (on a turnover of £600,000) was found to be an excepted asset in that it was not needed for the future purposes of the business at the date of the shareholder's death. Evidence is all important.

There are known to be occasional problems in connection with replacement of business assets by the transferee [*IHTA 1984, s 113B*]. There will be capital gains tax problems because the existence of 100% relief will mean that no valuation has to be 'ascertained' for probate purposes (see 7.25 above) and this can leave the acquisition value open to discussion.

Agricultural property relief was substantially improved in 1992, in line with business property relief. From 10 March 1992 agricultural property with vacant possession (or the right to it within 12 or by concession 24 months) has qualified for 100% relief. Other agricultural properties

14.7 *Inheritance Tax—Administrative Matters*

attracted 50% relief, except where they were the reversion to a tenancy commencing before 10 March 1981 and remain protected by the transitional 'working farmer' provision. However, where the tenancy starts after 31 August 1995 the 50% relief becomes 100%. This is expected to increase the number of tenancies being granted because the 1992 rates of relief did work against tenancies. From 6 April 1995 the cultivation of short rotation coppice qualifies as an agricultural purpose. Previously this was forestry. These changes stem from *FA 1995, ss 154, 155*. *The Finance Act 1997 s 94* enacted a new *section 124C* for the *Inheritance Tax Act*. As a result, from 26 November 1996 land taken out of agricultural use and dedicated as a wildlife habitat can qualify as agricultural property.

14.7 It is to be expected that families with landed estates or with a family company will use settlements. If there is a settlement of such assets then the valuation reliefs are extremely important and the trustees should exercise great care during the first seven years of their ownership to avoid the operation of the notorious claw-back rules. There are sections [*IHTA 1984, ss 113A, 113B, 124A, 124B*] dealing with the position where

(a)   there has been a PET;

(b)   at the time of the transfer a valuation relief was available;

(c)   the transferor had died before the seven years has expired;

(d)   the property transferred has been sold.

Unless the property has been replaced by other property qualifying for a valuation relief the tax on death is calculated as if no relief was due. The provisions relating to replacement property are not straightforward. Where a company changes character (e.g. from being unlisted to being listed) that is ignored. [*IHTA 1984, s 113A (3)(b)(3A)*].

There was a concern that, where business property replaced agricultural property (or vice versa) within the seven-year period, there would necessarily be a claw-back problem on the donor's death within that period. However, publication of an article in Inland Revenue Tax Bulletin December 1994 (Issue 14) indicates that 'mix and match' may be allowed, subject to satisfying certain conditions. However, the position is not completely straightforward and, if trustees are given property which attracts either of the valuation reliefs and they wish to reinvest or change the use of the property, they should first look carefully at the replacement provisions as amplified by the Tax Bulletin article.

There is also a risk for capital gains tax. So long as the trustees have property which attracts a valuation relief or which produces a proportionate charge if passed to a beneficiary, it is nearly certain that they have the right to hold over a capital gain under *TCGA 1992, ss 165* or *260*. They must not lose this privilege without being aware of it. If the disposal is a chargeable transfer for inheritance tax as well as a disposal for capital gains tax, CGT holdover relief should be available under *TCGA 1992, s 260*.

Inheritance Tax—Administrative Matters **14.9**

14.8 There is a seeming anomaly where a PET is made to an accumulation and maintenance settlement for older children and the settlor dies within seven years. If by then the settled shares etc. have vested in the children, whether on interests in possession or on absolute interests, by reason of their having attained the age of 25 etc., there has been a change of ownership. Because the donee is required to be the same, both when the gift is made and when the premature death occurs, business or agricultural property relief is lost. The official view seems to be that the children are likely to be adults when the gift is made and therefore the settlement is slightly artificial as compared with an outright gift.

14.9 The consequences of premature death causing a loss of business property relief etc. can be serious. The more complex case is where there has been a gift of business etc. property to a discretionary trust, no tax being paid on commencement and tax falling due on the premature death of the settlor.

Example

			£
(a) May 2000	Settlement of shares		400,000
	Less: 100% business property relief (BPR)		400,000
	Transfer of value		NIL

NB: Assume that no CGT holdover election is made

(b) July 2000 Following a bid for the company the shares are sold for £400,000 (i.e. the same figure as in May of the same year). The cash remains on deposit.

(c) Sept. 2000 The settlor dies. Therefore, there is an additional charge upon the trustees. [*IHTA 1984, s 7(4)*]. The business property relief is no longer available. [*IHTA 1984, s 113A(2)*].

The tax is calculated as follows.   £

Original chargeable transfer net of BPR	NIL
Add back BPR	£400,000
	£400,000

	£
£234,000 @ nil	–
£166,000 @ 40%	66,400
	66,400
Extra tax	£66,400

The cumulative total of chargeable transfers of the deceased is not affected.

14.10 *Inheritance Tax—Administrative Matters*

It seems clear that, in July, the trustees should have considered term assurance unless they were going to invest in business property. What is more, a very different result arises if the company sells the business and retains the cash whilst looking for another business (Brown's executor's case in 14.6).

14.10 There can be no quick succession relief so far as trustees of discretionary settlements are concerned. However, if the proportionate charge is paid when property leaves the settlement and vests in an individual, then a second charge by reason of the deemed transfer on his death can attract quick succession relief if it happens within five years of the transfer from the discretionary settlement. [*IHTA 1984, ss 2(3), 141*].

14.11 A valuation point which might be of passing interest to trustees, mentioned principally because it has been explored only in recent years, is the value to the tenant of a non-assignable agricultural tenancy. There is value in such a tenancy but there is no market. A market has to be imagined. See *Gray (surviving exor of Lady Fox) v CIR CA [1994] STC 360* and *Baird's executors v CIR, Lands Tribunal for Scotland 1990 (1991) 09 EG, 10 EG 153* and also *Walton (Exor of Walton deceased) v CIR CA [1996] STC 68*.

14.12 The introduction of the AIM has increased the range of companies in which to invest for tax saving. Trustees do not have such a wide range of tax saving investments as do individuals. They cannot claim losses under *ICTA 1988, ss 573–576*. In other directions there are worthwhile inheritance tax and capital gains tax savings. Firstly there is business property relief. This is 50% for a control holding in a listed company but is 100% for holdings in AIM and unlisted companies engaged in business, rather than in property or investments. For capital gains tax there is hold-over relief for gifts of business assets (*TCGA 1992, s 165* and 7.12 above) where shares are listed on the AIM or are unlisted. Further, trustees can defer a capital gains tax liability by subscribing for EIS shares from 6 April 1998 (*TCGA 1992, 5B Sch 17*). This facility is also open to trustees of a 'settlor-interested' trust (resident in the UK) where the gains are assessed on the settlor under section 77.

Payment of tax by instalments

14.13 A useful relief is that of payment of tax by instalments. Where inheritance tax has been charged on instalment assets, tax may be paid by ten equal annual instalments. Where the premature death of the settlor causes a charge on assets contained in a PET to a settlement, then the transfer must have been of instalment assets still held by the trustees at the death (i.e. the property is tested twice, once on the gift and again on the death). In general, no interest is charged on the outstanding instalments unless they are paid late, though see 14.14 below for exceptions to this rule. [*IHTA 1984, ss 227, 234*].

Inheritance Tax—Administrative Matters **14.14**

14.14 Instalment assets are as follows.

(*a*) Land of any description and in any country. This item does not carry the interest relief mentioned in 14.13 above, unless the land can be included under one of the other heads below (i.e. (*d*) or (*e*)).

(*b*) A controlling holding in a company. This could be a public company but it is unlikely that many trustees could control a listed company. An AIM company might be so controlled. Note that the related property provisions of *IHTA 1984, s 161* work in one direction, so as to relate property contained in certain favoured trusts to that contained in an individual's estate, not to relate his property to that contained in one of those trusts. However, the deemed ownership accorded, by *IHTA 1984, s 49(1)*, to an income beneficiary of an interest in possession settlement counts as ownership for this purpose.

(*c*) Shares or securities of a company which is not controlled by the trustees and which is not listed, where:

(i) the Inland Revenue accept that payment in one sum would cause *undue* hardship; or

(ii) the value of the shares transferred exceeds £20,000 and the shareholding is at least 10% of the nominal share capital of the company or, if the shares are ordinary shares, it is at least 10% of the ordinary share capital.

(*d*) The net value of a business or of an interest in a business. This is the interest of a proprietor rather than that of a creditor. The question whether it is a business is decided without reference to income tax legislation and therefore the fact that it produces 'unearned' income is not decisive. The classic example unfortunately has little to do with settlements. It is that of the Lloyds' underwriter who although not in any way concerned with the work of the syndicate, is nevertheless a proprietor. Therefore he has an interest in a business although it produces 'unearned' income.

(*e*) Land on which agricultural property relief is due.

(*f*) Standing timber, in certain circumstances.

[*IHTA 1984, ss 227–229*].

Note that shares quoted on the AIM are unlisted for this purpose.

The interest relief (see 14.13 above) for (*b*) and (*c*) above does not apply to shares and securities of every company. Shares etc. in a company dealing in securities, stocks, shares, land or buildings and one making or holding investments will not qualify unless either the company's business is holding land which qualifies for agricultural property relief or the company is a holding company for one or more ordinary trading companies or it is a UK market maker or discount house. The words 'market maker' were introduced by *FA 1986*. They mean a dealer in

14.15 *Inheritance Tax—Administrative Matters*

Stock Exchange securities and apply from the date when one person can be both a broker and a jobber. Until that date, jobbers qualified. [*IHTA 1984, s 234*]. There is some similarity with the valuation reliefs. However, the privilege of paying by instalments is for a different reason. These are cases where the tax cannot be found quickly.

14.15 Where the instalment property is sold while instalments are still outstanding, the balance of the tax is payable immediately. [*IHTA 1984, s 227(4)*].

14.16 The facility to pay tax by instalments is available for the ten-year charge on discretionary settlements as well as for the proportionate charge. To qualify, either the instalment assets must continue to be comprised in the settlement or the beneficiary must pay the tax. The person paying the tax must give notice in writing to the Board that he wishes to pay by instalments. [*IHTA 1984, s 227(1)*]. There is a space for this in the inheritance tax account. The first instalment is normally due six months after the end of the month in which the chargeable event occurs. [*IHTA 1984, s 227(3)*]. The interest relief has already been mentioned (see 14.13 above). This would not apply to land unless it were part of a business, so the discretionary trustees who are in business have an advantage. Farmland where the trustees are in possession and land on which commercial woodlands stand are examples of land forming part of a business. They would be eligible for the interest relief under 14.14(*a*) above as also being within 14.14(*d*) or (*e*)) and so would be instalment assets *with* the interest relief.

Liability for tax

14.17 In the first instance, the persons liable to pay the inheritance tax are the trustees. Where property leaves a discretionary settlement, the individual who benefits can be liable if the trustees do not pay. [*IHTA 1984, s 201*]. The Inland Revenue charge applies so that the Inland Revenue can have recourse to the property. [*IHTA 1984, s 237*].

14.18 Certificates of discharge can be obtained. [*IHTA 1984, s 239*]. The first discharges the property from tax, the second discharges the taxpayer. Applications are made on Form IHT 30 and, bearing in mind that trustees must act with extreme caution, it must be recommended that certificates of discharge are obtained. Even though a discharge has been obtained that is not the end of the matter if some failure to disclose material facts is discovered. [*IHTA 1984, s 239(4)*]. The obvious danger is a failed PET not reported by the family.

14.19 Certificates of tax deposit can be used by trustees. If surrendered in payment of inheritance tax, the interest on the certificate and any interest on unpaid tax cancel each other out. If encashed, interest is paid which is chargeable to income tax. Therefore it is possible to buy certificates for an amount exceeding the first estimate of tax, in the knowledge that there can be no interest on the likely amount of tax and that interest

Inheritance Tax—Administrative Matters **14.22**

will be received on any balance from the certificates. The interest rates change from time to time. The current rates (February 2000) range from 2.5% to 5.25% if used to settle a tax liability and 1.25% to 2.75% if encashed.

14.20 Deposits on account of tax due can be made by direct payment. In this case interest will be received on any overpayment (but see 14.3 above) and it will be tax exempt. [*IHTA 1984, s 235*].

14.21 National heritage property is a specialised subject. For many years the Inland Revenue Library at Somerset House sold a very useful guide. This is obsolete from 17 March 1998 as regards gifts to charities and conditional exemptions (*FA 1998, s 143, 25 Sch*).

14.22 Where compensation is received in respect of the shortfall in pension because of mis-selling any amount due to the estate of a deceased person bears neither income tax nor inheritance tax.

Chapter 15

The Use of Discretionary Settlements

The examples in this chapter assume a nil rate band of £234,000 for inheritance tax, i.e. as in 2000/01.

Avoiding aggregation

15.1 Given a progressive tax, avoiding the aggregation of two funds intended to benefit the same family must always be beneficial except for those cases where 100% business property relief or agricultural property relief is available.

If one accepts that £234,000 is not a significant fortune nowadays (e.g. house with the mortgage paid off plus a death benefit under a pension scheme), consider the effect of a legacy of £234,000 to someone who either has £234,000 already or will have that sum in his estate on death. Ignoring the use of the spouse exemption, the inheritance tax on the death of someone

with £234,000 is Nil;

with £468,000 is £93,600.

However, if the legacy were on discretionary terms, the tax on the original estate of £234,000 would not be altered.

A ten-year charge on £468,000 is £14,040 (£468,000 − £234,000 = £234,000 × 20% × 30%). If a settlement of £468,000 was made on a beneficiary whose own estate was already £468,000, the additional tax in prospect on the beneficiary's death is £187,200. As £187,200 is more than 13 times the £14,040 ten-year charge, it would seem very much better to make discretionary settlements and pay the relatively modest ten-year charges. This has been one of the incentives to use post-death deeds of variation. At the lower end, where a legacy of £100,000 might be received by someone with free estate of a similar figure, there is no point in using a settlement. The illustration where two sums of £234,000 come together shows the dramatic effect where the figures are in that part of the tax where the death rate is a flat 40%, and the nil rate band is still a major element in the arithmetic. Presumably, the sophisticated donee will argue in favour of discretionary settlements which can benefit him, whilst the donor will wish the gift to be outright so as to have a PET.

138

Fast-growing asset

15.2 The next use of discretionary settlements which is worth considering is to shield a fast-growing asset from inheritance tax where the owner's expectation of life exceeds three years (less if the asset grows really quickly). Sometimes an asset can be created which has a special possibility of growth. For many years it was held that deferred shares were of this sort. That is to say, shares with a derisory profit share and perhaps no votes but which in ten years' time rank pari passu with the other issued shares. The Revenue now consider (albeit not universally accepted) that the change in the rights at the end of the ten years is within *IHTA 1984, s 98* so that there is a deemed disposition. Perhaps business property relief will make this acceptable. The change in approach came in 1991 and deferred share schemes set up on or before 5 August 1991 will be allowed to save tax.

15.3 The point has already been made that, if the settlor dies prematurely, then any consequent charge to inheritance tax is on the value at the date of transfer. This is value freezing. Whether a PET is being considered or alternatively a chargeable transfer to a discretionary trust, the taxpayer is looking at seven-year planning, where the downside risk is tax at some future lesser rate of tax (one hopes) on today's value or, if the value falls, on the value at the date of death, but only to the extent that it exceeded the nil rate band (see *IHTA 1984, s 131*).

15.4 If growth is likely then, with one eye upon the ten-year charge, one makes multiple settlements.

Example

A would-be settlor believes his gift will treble in value in ten years' time. He has not used his £3,000 annual exemption for this year (2000/01) or last. He wishes to settle £234,000 on discretionary trusts. BPR is not available.

	Deemed cumulative total £000's A	Amount settled £000's B	Possible Growth within Nil Rate band £000's C (= 234K − (A+B))
Monday	–	56	178
Tuesday	50	50	134
Wednesday	100	50	84
Thursday	150	50	34
Friday	200	34	–
		240	430

Had everything been within one settlement there would have been no possibility of growth within the nil rate band.

15.5 The Use of Discretionary Settlements

It is possible that a case will go to the High Court where the Inland Revenue will argue that there is only one settlement and that the later instalments of the scheme are associated operations. Therefore, the example is not to be adopted in such a provocative way. Certainly, if a number of settlements are to be made on successive days, steps should be taken to differentiate the settlements, to minimise the chances of a successful attack under *IHTA 1984, s 268* (associated operations). For example, there could be differences in trustees, beneficiaries, ultimate default trusts, perpetuity periods and administrative provisions, such that as a matter of trust law (at least) the settlements cannot be regarded as one.

When a number of small settlements are made on the same day and further capital is phased in over a period, the Inland Revenue will aggregate them.

Elderly people

15.5 One advantage of discretionary settlements is that they never pay the full rate of inheritance tax which is borne by an individual's estate upon his death. Therefore, if a gift is intended for elderly people it may suffer less tax if settled on discretionary terms and the income voted to them by the trustees.

Example 1

The donor, having used all annual exemptions gives £300,000 to donee 1 who has no other assets. Donee 1 dies after six years and leaves his estate to his brother, donee 2, who dies after a further six years also without other estate. The donor survives so that he has successfully made a PET. At 2000/01 rates, the inheritance tax will be as follows.

	£
Death of donee 1	
Tax on £300,000	26,400
Death of donee 2	
Tax on £273,600 (£300,000 – £26,400)	15,840
Total Tax	£42,240

Example 2

The trustees pay the tax, hence grossing up is required. The gift is as in Example 1 but using a discretionary settlement as a vehicle. The inheritance tax will be as follows.

	£
Donor's chargeable transfer is £316,500. Tax =	16,500
Ten-year charge on £300,000	3,960
Total tax	£20,460

This sort of example produces superior figures with more than one beneficiary, each with a modest to poor life expectation. However, it can still demonstrate worthwhile savings if there is only one beneficiary where he has a modest free estate of his own.

Married couples

15.6 Another use for discretionary settlements is in the planning of wills. The couple who use the spouse exemption on the first death (i.e. by having reciprocal wills) do not use that spouse's nil rate band. At one time the equalisation of estates played a part in inheritance tax planning but this is pointless if the estate of each spouse exceeds £234,000 as the marginal rate of tax is 40% for each of them. If ever we suffer a more progressive table of rates then equalisation may be useful again. For each to leave £234,000 to the children may be good tax planning but it will leave the survivor exposed unless the couple are quite well off. Given inflation, even if only modest, and the general uncertainties of the economic climate, it must be very difficult to extract capital from the wealth available to the second spouse, just to save inheritance tax. If proper provision for the widow(er) is the first purpose of the arrangement, then most people would baulk at these schemes unless the joint fortune is well in excess of (say) £750,000. The standard solution is to incorporate a legacy of £234,000 on discretionary terms in each will, with the surviving spouse as one of the trustees and, also, an object of the discretion. Interestingly, this device is relevant to people with little wealth, people who might not think about death duties.

Example

H1 (husband) and W1 (wife) have estates as follows.

	H1 £	W1 £
House (joint names)	90,000	90,000
Less: mortgage	15,000	15,000
	75,000	75,000
Maturity value of mortgage protection policy	15,000	15,000
Chattels	3,000	2,000
National Savings, bank balance etc.	11,000	11,000
Life policy (maturity value)	20,000	
Death in service benefit from employer	70,000	
	£194,000	£103,000

H1 dies, leaving his estate to W1, and the spouse exemption prevents a tax charge. If values and tax rates do not change by the time of her death, the tax on W1's death is as follows.

Estate	£297,000
Tax	£25,200

15.6 *The Use of Discretionary Settlements*

H2 and W2 are in the same position and die in the same order but H2's will includes the recommended nil rate band legacy on discretionary terms. The residue is left to W2. There is no tax on H2's death. On the death of W2, the position is as follows.

Her estate–as above	£103,000
A discretionary will trust of	£194,000

W2's free estate is within her nil rate band and the death of a beneficiary is not an occasion of charge for a discretionary trust. H2 and W2 save £25,200 in tax. The objects of the discretion in the husband's settlement could not have included the husband himself (and vice versa) as that would have produced a gift with reservation. [*FA 1986, s 102*]. The practical difficulty is that it would not be possible to give the widow a non-exclusive occupation of the matrimonial home. Once she has exclusive occupation, then to that extent her late husband's discretionary legacy could be regarded by the Capital Taxes Office as having become an interest in possession (under Statement of Practice SP 10/79 — see Appendix A). As a precaution, it is as well for the executors to be in a position to sell their half interest in the matrimonial home to the widow and then, if she has funds, she can buy the executors out. If she is an executor then a self-dealing clause in the will is necessary. The Capital Taxes Office have been known to track estates where the discretionary settled legacy includes part of the matrimonial home. Then, upon the death of the second spouse they may look for inheritance tax on that part. There are arguments against this analysis but so far there has been no reported case. The *Trusts of Land and Appointment of Trustees Act 1996* includes a power for the trustees to charge rent, though this is not thought to affect the position. Draftsmanship is important. Rather than give a settled legacy of £234,000 on discretionary terms, an oblique formula will be used such as 'such sum as can be given within the nil rate band'. This may cover the problem where lifetime gifts after the signing of the will but within seven years of death reduce the nil rate band. However, the estate may well include relevant business property or agricultural property.

A recent case related to the wife's share of the matrimonial home. The house was owned by the husband and wife as tenants in common in equal shares. The wife died. Her will provided that her trustees should not object to her husband's continued residence and should not enforce the trust for sale on which the property was held. After the husband's death, their daughter would inherit. When heard by the Special Commissioner it was held that the death of the wife could not have determined the husband's right of residence which derived from the tenancy in common and her will did not give him an interest in possession. In the High Court it was held that there was such an interest, because in substance the wife's will created interests in succession within the statutory definition of 'settlement' in *IHTA 1984, s 43(2)*. *Lloyds Private Banking Ltd v CIR, Ch D [1998] STC 559*.

15.7 In real life, the value of the house and of the investments would change. Presumably they would increase. This in turn must lead to the thought that some couples might set up two discretionary settlements now, each of £234,000 with the intention of keeping some capital growth out of their estates. The general idea would be to look for assets which need little administration unless the couple possessed the skills necessary to run a discretionary settlement themselves. To involve professional assistance on an annual basis would be too expensive for most people unless the settlements were rather wealthier. This question of costs is very real. The discretionary nil rate band legacy has been around for quite a few years. The nil rate band has increased over the years and so it was £110,000 in 1988/89 and reached £154,000 in 1995/96. There must be any number of settled legacies of this sort, well below £200,000. Current professional charge-out rates would bear quite heavily on the income of such small settlements, even though there is a worthwhile inheritance tax saving on the second death. Note the effect of business property relief if shares are to be settled.

Taking all taxes together, it is highly unlikely that the wife would be an object of discretion in the husband's settlement during his lifetime. Therefore it would be important to know that these sums could be spared without risk of discomfort to the couple. One thing which might make it easier would be to allow the wife to benefit from the husband's settlement after his death and vice versa. One would expect the income of the household to be adequate whilst both were alive but there would be a fall (e.g. loss of one pension) when the first spouse died. Hence the desirability of allowing the surviving spouse some help from the discretionary settlement of the first to die.

Incidentally, where a couple have conventional wills, each leaving his or her estate for the benefit of the other, it is still possible to obtain the benefits of a discretionary settlement of £234,000 so as to preserve the nil rate band of the first to die. This would have to be done within the provisions of *IHTA 1984, s 142* which allows for deeds of variation and disclaimers. *Section 142* is not liked by the Inland Revenue and although it has been part of the legislation for years, some narrowing down is to be expected in a future Finance Bill. There has been one attempt to have it repealed, in 1989. However, the facility remains for the moment. 'Double death' variations are possible: if within a short space of time both spouses die and the second inherits the whole of the estate of the first, the executors (and, probably, the beneficiaries) of the second can vary the will of the first (within two years after the first death). This will maximise use of the nil rate band in the estate of the first. This mechanism is accepted by the Capital Taxes Office, even if the assets concerned end up in exactly the same hands, albeit by a different route.

Having your cake

15.8 Before 18 March 1986, it was possible for the settlor to be an object of the discretion. Therefore small settlements like those described in 15.7 above were set up but with both settlor and spouse as objects of

15.9 *The Use of Discretionary Settlements*

the discretion. *FA 1986, s 102* (gifts with reservation) applies only where the settlement is made on or after 18 March 1986. Therefore, these older settlements still work as intended but they must not receive further capital from the settlor etc. If this device has been set up, there is always the question as to whether the trustees may accidentally convert the settlement into one with an interest in possession. For instance, if they resolve formally that all income shall be paid to the settlor until the resolution is countermanded, have they created a defeasible interest in possession (see 8.3 above)? For safety's sake it is better not to make such resolutions.

Family companies

15.9 There are now three sorts of family company so far as trustees and their taxation is concerned. There are those where the shares qualify for 100% business property or agricultural property relief, those where (exceptionally) business property relief is 50% and those which are not or are not wholly eligible for these valuation reliefs. The shares which do not qualify could still be shares in a trading or farming company but either:

(*a*) they do not qualify as relevant business property or as agricultural property (e.g. they fail the two-year ownership test or the two-year occupation or seven-year ownership tests for agricultural property), or

(*b*) some of their assets are 'excepted assets'. [*IHTA 1984, s 112*].

The rules for the valuation of shares in family companies are of long standing. They date back to the invention of estate duty in 1894 and have remained virtually unchanged since. Therefore, it would seem reasonable to expect these rules to be the basis of fiscal valuation for some time to come. These rules favour small minority holdings, each owned by a different taxpayer as compared with influential holdings. (Between 6 April 1998 and 5 April 2000, the taper relief from capital gains tax encouraged the ownership by trustees of at least 25% of a trading company, so as to qualify for the higher rate of business taper. Alternatively, within an interest in possession trust where the life tenant is a full-time working officer or employee, the trustees could hold just 5%. Now, however, with the new improved regime of business taper from 6 April 2000, it does not matter how few shares the trustees own in a qualifying trading company. They will still qualify for the business assets rate of taper. Note, however, the trap presented by the apportionment rules in a case where the shares or other asset concerned attracted the non-business rate between 6 April 1998 and 5 April 2000 and the business rate thereafter: see 10.12(c) above.

The next example is one where the valuation reliefs are not important but the valuation rules are. The example could relate to a successful investor in property.

Example

An entrepreneur aged 30 feels that he has financial responsibility not only for his wife and one-year old child but also for his parents who live on social security and on gifts from him. He wishes to start a new company with £3,000. He has made no previous chargeable transfers and can give away £3,000 within his annual exemption. He makes six settlements each of £500 on discretionary trusts for his father, mother, his present child and any further children born in the next 30 years. After his death, his widow can benefit. The trustees of the settlements subscribe the entire £3,000 share capital of his new company (which is denominated into 3,000 £1 nominal value shares). He dies at the age of 60 when inheritance tax rates etc. are the same as in 2000/01. The company could be worth, say, £2,500,000 on a takeover. One-sixth of its shares put on the market as a single parcel would be worth, say, £200,000. Therefore the total settled shares are

(a) worth £2,500,000, and

(b) valued at £1,200,000 (= £200,000 × 6)

and each settlement can distribute its holdings without tax, as follows.

	£
Valuation of 500 shares	200,000
5 related settlements valued at commencement	2,500
Chargeable to inheritance tax	£202,500

Inheritance tax is nil.

There will, in the meantime, have been three ten-year charges but there can have been no tax unless the valuations on those occasions exceeded £234,000. An equally satisfactory result could probably have been obtained by the use of accumulation and maintenance settlements had it not been for the desire to protect the older generation. If the company were one whose shares were relevant business property there would be no tax (whatever the number of shares and whether or not there were several settlements, for so long as the present rules subsist).

Where there are management reasons for keeping a block of shares intact but there are several people who should benefit, then a discretionary trust is the obvious solution. Perhaps a testator owns such a block of shares and has several children. His will could dispose of them by way of a settled legacy on discretionary terms to benefit his issue. Alternatively if there are no strong CGT reasons for his retention of the shares he could settle them now.

It might be necessary for the settlor to be a trustee. This would permit him to be involved in the management of the trusts and so in the exercise of the voting rights. Unless the Articles of the company are most unusual, the votes of shares which are jointly held are offered by the first-named. This means that the company secretary does not have to consider the form of ownership of the shares and, if he were to discover that they were held within a trust, he does not have to enquire whether the vote is offered in the manner laid down by the trust instrument. However, this is simply a matter of company law. As a matter of trust law, the trustees should normally discuss how their vote is

15.10 *The Use of Discretionary Settlements*

to be used and, once they have reached unanimity (subject to any provision to the contrary in the trust instrument), the first-named would be instructed as to how their vote should be offered. Therefore, the second or third-named trustee has just as much influence over the way in which the vote is cast as does the first-named. Although it is difficult to say why the settlor should not be the first-named trustee, many draftsmen feel happier if he is not. As it is only the question of offering a vote and receiving circulars, notices etc. which turns on this, it is often easier to have the trust instrument show someone other than the settlor as the first-named. Once the settlor has some way of influencing the vote, he will normally raise little objection to very substantial holdings being put in trust if his professional advisers can find sound reason for so doing. After all, to the extent that the company is successful, he should be able to achieve reasonable remuneration and perhaps a substantial retirement scheme, and so should not need the shares.

The usual warning about unreasonable remuneration is necessary. Anybody giving away shares and remaining as a director could be making a gift with the reservation of a benefit. As has been mentioned (see 10.12 above) this point is not likely to be taken by the Capital Taxes Office unless they are provoked by unreasonable remuneration. No trustee-director should be in a position where he relies upon the votes of the trustees for his appointment.

Provided there is no problem over the remuneration of the settlor, it would only be if he wanted to sell the company at some time and live on the proceeds that he would have any need to own the shares himself.

15.10 The reader might now wish to consider the problems of trustees where shares in a family company are settled. The major problem is the 'loss to donor' principle for inheritance tax. The next example shows one pitfall, in that the trustees cannot divide their holding of shares into two halves unless the division is done on the same day. There would be no problem were the shares to qualify for a 100% valuation relief.

Example

	£
Value of trust property	
66⅔% of the capital of a family company	500,000
Liquid assets	100,000
	£600,000

The trustees appoint half their holding of shares for the adult children of brother A. A similar appointment of the rest of the shares will be made when brother B's family is of age.

	£
Fall in value of the holding	
From 66⅔% worth	500,000
To 33⅓% worth (say)	200,000
Fall in value (chargeable to inheritance tax)	£300,000

In a year's time, brother B's family takes the rest and the remaining half of the original holding is appointed. Values have not changed.

33⅓% holding worth (being the amount chargeable
to inheritance tax)   £200,000

It will already be clear to the reader that the division must take place on the same day if the inheritance tax on each half of the fund is to be equal. Therefore, it is unnecessary to show the calculation of the tax with grossing-up and the depletion of the £100,000 liquid assets.

Business property

15.11 The extension of 100% business property relief to holdings of 25% or less of unlisted shares in trading companies on 6 April 1996 gives considerable flexibility to those concerned with family companies. There is no inheritance tax to pay on giving away these shares although there can be a problem if the shares are realised within seven years (see 14.9 above). There is a capital gains tax position but often enough, re-basing to March 1982, indexation allowance and retirement relief cover the gain. In the alternative there is holdover relief which holds over the gain not already covered by retirement relief, etc. Retirement relief is still a significant figure (up to 100% relief for gains of £150,000 in 2000/01 and 50% for the next £450,000 of chargeable gains) although it is being run down. See 14.6 above for cases where companies are concerned.

The fact that a settlement does not contain business property or agricultural property does not prevent its trustees grooming it, as it were, so that it does contain such property in time for the ten-year anniversary. Theoretically, they could go in and out of business etc. property so as to get the best yields or capital appreciation and the best tax treatment. However, one cannot imagine this in real life.

15.12 Much more possible is the case where someone has business or agricultural property with 100% relief and some time ago he has settled capital on discretionary terms. Best of all would be a discretionary settlement with only two or three years to go to its ten-year anniversary. If the taxpayer were to transfer the property with the valuation relief to the trustees of the discretionary settlement then the increase in the ten-year charge should be nothing (i.e. the added property qualifies for 100% relief). There should be no tax by reason of the transfer to the trustees. The point of the exercise would be to ensure that if the valuation reliefs were reduced after the next ten-year charge, then that which was added to the settlement would be protected for ten extra years. This is because the rate for a proportionate charge is based on the rate at the commencement of the ten-year period. Of course, on present tax rates, there need be no reason to move the asset out of the trust, even if the valuation reliefs were diminished because the rate of tax on a ten-year charge is a reasonable one. The idea behind this paragraph is that some future

15.13 *The Use of Discretionary Settlements*

Chancellor might find the valuation reliefs too generous. That must be a possibility so the taxpayer should consider how his business, etc. assets should be owned before any such change is likely.

15.13 Until the 100% business property relief was introduced it was standard estate planning to split large holdings so that the valuations were always valuations of tiny minority holdings.

Then it became better to have larger holdings because the 100% relief was given on holdings larger than 25% and the smaller holdings attracted just 50%. Now that, from 6 April 1996, any size of holding attracts 100% relief, tax strategies do not come into the matter at all.

Future considerations

15.14 One of the biggest problems in using discretionary settlements where one strays outside the nil rate band is the question of funding the ten-year charge. The cash which will be needed to pay the inheritance tax is capital. Most settlements are fully invested and if the assets are dear to the family as with the holding of shares in a family company, the power to accumulate is essential in order to provide cash. However, this power will run for only 21 years in most cases. Perhaps by then some other means will have been found of providing cash. The solution is not likely to be for the company to buy its own shares. Much more likely would be finding some other person within the family who would buy a few shares from time to time. This could, however, lead to problems. *IHTA 1984, s 65(1)(b)* ensures that a disposition by the trustees which lessens the value of property within the discretionary regime is itself an occasion of charge. The sale of a few shares would normally take place at a value appropriate to a minority holding. However, if the shares came from an influential holding, the fall in value would exceed the price. In order to avoid the resultant charge to inheritance tax, the trustees might attempt to sell at the price appropriate to a substantial holding. In that case, the purchaser may be making a chargeable transfer himself because he pays more than the market value. However, this is a problem which the trustees of a modern settlement can defer until their accumulation period runs out in, say, 21 years. If at that time there are still infants who could benefit from the settlement, then it may be possible to go to the court for a variation of trust, that variation being the creation of an additional period of accumulation.

15.15 The holdover reliefs for capital gains tax still make it relatively easy to put shares and land into settlement and entrepreneurial families now have an infinite variety of plans open to them to prevent death causing a financial crisis.

In circumstances where the asset proposed to be settled is not a business asset attracting hold-over relief under *TCGA 1992, s 165*, the alternative relief under *section 260* (for, typically, gifts into a discretionary settlement) means that any value transferred to the trustees over and above the settlor's nil rate band attracts an immediate charge to inheritance tax of 20%. A prospective settlor of such an asset, wanting to obtain the benefits of hold-over relief, might seek to devalue the amount of the chargeable transfer, so as to bring it within his nil rate band, when putting into settlement property that is very valuable. This could be achieved by reserving to himself a right to require the trustees to return the settled property to him once 90 days had expired from the date of the gift. This would of course entail the settlor being a beneficiary and the gift would be caught by the reservation of benefit provisions. However, it would then be open for the trustees to exercise powers in the settlement to exclude the settlor from benefit, thus deeming him to make a potentially exempt transfer under *FA 1986, s 102(4)*, which will become exempt upon his survival for seven years. The question has been whether or not this stratagem is effective, to devalue the initial transfer of value. The High Court has recently decided in *Melville and others v IRC [2000] STC 628* that it is. The right of the settlor to require the property to be transferred back to him was held to be 'property' within the meaning of *IHTA 1984, s 272* and therefore very significantly devalues the amount transferred by the gift into settlement, to within the nil rate band. No doubt an appeal by the Revenue can be expected, given that it is paid within 30 days after execution.

15.16 The repeal of Stamp Duty on gifts in 1985 leaves the greatest damage this tax can do as £5 per document (from 1 October 1999, previously 50p).

15.17 The rate of capital gains tax for discretionary settlements is 34%. The rates for an individual will be 40% or 20% (23% up to and including 1998/99) in most cases. Therefore there could be some attractions in this area.

Comparisons with accumulation and maintenance settlements

15.18 The discretionary settlement which never goes outside the nil rate band is just as effective as an accumulation and maintenance settlement and it can have advantages (e.g. a wider range of beneficiaries, a better accumulation period).

The gift to an accumulation and maintenance trust is a PET and is the better vehicle for gifts where the settlor wishes to give away a few hundreds of thousands of pounds. If he thinks that, during the next seven years, his only major gifts will be within the £234,000 nil rate band, he would generally be better off with a discretionary settlement. One imaginative variation would be a gift of £3,000 (the annual exemption) to discretionary settlement No 1, followed by the settlement of £234,000 (No 2), followed in turn by annual additions of £3,000 to settlement No 1. Note that this order is essential if settlement No 1 is to have no deemed cumulative total. The settlements should not be made on the

15.19 *The Use of Discretionary Settlements*

same day, because of the related settlement rules (see 11.18 above). It would be essential for the trustees to do the bookkeeping, filing of tax returns etc. themselves, because neither settlement could pay for much professional assistance.

The rate of capital gains tax on trusts is now 34% regardless of the type of trust. Therefore, if the beneficiaries' shares in an accumulation and maintenance settlement continue settled after they attain 25 (or other designated age), the rate will not change. The beneficiaries' rates could easily be lower.

Protection from foreign legislation

15.19 Anybody leaving the UK for permanent residence overseas, perhaps on marrying a foreigner, perhaps when retiring, should consider the political and fiscal situation in his new country. If there could be any attack on his capital then it would be better settled either in the UK or in one of our offshore tax havens. There are snags because by this time he is not likely to have assets qualifying for 100% business or agricultural property relief. Unless the migrant settles his capital on himself there is a chargeable transfer. Capital gains tax is a major hurdle if the principal asset is shares in a family company already held for a long period. Nevertheless these protective settlements are common. Where cash can be settled, an offshore investment holding company may be of use. It would have a nominal capital (say £100) and so most of the investment by the trustees would be on loan account. Then money in the company (presumably its investment income) can be paid up to the offshore trustees as dividend or as a partial repayment of the loan, as may be desired.

15.20 UK discretionary settlements with powers to trade can be used by trading families originating in foreign countries with stringent exchange control. Given a modest capital provided by the English branch of the family, the trustees could trade, guided by the family and so accumulate income. When the accumulations made a ten-year charge possible, the trustees of that settlement would then cease to trade, having a decent sum of money with which to make provision for any member of the family visiting the UK. Income tax would, of course, be paid on the income as it accumulated, but only at a total of 34% (under *ICTA 1988*, s 686).

Income tax planning

15.21 The possibility of using a settlement as a reservoir for income, leaking it out as is convenient has already been explained (see 6.32 above). Stripping old settlements is explained in 6.34 above. Apart from these possibilities, in a very wealthy family, accumulation will be acceptable whether taxed at 34% or, in 2000/01, at 25% (on dividends). If recourse is had to accumulations and the numbers are particularly large, it would be prudent to take expert opinion as to whether the payments will be income in the hands of the beneficiary (see 6.35 above).

The attractions of setting up discretionary and accumulation settlements as a conduit for income to members of the family paying less than 40% have been reduced by the introduction of the 10% and 20% rates for income from savings. This has been touched on in 6.21 above. The tax system for 1999/2000 and later years will work against the income of discretionary settlements, etc. The tax credit on dividends is now 10% and the trustees have to pay an extra 15% rather than the 14% they paid in 1998/99. They have to deduct 34% from payments to beneficiaries. Perhaps a new trend will emerge and companies will resort more to interest bearing loan stocks than they do at present. Certainly, the prospect of using discretionary settlements and accumulation settlements as a conduit for dividend income has effectively disappeared, now that a higher rate beneficiary receiving income distributions funded out of dividend income will suffer an effective rate of rather more than 40% (in the absence of a brought forward tax pool in the trust).

The flexibility provided by a discretionary settlement

15.22 A discretionary settlement can normally run for 80 years in England although different periods are possible in other parts of the UK: there is no perpetuity limit for a Scottish discretionary settlement. The power to accumulate can normally be exercised for the first 21 years.

It is not easy for trustees to re-settle trust property. The new trustees could be irresponsible and this could render the original trustees susceptible to action by the beneficiaries. However, in a discretionary settlement, there are usually powers to appoint property in the form of a sub-trust. This is done by a clause empowering the trustees to declare trusts of all or part of the settled property provided those trusts are for the benefit of objects of the discretion. Such appointments are made by deed. They may be revocable or irrevocable.

Provided the appointment can be regarded as the trustees filling in blanks in the instructions given to them by their trust instrument, then the sub-trust is not a new trust. The importance of this distinction was illustrated in the case of *Hart v Briscoe and Others, Ch D 1977 [1978] STC 89*. In that case, there were two completely separate settlements, one made in 1955, another in 1972. The trustees were the same. As trustees of the 1955 settlement, they declared that certain assets in the 1955 settlement would thenceforth be held on the trusts of the 1972 settlement. The result was an argument about capital gains tax which went in favour of the Inland Revenue. The two settlements were separate and there had been an occasion of charge because assets had left the 1955 settlement and gone into the 1972 settlement. [*TCGA 1992, s 71(1)*]. As a consequence, the Board of Inland Revenue issued a Statement of Practice SP9/81 on 23 September 1981. This has been superseded by SP7/84 (see Appendix A),

15.23 *The Use of Discretionary Settlements*

following *Bond v Pickford, CA [1983] STC 517*, explaining how the Board would distinguish between appointments that created sub-trusts and those transactions where there had been a transfer to a new settlement.

15.23 A standard use of powers of appointment is to create an 'accumulation and maintenance settlement' out of a settlement which originally was completely discretionary. Given modern precedents and good draftsmanship, it is standard practice to take power to declare fresh trusts of property within the discretionary regime so as to take the capital into a different regime, and to be able to revoke those trusts and redirect the property without capital ever leaving the main settlement.

Anti-avoidance

15.24 As will have been seen from the chapters on discretionary settlements, there has been anti-avoidance legislation, as interpreted by the courts, against stratagems. The case of *CIR v McGuckian, HL [1997] STC 908* (see 4.19 above) shows that artificial schemes carry considerable risk. The Labour government's promise to promote general anti-avoidance clauses (although now dropped) points in the same direction.

15.25 The legislation includes the catch-all of 'associated operations' (defined in *IHTA 1984, s 268* and incorporated in the charging sections by *section 10(3)*) and this is a powerful deterrent to artificiality. The Capital Taxes Office may regard the making of a loan followed by annual writing off within the annual exemption as being associated operations, although this should be in order provided that the annual releases are effected by deed. If a family settlement contains important assets and is intended to be an enduring part of the family's planning the risk of using sophisticated schemes which could turn out to be associated operations is obvious. Therefore, the estate planner using settlements will usually prefer a solution unlikely to be attacked by the Inland Revenue under present legislation or anything likely to be used as a weapon by them in the foreseeable future.

15.26 There may be room for the decision in *Furniss v Dawson, HL [1984] STC 153* to affect inheritance tax saving schemes. However, as has been explained in 15.26 above, the legislation is already tight enough to cope with artificial schemes, although 'associated operations' were never mentioned in *Cholmondeley and Another v CIR, Ch D [1986] STC 384* where an appointment on 11 June 1979 followed by an advancement on the following day were treated as one. 'In my view, so far as the three farms are concerned, the deed of appointment and the deed of advancement should be read together'. (Scott J, p 392).

Another case which shows a willingness in the courts to limit the effect of *Furniss v Dawson* is that of *Countess Fitzwilliam and Others v CIR, Ch D [1990] STC 65* where, following the death of the tenth Earl Fitzwilliam in 1979, an artificial scheme was used with the intention of reducing capital

The Use of Discretionary Settlements **15.28**

transfer tax. The Inland Revenue lost in the court of first instance. The time for serving notices of appeal ran out in December 1989. The Inland Revenue served notice out of time and in *Countess Fitzwilliam and Others v CIR, CA [1991] STI 158* were allowed an extension. The Court of Appeal pronounced on the case in February 1992 and the High Court decision was confirmed (*1992 STC 185*). On appeal to the Lords, the Inland Revenue lost again. There were five steps in the family's transactions. Although steps 2 to 5 constituted a preplanned tax avoidance scheme, the first step did not. The steps did appear to be separate transactions and there was no question of running them together as in *Furniss v Dawson* nor of disregarding any one or more of them (*Countess Fitzwilliam & Others v CIR, HL [1993] STC 502*). Another case confirming the judicial approach to artificial schemes is *Hatton v CIR, Ch D [1992] STC 140*. Mrs Cole granted a power of attorney 18 days before she died in August 1978 and expressly authorised gratuitous dispositions in favour of her family. Two settlements were made, one by the attorneys on 10 August and another by Mrs Cole's daughter on the next day. Under the law as it was then, if the settlement had been two separate transactions tax would have been saved. The Inland Revenue won the case. See also 15.28 below.

15.27 The Finance Act 1986 reintroduced the concept of gifts with reservation of benefit. [*FA 1986, s 102*]. This was part of the anti-avoidance legislation of Estate Duty. It is interesting to see that the phrase 'to the entire exclusion of the donor' in *FA 1986, s 102(1)(b)* derives from the *Customs and Inland Revenue Act, 1881, s 38(2)(A)*. Because the gift with reservation of benefit was part of the UK tax system until the repeal of Estate Duty, there is case law and the concept is well understood. Obviously, nobody will knowingly create a settlement now where there is a benefit reserved. Perhaps there is a case for settled gifts with reservation of benefit because the renunciation of the benefit counts as a potentially exempt transfer.

15.28 The slimming down of estates with properties in them which owners still want to occupy has occupied estate planners for many years. A case on these lines has just completed its passage through the Courts [*Ingram and another (executors of Lady Ingram dec'd) v CIR, HL [1999] STC 37*]. In March 1987 Lady Ingram transferred property to a nominee. That nominee purported to grant her two leases giving her the property rent free for 20 years. He then transferred the property subject to the leases to a settlement of which Lady Ingram was not a beneficiary. She died in February 1989. The High Court found in favour of the taxpayer on the grounds that valid leases had been made in equity subject to which the reversionary interest had been given away from which Lady Ingram was excluded from benefit. That decision was reversed by the Court of Appeal. However, the House of Lords decided in favour of the taxpayer on 10 December 1998, finding both that the leases to a nominee were effective and also that the subject matter of the gift made by Lady Ingram, namely the reversions, was enjoyed to her entire exclusion. That decision has been reversed, substantially at least, by *FA 1999, s 104*.

15.29 *The Use of Discretionary Settlements*

15.29 Regulations for the avoidance of double charges have been made. This is because the same property could be charged twice, once as a chargeable transfer and once as a gift with a reservation of benefit. The regulations are in *SI 1987, No 1130*. They cover situations where:

(*a*) a potentially exempt transfer has become chargeable and the estate of the deceased includes property given to him by the recipient of the original transfer; or

(*b*) there is both a chargeable transfer and a gift with reservation in respect of the same property; or

(*c*) the deceased owed money to a former donee, the debt is abated by *FA 1986, s 103* and the deceased had made a transfer of value to his creditor; or

(*d*) the deceased died within seven years of making a chargeable transfer and the property had returned to him, during his lifetime and other than for full consideration, so as to form part of his estate on death.

Chapter 16

The Use of Non-Discretionary Settlements

16.1 In many cases assets are settled so as to ensure proper management. Certainly, gifts to children or young adults are better settled. In fact it may be necessary for them to be settled if they are minors. Apart from this question of management, many wealthy people do feel better if they have settled much of their capital, whether by will or by *inter vivos* settlement. They wish to lay down rules for the next generation or perhaps to ensure that family wealth follows the blood-line and is not inherited by in-laws. The increase in the rate of capital gains tax to 34% (*FA 1998, s 120*) upsets the idea of a level playing field. The traditional provision for a widow in her husband's will was a life interest with remainder over to the children (though a wife might also similarly provide in her will for her husband). If tax is the only thing at stake, all such structures for residue could be varied so as to give the widow an absolute interest. That said, interests in possession can have tax advantages over absolute ownership (see 9.10 and 9.11 above).

16.2 General factors apart, trusts are used for tax planning. Discretionary settlements have their own inheritance tax regime which is very reasonable where property is settled for the benefit of adults. Discretionary settlements can achieve just about the same as accumulation and maintenance or an interest in possession settlement. Settlements of business property are generally good planning in that there need be no capital taxation on the making of the settlement. Interest in possession settlements are interesting because they can receive and make potentially exempt transfers. They have their own charging clause. Unfortunately they bring capital into charge on a death, in contrast with discretionary settlements where there is only the ten-year charge and the derivative proportionate charge.

16.3 One of the oldest methods of estate planning is generation skipping. Gifts to infants have to be settled. The usual vehicle would be an accumulation and maintenance settlement. Such a settlement (unless made by a parent) can provide income for the infant and so, perhaps, make use of his/her personal allowance for income tax. As deeds of covenant for children no longer work this is quite an advantage. The capital gains tax rate will be 34%. A settlement can keep together shares which qualify for 100% business property relief. There may be no obvious tax savings but it can be important for a family's holding to be

16.4 The Use of Non-Discretionary Settlements

kept together for voting, etc. and, perhaps, as part of the game of guessing what the Chancellor might do next. An accumulation and maintenance settlement can be a class gift, e.g. 'to such of my grandchildren as attain the age of 21, if more than one, in equal shares'. So there can be unborn beneficiaries. Further, an accumulation and maintenance settlement will constitute a PET. There are occasions when a trust would not be used. For example a gift of relevant business property with 100% business property relief might be made with a capital gain held over, the gift being to an elderly member of the family. The death of the donee would wash out the held over gain and the 100% relief would prevent any charge to inheritance tax. Had the gift been settled, giving the donee an interest in possession, then his death would have caused the clawback of the gain held over, albeit perhaps with the opportunity to hold over yet again [*TCGA 1992, s 74*]. One would hope that the will of the deceased donee would settle the property on the youngest member of the family.

16.4 Any settlement can give dispositive powers to the trustees (e.g. to revoke a life interest) so that they can remove all benefits from anybody who has behaved badly. That can be a PET deemed to have been made by the excluded beneficiary. It is possible to move a transfer from one individual's computations to another's. For instance, were a will to give the widow a life interest, that would be an exempt transfer by the deceased. Were there some machinery in the will to move wealth away after the widow had become a life tenant, then that second transfer would be attributed to the widow for computational purposes. Probably the commonest such transfer is where the widow's interest is given to her during widowhood. So her remarriage would bring her interest to an end and, quite probably, that would be a PET. This is purely an illustration and going on from there, a skilful draftsman could give the trustees powers to revoke part of the life interest so as to benefit the children if they were clear that there was ample provision for the widow. Of course, she could do this herself by a partial renunciation of her interest, etc.

16.5 Interest in possession settlements have a separate charging section for inheritance tax [*IHTA 1984, s 52(1)*] and the valuation can be unexpectedly low. This has been explained in Chapter 9.

16.6 Sometimes where trustees have power to accumulate, shares in a family company may be settled and a generous dividend paid, perhaps enhanced by dividend waivers by other shareholders. The waivers could be attacked under the anti-avoidance rules. The accumulation will not be so tax efficient now because the tax credit has fallen to 10% and the additional tax will be 15%. Nevertheless, in a family of 40% taxpayers that might be acceptable. Note that there are anti-avoidance sections where an enhanced dividend is paid out of profits earned prior to the acquisition of the shares and where the recipient could recover tax (e.g. a charity).

16.7 Sometimes it may be desired to extract surplus cash from a family company and yet not to have the cash spread around the family. In such a

The Use of Non-Discretionary Settlements **16.12**

case it might be possible for the company to buy back its own shares, the only shareholders selling shares being trustees. The buy-back would be structured so that the payment by the company would be a qualifying distribution. The trustees would have to pay a further 14% to bring the tax up to the 'rate applicable in accordance with *sub-section (1AA)*'. The tax credit for a qualifying distribution is 20% as for a dividend.

16.8 Where there is an interest in possession then the reversionary interest is excluded property. The reversioner can therefore pass on his interest with no tax repercussions at all.

16.9 Where a will or intestacy is not acceptable to the family and they decide upon a deed of variation it is often the case that settlements will emerge. Following the decision in *Marshall v Kerr* (see 7.9 above) it is likely that wills will be drafted so as to enable the trustees to make an appointment out of a discretionary trust of residue. That is to say that the variation intended by Mrs Kerr may in future in effect be made by the trustees of the will, albeit under *IHTA 1984, s 144* rather than *section 142*.

16.10 Quite often when shares in a family company are to be given away or settled, the professional advisers must be sure that there is adequate provision for the donor. This usually causes a review of his retirement arrangements. If found wanting, a substantial premium to cover back service etc. may be paid perhaps to the trustees of a self-administered pension fund. Such a premium may not be allowed as a corporation tax deduction in the year of payment but it will be allowed over a period.

16.11 The interest of a remainderman is typically excluded property for inheritance tax purposes. In those few occasions provided by *IHTA 1984, s 48(1)(2)* where excluded property treatment is denied, this will not apply if the remainderman is not domiciled here (see 22.6 below). The disposal of a reversionary interest is (usually) exempt from capital gains tax under *TCGA 1992, s 76*. The capital gains tax exemption depends upon the trustees never having been resident outside the UK. [*TCGA 1992, ss 76(1A)(1B), 85*]. This provides a painless route for the son whose inheritance from his father is subject to his mother's life interest to resettle his interest for the benefit of his children.

16.12 Although stratagems used by the life assurance industry alone are not covered in this book, attention has recently been drawn to the so-called inheritance trusts which are one standard ploy. A single premium bond (i.e. a non-qualifying life policy) is issued to trustees. The beneficiaries are the intended donees. The settlor lends a substantial sum to the trustees of the bond who then effect a second similar single premium bond on the settlor's life. Each year a fraction of the second bond (typically, up to 5%, to defer higher rate income tax under the chargeable events rules in ICTA 1988, ch XIII part II) is encashed to pay off the settlor. The expectation is that there will be investment gains in the bond and these will be outside the settlor's estate. The annual loan repayments will typically have been spent as income and so the settlor's estate is

16.13 *The Use of Non-Discretionary Settlements*

diminished. In the *Finance Bill 1995* it was proposed that the settlor be taxed for income tax on interest deemed to have been earned at an arbitrary official rate. The clause never reached the statute book but one wonders whether some future Bill will contain some similar provision.

16.13 There are settlors willing to give shares in a growing asset to settlements for the benefit of children and grandchildren, excluding themselves and spouses from benefit. The ability to hold over the gain on settling the shares depends upon their qualifying as business assets under *TCGA 1992, s 165* and *7 Sch*. If the children are the life tenants and if the shares are sold at a worthwhile profit then the rate for capital gains tax is 34%.

Chapter 17

Charities

Introduction

17.1 A charity is generally exempt from taxes and so are transfers to one. See 2.21 above for the definition of a charity. This chapter contains a brief outline of the main taxation provisions concerning charities. Charities are of importance in any trust and estate practice. The Charity Commission, in their latest annual report show £19.7 billion of charitable income in 1998: the 1999 report will not be available until November 2000. That will not include the income of charities which do not have to register (e.g. schools, charities in Scotland). Strangely this is one of the commonest areas for mistakes when filling in IHT 200 (the Inland Revenue Account) and it has been reported that the forms for as many as 17% of estates with charitable legacies do not reveal that fact. As a result tax is overpaid and has to be repaid later.

Exemptions on setting up charities

When setting up a charity, the following exemptions are relevant.

Stamp duty

17.2 No duty is charged on conveyances or other transfers to a charity. The document of transfer must be adjudicated. [*FA 1982, s 129*]. The Stamp Office has published a three page leaflet (SO 11).

Inheritance tax

17.3 Gifts and legacies to charities are exempt transfers. [*IHTA 1984, s 23*]. This extends to transfers from discretionary settlements. [*IHTA 1984, s 76*].

At one time there were monetary limits on the exemption but this came to an end in 1983. There are anti-avoidance provisions.

Capital gains tax

17.4 A gift to a charity which involves a disposal of a chargeable asset is exempt. [*TCGA 1992, s 257*].

17.5 Charities

Income tax

17.5 Settlements of income (e.g. deeds of covenant) generate a tax recovery for the charity. Payroll giving [*ICTA 1988, s 202*] is not counted as taxable income of the individual and therefore reaches the charity as a gross sum. The annual limit for any one donor in 1999/2000 was a total of £1,200: the limit has been abolished from 6 April 2000. FA 2000, s 38 has also increased the benefit of certain payroll giving schemes through a 10% supplement paid by the Treasury. Gift aid was introduced with effect from 1 October 1990 for one-off gifts of £600 or more. [*FA 1990, s 25*]. Having been reduced to £400, the limit was £250 from 16 March 1993 until 5 April 2000. [*FA 1993, s 67*]. As from 6 April 2000, there is no minimum: the Gift Aid Declaration (which covers all gifts by an individual to a charity) simply acknowledges that the donor has sufficient liability to income tax or capital gains tax to frank the gift(s). Generally, gift aid made the deposited deed of covenant redundant. The donor is treated as having deducted basic rate tax which the charity recovers. The gift is relieved against the donor's higher rate tax. Gift aid is also available to companies supporting charity. Non-close companies do not have a minimum restriction.

UK charities can raise funds from 31 July 1998 under the millennium gift aid scheme. They will support anti-poverty or educational projects in one or more of eighty poor countries. They must register with FICO (Charities) at Bootle who will send a guidance pack.

The reduction of the tax credit on dividends from 20% to 10% in 1999/2000 would have been a serious blow to charities. Therefore compensation will be given by payments of 21% of dividends received in 1999/2000 reducing to 17%, 13%, 8% and 4% over the following years.

FA 1992, s 27 permits deeds of covenant to be drafted which run for a minimum of four years and continue thereafter until cancelled. Payments under a deed of covenant which commenced before 6 April 2000 may continue without the new Gift Aid Declaration. While there is no tax reason for making a deed of covenant now, such deeds will be welcomed by charities as ensuring some continuity in giving. If a deed of covenant is made on or after 6 April 2000, the donor must still complete the relative Gift Aid Declaration to enable recovery of tax by the charity.

Transfer of shareholdings to charities

17.6 As outlined above, there are no tax costs in setting up a charity. Further, the income of a charity will normally be exempt. So will its capital gains. Therefore, a benevolent family with a family company could easily use a charity as the vehicle for ownership of an important minority holding in the company. The trustees would be drawn from the family. It is hard to envisage circumstances in which the trustees would need to vote in opposition to the rest of the family. Of course, this can happen now and again and it is only a few years ago that trustees of just such a charity had to seek a takeover bid for a family company (a PLC) because it made losses. In that case, the block of shares held by the charity was influential. The gift of a holding of shares would satisfy the charitable instincts of the family, particularly if there were dividends which could fund annual donations. There will be some compliance costs if income is taken from the company because the *Charities Act 1993* requires an audit or similar if the charity has a decent income.

Bearing in mind the difference between the valuation of shares in, for instance, a 51% holding and those in a 49% holding the Capital Taxes Office needs protection for inheritance tax. As a generalisation this is still true, despite the generous business and agricultural property reliefs introduced in *F(No 2)A 1992* and subsequently further extended. Hence assets transferred to a charity are within the 'related property' provisions. This does not affect the trustees, but it does affect the estate planning of the donor. If the shares would be valued at a higher figure if the holdings of the charity and the donor were aggregated, then that is done for the calculation of any inheritance tax on the donor's estate. Therefore, if the donor had 49% and the charity 2% the donor's shares would be valued as if they formed part of a 51% holding (i.e. 49/51 × 51%). Transfers to charities before 16 April 1976 are ignored. This 'relating' of the two holdings is applied not only to shares transferred by the donor but also by his spouse. If the trustees dispose of the shares they remain 'related property' so far as the donor is concerned for a further five years. [*IHTA 1984, s 161*].

17.7 There is no parallel legislation for capital gains tax. That tax depends upon the size of the holding which is disposed of rather than the 'loss to donor' principle which is behind much of inheritance tax. Any protection needed against breaking shareholdings down is contained in *TCGA 1992, s 19* (assets disposed of in a series of transactions).

Tax exemptions for charities

17.8 Once set up, the tax exemptions which can be claimed by the trustees of a charity on money received by them depend upon it having been spent or accumulated for charitable purposes. The exemptions extend to the following.

(i) Rents and anything else received from properties which would otherwise be assessed under Schedule A or Schedule D, Case VI.

(ii) Interest and dividends, including income from a common deposit scheme under *Charities Act 1993, s 25*.

(iii) Covenanted payments.

(iv) The trading profits of the charity if either

   (*a*) that trade is part of a primary purpose of the charity, e.g. running a school, or

17.9 *Charities*

(b) the work in connection with the trade is carried out by beneficiaries, e.g. work for disabled people.

See also below.

[*ICTA 1988, s 505(1)*].

(v) Donations from another charity (see 17.12 below). [*ICTA 1988, s 505(2)*].

(vi) Single gifts by companies from which tax has been deducted. [*ICTA 1988, s 339*].

(vii) Chargeable gains. [*TCGA 1992, s 256*].

Note that quite a number of trades could involve a charity in tax (e.g. sale of christmas cards). The trustees should then consider setting up their own company to carry on such a trade and arrange for it to covenant its income back. Among various fiscal incentives to charitable giving and to charities generally, proposed in the Chancellor's Statement on 9 November 1999 and Budget 2000, *FA 2000, s 46* has removed the need for small charities to have to set up a subsidiary company to run their fundraising trades. There is now a tax exemption to all trading by a charity with a turnover of less than £5,000 and where the trading turnover represents less than 25% of the charity's total income, up to a maximum of £50,000. A technical problem where a lottery was promoted for a charity was revealed in July 1994. Apparently the profits were taxable. Relief was given by extra-statutory concession and amending legislation was introduced by *FA 1995, s 138(1)* which introduced *ICTA 1988, s 505(1)(f)*. If the finance required to set up a trading subsidiary could be a drain on the charity's finances the Charity Commission could object. They would suggest that the investment is inappropriate and damaging to charitable status. By concession, subject to certain conditions, assessments are not raised on the profits of bazaars, jumble sales, gymkhanas and the like (extra-statutory concession C4). There have been difficulties in obtaining refunds of tax when discretionary payments of income have been made to charities by personal representatives. This has been cleared up by SP4/93 (see Appendix A). It is to be noted that claims previously refused will now be repaid. A minor technical amendment was made to the concession in March 1994 and the Inland Revenue issued a free booklet on how they treat fund raising for charities. 'Fund raising for Charity' from Inland Revenue, FICO (Trusts and Charities), St John's House, Merton Road, Bootle, L69 9BB or FICO (Scotland), Trinity Park House, South Trinity Road, Edinburgh EH5 3SD.

Anti-avoidance

17.9 The fact that charities are generally tax exempt has always attracted tax planners. By 1986 the Inland Revenue found itself in a position where protection was needed. By way of illustration, at least one of the Rossminster schemes required a charity as one of the players and other scheme advisers followed suit. The *Helen Slater* case (*CIR v Helen Slater Charitable Trust Limited, CA 1981, 55 TC 230*) had gone against the Revenue. That case showed that if one 'family charity' paid income to another or made a donation to another, that satisfied the requirement to apply income to charitable purposes. The donee charity could then use the donation to invest in some family venture, perhaps even by way of loan to an overseas company and so on.

There were too many tricks being played. The consequence was a substantial body of anti-avoidance legislation in *FA 1986*. This is now incorporated in *ICTA 1988, ss 505, 506, 20 Sch*.

The anti-avoidance legislation has its own jargon as follows.

(i) Relevant income and gains. This is income which is taxable or would be taxable were it not for the exemptions in *section 505(1)* (see 17.8 above), and capital gains, whether relieved by *TCGA 1992, s 256* or not.

(ii) Qualifying expenditure is that which is incurred for charitable purposes only. It includes administrative costs which are reasonable. It does not include investments or loans.

(iii) Non-qualifying expenditure is that which is not for charitable purposes only, and, what is more, money invested in investments which are not qualifying investments. Payments to overseas bodies are non-qualifying expenditure unless it is reasonably certain that they will be used for charitable purposes.

(iv) Qualifying investments are, broadly, anything to which a reputable broker would introduce you. Loans and investments in unlisted companies, or which could assist in the avoidance of tax etc. do not qualify.

(v) Chargeable period is an accounting period if the charity is a company. Otherwise it is the fiscal year. [*ICTA 1988, s 832(1)*].

Those who set up charities must ensure that the trustees know what they are about. The Charity Commissioners, having been vastly under-resourced, are making an effort to enforce the law. The results include inquiries which have looked at national charities such as War on Want, Oxfam and the Royal British Legion. The inquirers were critical but no punishments were made. The *Charities Act 1993* contains a volume of legislation relating to administrative, financial and accounting matters. The Charity Commission report that in 1998 they used their protective powers on 318 occasions. They froze 37 bank accounts, appointed 18 receivers and managers and removed and suspended 11 trustees.

17.10 There is a *de minimis* provision in that a charity with less than £10,000 by way of relevant income and gains in the chargeable period is not within the anti-avoidance legislation. It still has to apply its receipts to charitable purposes if it is to claim exemption.

17.11 Having eliminated small cases, the legislation goes on to attack any 'relevant income and gains' which is in excess of the 'qualifying expendi-

17.12 *Charities*

ture' and is expended on 'non-qualifying expenditure'. There are provisions to catch teeming and lading between different years. This should be enough to prevent charities from investing money in family companies or projects more beneficial to the sponsors than to a charitable purpose.

17.12 The final part of the anti-avoidance legislation relates to grants made by one charity to another. Such grants are chargeable to tax on the charity which receives them, unless used for charitable purposes.

17.13 Obviously a key question is what are charitable purposes? There should be no problem about payments which are charged against income. They will be proper administrative expenses, grants to other charities or money expended on the work for the charity. This leaves what one may describe as capital payments. It is quite possible to apply funds to building projects which will appear in the trust Balance Sheet (e.g. a charity may build new classrooms or buy playing fields if it is a school). Saving up for a few years for some charitable project which requires a lump sum, or paying off a loan incurred for such a project, are charitable purposes. Therefore, there are times when the Inland Revenue will, quite correctly, take a long view and there will be times when they view a capital project as completely charitable.

17.14 The *Charities Act 1993, s 10* (formerly *Charities Act 1992, s 52*) provides for the disclosure of information to the Charity Commissioners by Customs and Excise and the Inland Revenue. This section only applies to charities in England and Wales.

17.15 There are several sections aimed at stratagems which could involve any gross fund. *ICTA 1988, ss 703–709* deal with abnormal dividends which follow a transaction in securities and where there is a tax advantage. A recent case (*Sheppard and Another (Trustees of the Woodland Trust) v CIR (No 2) Ch D, [1993] STC 240*) illustrates the problem. The Woodland Trust is a charity. The Sheppard family had a prosperous family company. A bonus issue was renounced in favour of the charity, dividend waivers were lodged by the family and a substantial dividend paid to the charity so that it could reclaim tax. Plainly the profits out of which the dividend came had been earned to a large extent prior to the charity becoming a shareholder. Aldous J did not see a tax advantage within the meaning of *section 709* (which is restricted) and so the appeal by the charity succeeded. There had been a transaction in securities. *ICTA 1988, s 235* ensured that no refund could be claimed in respect of the pre-acquisition profits paid up by way of dividend. The Inland Revenue have said that, but for a technical point relating to the assessment, they would have appealed. In their Tax Bulletin of August 1993, at page 90, the Inland Revenue warned that they would continue to reject claims in similar circumstances. One of the claims rejected was discussed in *CIR v Universities Superannuation Scheme Ltd, Ch D [1997] STC 1* when a decision by the Special Commissioners favourable to the taxpayer was referred back to a tribunal under *s 705(2)*. One of the provisions of the *1995 Finance Bill* which never became law related to

Charities **17.18**

interest free loans and would have caused interest to be attributed to them and assessed upon the lender. The clause was abandoned partly out of concern for its effect upon charities.

Time charities

17.16 Time charities have been mentioned (see 2.22 above). These should be able to claim income tax relief and should be free from the ten-year charge etc. for inheritance tax. However, they lack inheritance tax exemptions when they are set up and they pay a special inheritance tax charge [*IHTA 1984, s 70*] when they come to an end.

Inland Revenue administration

17.17 The Inland Revenue have two offices designated to attend to the income tax of charities. These are the Financial Intermediaries and Claims Offices (FICO) at Bootle and at Edinburgh. These used to be known as Claims Branch. At Bootle there is a separate sub-branch (FICO (Trusts and Charities)). District Inspectors are involved, to a very limited extent, because, if a charity ceased to be charitable or carried on non-exempt activity, the District would be involved. Where a District Inspector receives a claim that a charitable trust or a disaster fund has been set up he will refer the matter to FICO (TM 2040 and 2045).

It used to be the case that charities sent their accounts to FICO as a routine so that it could be seen that their income was being used for charitable purposes. From 4 March 1998 this is not necessary. FICO will ask for accounts when they want to see them.

Value added tax

17.18 For the sake of completeness, VAT must be mentioned. Firstly, if a charity has any activities which look like a business (e.g. first-aid classes where fees are taken from those who attend, provision of food to employees in a canteen, sales of second-hand goods) it has always had to consider registration for VAT. Now, following *FA 1989*, property transactions can result in a charge to VAT. The charity's main problem will be for the volunteers to realise that they are doing something which is taxable. Secondly, there is normally a shortage of inputs which can be related to the chargeable activity. There are reliefs for charities in that a number of different types of supply to them are zero-rated. To the extent that charities are concerned with listed buildings there are concessions in respect of building works. The VAT angle must be considered not only when a building is an investment but also when there is self-supply.

Among ameliorating VAT changes for charities proposed by the Chancellor in his Statement on 9 November 1999 are:

17.19 *Charities*

(*a*) an extension and alignment of the income tax and VAT exemptions for charity fundraising events;

(*b*) a significant extension to the VAT zero rating of advertisements bought by charities;

(*c*) raising from £250 to £1,000 the *de minimis* limit below which charities and other businesses do not have to account for VAT when they de-register.

Disaster funds

17.19 Public appeals following some tragedy attracting immediate sympathy may or may not be charitable. Those which are charitable can offer tax savings to donors and have tax exemptions themselves. However, they are subject to the scrutiny of the Charity Commissioners and cannot give money to an individual without limit. Any grant in excess of that which an individual needs must be non-charitable. An appeal fund which is not charitable escapes this restriction. However, the disposal of any surplus funds becomes a problem—they belong to the donors. There is also the question of inheritance tax because the appeal fund which is not charitable will be a trust of some sort and it could be discretionary.

The Inland Revenue and Customs and Excise jointly issued, in November 1989, a free leaflet giving guidelines on the tax treatment of disaster funds (see Inland Revenue Press Release 23 November 1989). The Charity Commission have a helpful leaflet CC40 'Disaster Appeals — Attorney General's Guidelines'. It would be very easy to set up a charitable disaster fund and then, in ignorance, contravene *Charities Act 1993* in relation to collections.

Miscellaneous

17.20 The *Charities Act 1992*, parts of the 1960 Act and some earlier legislation have been codified into *Charities Act 1993*.

17.21 There can be problems when land given for educational or other charitable purposes ceases to be so used. The land could then revert under the *Reverter of Sites Act 1987* or pursuant to the *Education Act 1973, s 2* or under some other provision. The result would be a chargeable gain under *TCGA 1992, s 256(2)*. However, where, within six years, the land is again held for charitable purposes income tax and capital gains tax will be discharged. Apparently, there were benefactors in early Victorian times who would give land and buildings for educational purposes but would want them back if the education ceased.

If the revertee cannot be identified tax may be postponed until he is identified (Press Release 9.3.94).

17.22 School fee payment plans arranged with educational trusts suffered a reverse in 1996. Their charitable status was removed. In a written parliamentary answer on 29 October 1996 it was said that there would be no change with regard to payments made in plans in existence on 20 June 1996.

Chapter 18

Self-assessment

Commencement

18.1 Self-assessment commenced in 1996/97. As a consequence:
(i) income is now assessed on a current year basis; and
(ii) the dates for payment of tax have changed.

The forms are voluminous. The return for 1999/2000 is 12 pages and the guide to filling it in runs to another 26. The tax calculation form takes 11 pages. Supplementary schedules add to the number. Because we are required to self-assess, the forms must be filled in correctly to avoid the risk of becoming a back duty case by accident. If there is no tax to collect the Return is simple. So, if the trust is an interest in possession trust of which the income is mandated to the life tenant, or all the income is taxed at source, etc. the form only requires a few ticks and a signature. If there is tax to collect then details of income are required. If there are capital gains and losses these will usually have to be reported. The losses will have to be calculated whether there is any chance of using them or not. The reporting of a loss in this way would seem to satisfy the requirement of *TCGA 1992, s 16(2A)* that notice be given.

18.2 The trustee is not asked to forward vouchers but he will have to retain them. As has been mentioned in 18.1 the forms are voluminous. If, in the course of a year, an estate is administered by personal representatives and then becomes a trust, two returns are needed. If it is office policy to take copies of everything, then there could be a storage problem. When schedules are required the forms are requested from a helpline. It is important to mention that the trust form is required.

18.3 New rules have been brought in for income tax under *Sch A* and *Sch D* but these are general and not specific to trusts. The opportunity has been taken to simplify the method of computation so that for instance, *Sch A* now treats the whole of a landlord's income as if his holdings were a business. The Schedule A business will usually be that of the trustees, unless in the case of an interest in possession trust they have delegated their powers of management to the life tenant (in which event it will be his). There are new rules for personal representatives where the estate is in course of administration. These date back to 6 April 1995. Interestingly enough, there is now a specialist unit at FICO (Scotland) working on nothing other than estates in course of administration. Relatively small estates are left with the Districts but anything large will go to Scotland.

18.4 The Return form is straightforward but does require care and attention. The tax computation is difficult and, at modern charge out rates, might be expensive to complete. This in itself is a good enough reason to file all Returns on or before 30 September, the first send back date. It will then be the Inland Revenue's job to calculate the tax which the practitioner can then check. In any event the beneficiaries will want their tax vouchers early so that they, too, can file their Returns on or before 30 September. If there is any obvious error in the Return or anything incomplete then it will be returned and treated as if it had not been sent. This will mean that some taxpayers filing Returns at the last minute will be caught out and will have to compute their own tax. The second (and last) send back date is 31 January and anybody using that date has to calculate their own tax.

18.5 There is now no form R59 so that the practitioner will have to work out the beneficiaries' income on his own forms. The tax vouchers for beneficiaries have been redesigned. They seem to be in short supply but a xeroxed form is acceptable.

18.6 If the trustee has arranged matters so that the calculation of the tax is done for him, he will want to check it. This could be much quicker if he uses the old method of calculation as in Appendix C.

Notification of liability

18.7 Taxpayers must notify liability within six months of the end of the year of assessment. This is a shorter period than before self-assessment.

18.8 As has been mentioned the last send back date is normally 31 January. If the Return is late then an alternative period is three months from the date of issue. In that case, if the Return is filed within two months of issue the Inland Revenue will calculate the tax.

18.9 The Inland Revenue can correct obvious errors in the taxpayer's calculations within nine months of filing. Taxpayers have twelve months to make a correction.

Payment of tax

18.10 There are two dates for payment of tax, namely 31 January and 31 July. Interest in possession settlements are hardly likely to be involved because their income is generally taxed at source. Discretionary and accumulation settlements are certain to have a liability.

The payments will be:

31 July 2000: second half of 1999/2000.
31 January 2001: CGT of 1999/2000, any balance of 1999/2000, first half of 2000/01.

The payments on account are estimated by reference to the prior year.

18.11 *Self-assessment*

18.11 There are *de minimis* rules so that where the tax is £500 or less or if 80% of the income is taxed at source the July payments on account will be left over.

Estimates

18.12 The Return specifically asks (Question 21.3) whether any provisional figures have been used. When a settlement includes unquoted investments or land and a disposal takes place it is highly likely that a provisional figure for the acquisition cost will be used. A new service is offered by the Inland Revenue from 1.4.97. The provisional figure can be checked by application on form CG34. This form is available at district offices. It should be submitted after the disposal but before filing the Return. The tax office will refer matters to Shares Valuation Division or to the District Valuer as may be appropriate. We are told that a minimum of 56 days is necessary for an official view of the provisional figure to be available. In fact it could easily be longer. It must be to the taxpayer's advantage to submit the form at the earliest moment with every detail, plan, etc. which might speed things up. Appeals to the Special Commissioners or the Lands Tribunal are still possible. This service is known as the 'pre-filing date valuation service'.

Penalties and interest

18.13 There is a system of automatic penalties and interest. If a return is filed late the penalty will be £100. If filed more than six months late then there is a further £100 and so on. An appeal is possible if the tax proves to be less than the penalties. Interest on tax paid late runs from the 28th day following the final balancing payment. This is doubled if anything is outstanding at the 31 July following. If a return is issued but the case has been closed, the form should be sent back with this explanation, otherwise automatic penalties would be triggered.

18.14 Where repayments of tax are made, interest may be added at a lower rate, however, than applies to tax paid late.

18.15 If the Inland Revenue find it necessary they will formally notify the taxpayer that they are commencing an enquiry. They can do so only in the twelve months following the due date for filing. In the absence of any such notification the self assessment is final and can be disturbed only if there is fraud, etc. Plainly personal representatives and trustees having wound up an estate will not want to wait for the tax return to be issued after the end of the tax year and then wait for twelve months from the filing date. In April 1996 the Inland Revenue announced that they would issue returns early in such cases (as to which there seems to be mixed experience, from Tax District to Tax District) and would confirm that they do not seek to enquire into the return (see Inland Revenue Press Release of 4 April 1996).

Clearance

18.16 If no enquiry is raised within 12 months of the statutory filing date, clearance is automatically given, subject to the obvious conditions protecting the Inland Revenue against fraud, etc. If the Return is filed late then the 12 months runs from the end of the quarter in which filing takes place. If earlier clearance is desired (e.g. to assist in winding up a trust) it will be available.

Policy for trustees

18.17 Trustees must look carefully at their programmes for filing returns and for quality control. A statutory requirement for the retention of records is to be found in *TMA 1970, s 12B*. This is a general provision and although there may be cases where trustees have to keep tax records for some 6 years the period will be shorter in most cases. This is purely to do with tax. There can be good non-tax reasons for keeping trust papers for long periods.

Their accounting records must be up to date.

The Inland Revenue recognises that the return may not be enough for them to be aware of any underassessment or excessive relief. It is open to the taxpayer to file additional documents so that adequate disclosure is made. Separate accounts are not expected where accounts are the basis of the assessment. Instead the standard accounts information will be appropriate. Provided the return and any supporting materials amount to full disclosure then the file for the year will be closed at the usual time (see 18.15 above, also *TMA 1970, ss 9A, 19A, 28A, 29*). This was confirmed in an Inland Revenue Press Release dated 31 May 1996.

Miscellaneous

18.18 Personal representatives will be dealt with by the deceased's tax district for the first year or so of the administration.

The beneficiaries

18.19 The beneficiaries have their own self-assessment returns and the same timetable as the trustees. Therefore the beneficiaries have to know the amount of trust income and whether it is 10%, 23% (or, for 2000/01, 22%), 20% or (up to 6 April 1999) foreign dividend income, etc. (see Appendix C).

18.20 *Self-assessment*

Because of this the figures have to be certain and the old system of re-working a life tenant's income at the end of the administration had to be abandoned. For 1995/96 and later years the income paid out by the personal representatives is the income of the beneficiary in the year of receipt (see 6.2 above). All this is a complete contrast to the calculation of the income of a beneficiary of a fixed interest trust which is done on a 'see through' basis, that is to say that the income of a particular tax year when received by the trustees remains income of that year in the beneficiary's computations whenever it is paid out. Whatever balance of income is outstanding at the end of the administration period will be the income of the year in which the end of that period falls, regardless of when the income was assessed upon the personal representatives. Given the width of the tax rate bands of individuals there may not be a lot of planning to do, but where there are beneficiaries who might recover tax or might be liable at 40%, the personal representatives should pass on the income regularly so as to avoid any bunching. A new term is introduced by *ICTA 1988, s 701(3A)* namely the 'applicable rate'. This enables 23% (or, for 2000/01, 22%) and 20% (and, from 1999/2000, 10%) income to be followed through the estate into the hands of the income beneficiary [*ICTA 1988, s 695(4)(a)*]. In this sort of calculation 23% (or 22%) income is deemed to be the first paid out.

18.20 Similar rules apply where there is an 'absolute interest' in an estate. That is to say that the beneficiary is entitled to income and capital. He, too, is treated as receiving income in the year it is paid to him, regardless of the year of receipt by the personal representatives. Running totals have to be kept totalling the estate income and the payments to him, so that he is taxed on the lesser of the cumulative estate income or the amounts actually paid. Again, whatever income is due at the close of the administration will be the income of the beneficiary for the year when the administration comes to an end. Again the 'applicable rate' is used to track the 23% (or 22%) and 20% (and, from 1999/2000, 10%) income to the beneficiary (see 6.2 above).

18.21 *ICTA 1988, s 700(5)* places a duty on the personal representatives to provide a tax voucher to the beneficiary, distinguishing 23% (or 22%) and 20% (and, from 1999/2000, 10%) income, etc. The forms have been re-designed to enable this to be done.

Trust income

18.22 The formula used for trust income is similar. First *TMA 1970, s 8A* imposes a duty on the trustees to make a return when required and to provide supporting information, etc. as may be required. This will include a self-assessment. Although one of the trustees will normally be treated as principal acting trustee and be issued with the return, the 'relevant trustee' legislation makes it possible for any trustee to be involved. This commenced in 1996/97 [*TMA 1970, s 107A*]. The change may seem trifling but under the old rules if the responsibility had to be transferred to a

Self-assessment **18.24**

different trustee, a new return form had to be issued in the new name, etc. The trustees must now be more self-reliant. They must decide matters for themselves as they fill in the return. For instance they will decide what is their country of residence and whether they are liable to the additional 11%/14% (or, for 2000/01, 12%/14%) under *ICTA 1988, s 686*. There will be decisions to take as to the acquisition value for capital gains tax and whether exemptions such as main residence relief will apply. *TMA 1970, s 42* explains how reliefs are to be claimed. Where effect will be given to a relief by carrying it back to an earlier year, a freestanding claim can be made, or else the claim can be included in the next return. Thus the self-assessment for the prior year need not be disturbed, the relief being given by adjusting the balancing payment of tax due for the year when the relief is claimed. Claims must be made on prescribed forms. Interest calculations are related to the normal filing date of the later year. If a claim involves a repayment of tax then the taxpayer has to have documentary proof of payment of tax (i.e. the official record of payment).

18.23 As part of the change to self-assessment and the current year basis the Inland Revenue have to deal with income which used to be assessed on the preceding year basis. As has been said, this is not specifically a problem of trustees, it is general. If there was a continuing source of Case III income for assessment which came to an end before 6 April 1998 the old cessation rules applied.

Points on completing the Trust and Estate Tax Return—SA900

18.24 These notes are a guide only and should be used in conjunction with the booklet SA950 *'Trust and Estate Tax Return Guide'*.

The notes on the front cover of the return should be read before starting to complete the return.

Page 2

*Step 1—These boxes are very important because if any one applies you do not need to complete the income boxes but merely consider pages 10 to 12. *The questions relate only to bare trusts, interest in possession settlements and personal representatives.* Only one box should be ticked.

Bare Trusts—Initially the Inland Revenue determined that such trusts did not fall within self assessment. They have now agreed that bare trustees can submit a Trust Return under *ICTA 1988, s 59*, settle the liability and vouch the income to the beneficiaries in the normal way. **It must be stressed, however, that any capital gains/losses arising must be entered on the personal tax returns of the beneficiaries and not on the Trust Return.**

*Step 3—Questions 1–7—if the trustees receive income which needs to be returned on one or more of the supplementary pages, then the

173

18.24 *Self-assessment*

appropriate box/es must be ticked and the supplementary pages obtained by means of the Inland Revenue 'Orderline'. **It is important when ordering the forms to stress that the supplementary return relates to a Trust/Estate.**

Page 3

Question 8—These boxes are important because they determine the rate at which the trust/estate will be charged to tax. If you get it wrong it could have serious consequences in the future.

Question 9—Whether the income needs to be entered will depend on the type of trust. For interest in possession settlements the notes should be read carefully. It may not be necessary to record all the income (e.g. where mandated to the life tenant). However where you wish to claim accrued income relief then the appropriate boxes must be completed. If for example the relief is from a 'gilt' then boxes 9.12 to 9.14 must be completed. The relief is obtained by reducing the gross interest in box 9.14 by the amount of the allowance.

For accumulation or discretionary settlements the whole of the income must be declared in the appropriate boxes.

The boxes are self explanatory.

Page 4

If trustees receive any income which does not fall to be entered in boxes 9.1 to 9.31 inclusive and is not proper to any of the supplementary pages, then boxes 9.32 to 9.40 inclusive should be used. [Pages 16 and 17 of the Guide explain in detail the type of income which qualifies under this section.]

The treatment of accrued income allowances has been dealt with earlier. Accrued income charges should be entered in box 9.38. This applies to both interest in possession and discretionary trusts as the liability on such charges is the rate applicable to trusts regardless of the type of trust.

This box should also be used for relevant discounted securities which have replaced those types of securities previously termed deep discount securities and deep gain securities.

Box 9.40 should also be used in cases where trustees receive a qualifying distribution following the re-purchase by a company of its own shares. In such cases box 9.39 should be used to enter the notional tax attached to the distribution. Under *FA 1997, 7 Sch* it must be remembered that all trusts are liable to the rate applicable to trusts where the distribution took place after 5 December 1996.

Page 5

Other charges—boxes 10.3–10.5
Where an annuity is paid to a beneficiary, the tax to be deducted is at the basic rate. This means that if the trustees receive only investment

Self-assessment **18.24**

income, then there is a shortfall, on 1999/2000 tax rates of 3% which must be paid by virtue of *ICTA 1988, s 350*. In interest in possession cases sufficient income must be included in the boxes on pages 3 and 4 to cover the amount of the annuity. If this is not done the tax calculation will claw back the full amount of tax deducted from the annuity. The amount of the annuity to be included under this heading is an amount equal to the total income received by the trustees. If the annuity exceeds the total income and the trustees have to revert to capital to make up the annuity, then the excess must be entered at boxes 11.1 to 11.3.

Page 6

Question 13—This section of the form starts with the question 'Is any part of the trust income not liable to tax at the rate applicable to trusts?' If the answer is yes, boxes 13.1 to 13.22 must be completed; if no, only boxes 13.13 to 13.22. This question has been somewhat modified in the last two tax years, helpfully one must say, in referring to specific amounts rather than (as it first did) to percentages of income. The various sub-questions distinguish between income chargeable at the 10% rate, the lower rate and at the basic rate and to trust management expenses applicable to each tranche of income. First, boxes 13.1 to 13.6 deal with income treated as that of the settlor. (Question 8(4) on page 10 of the Trust and Estate Tax Return Guide explains that income treated as that of the settlor is assessed on the trustees at the lower/basic rate only.) Then, boxes 13.7 to 13.11 require details of income which is not subject to the trustees' discretion. Boxes 13.12 to 13.18 request details of income allocated to specific purposes and their relative trust management expenses. This might include income applied towards redeeming a lease or a mortgage (but not income applied for the maintenance, education or benefit of minor beneficiaries). Box 13.18 requests the total amount of deductible trust management expenses, which is clarified by page 18 of the Guide. Page 20 of the Guide incorporates a Working Sheet for Question 13.

Box 13.22—Exceptional Deductions. There are certain items which are treated as income for tax purposes but which under trust law are capital. Such items are not chargeable at the rates above basic rate. The list of items can be found on page 21 of the guide.

Page 7

Question 14—The boxes should be completed only for discretionary payments. They must not be completed for payments made to beneficiaries who are absolutely entitled to the income as it arises.

The amount to be entered is the net payment. If the distribution is to the minor or unmarried child of the settlor and the settlor is alive, then the appropriate box must be ticked. This is because under the provisions of *ICTA 1988, s 660B* the distributed income will be treated as that of the settlor for that year of assessment and not as the income of any other person.

18.24 Self-assessment

Box 14.15—It is important that the 'tax pool' is computed each year and the amount entered in the box. The 'tax pool' is calculated on page 7 of the *Tax Calculation Guide For Trusts and Estates* under boxes T4.1 to T4.16 inclusive. This replaces Form 32 used for all years to 1995/96.

If you make no entry and payments are made to beneficiaries a charge under *ICTA 1988, s 687* will arise.

Question 15 asks whether the trustees have made any capital payments to or for the benefit of minor unmarried children of the settlor during the settlor's lifetime. If so, there will again be implications for the settlor under *ICTA 1988, s 660B*.

Page 8

Question 16 asks whether the trust has at any time been non-resident or received any capital from another trust, which is or at any time has been non-resident. If it has, details of capital payments made by the trustees to, or any benefits provided for, beneficiaries are required. If so, this will have capital gains tax implications under *TCGA 1992, s 87*.

Page 9

Question 17—When you reach this point of the return it is decision time. If you decide not to self-calculate then the return must be submitted to the Inland Revenue on or before 30 September. If this is done then the Revenue guarantee to calculate the liability in time for the correct payments to be made by 31 January.

If you decide to compute the liability then all the appropriate boxes must be completed. This is so that the Revenue can check to see whether the calculation is correct.

If you wish to reduce the payment on account tick box 17.6 and explain why in the 'Additional Information' box on page 11.

If the liability is below a certain figure, then payments on account for the following year are not required. If this is the case then box 17.7 must be ticked. Page 8 of the *Tax Calculation Guide For Trusts and Estates* explains the position.

If a repayment arises (e.g. because all the income is taxed at source and there is an accrued income allowance for the year) then the amount of the repayment will have been entered in box 17.1, in brackets.

If you wish to claim the repayment then Boxes 18.1A to Boxes 18.12 must be completed. The Inland Revenue will not repay if question 18 has been ignored. In such cases the repayment will be allocated against the next tax bill.

Self-assessment **18.24**

Page 10

Question 20—It is important to complete the appropriate boxes where there has either been a change of trustee or merely a change of address. It is advisable to notify the Trust Unit by letter as soon as the event takes place so that correspondence such as statements can be sent to the new trustee during the year. The boxes on the return must still be completed even though the information has already been sent to the Revenue.

Page 11

Question 21—Box 21.1 is important. If the trust or administration has ceased, enter the date. This will stop the issue of any further returns and unnecessary correspondence by the Revenue.

Page 12

Question 22—Tick the appropriate box for the return. If supplementary pages have been completed then tick those boxes also. When you are satisfied sign the declaration. If you fail to do so or you have failed to include the supplementary pages, the Revenue will send the return back to you with a covering letter.

The final comment is that the Trust Unit will assist you with any difficulties which may arise.

Part II:
Offshore Resident Trusts

by
Ian Ferrier MA Barrister TEP

Chapter 19

Residence, Ordinary Residence and Domicile

Introduction

19.1 The use of trusts in tax planning in England goes back to their origins in medieval times. Their use in an international context is more recent, deriving from the period after the First World War when levels of tax on income and estates reached punitive proportions. The addition of capital gains tax in 1965, levied for many years on largely inflationary gains, provided a new incentive to ensure that such gains accrued outside the UK tax net.

For their part, the authorities have sought over the years to prevent tax avoidance through the use of offshore structures, most of which involved trusts at some stage. The legislation has tended to be highly draconian in character, catching the unaware as well as those who harboured an intent to avoid tax. Trustees as well as beneficiaries may be penalised as a result, so that it behoves anyone who may be involved in whatever capacity with an offshore trust to be aware of the pitfalls.

Basic concepts

19.2 There are three important concepts in the UK tax code relating to liability for tax on income or capital outside the UK. These are residence, ordinary residence and domicile. In the context of trusts they may be relevant in relation to settlors, beneficiaries or trustees.

Residence

19.3 There are few legislative provisions regarding residence. Three *sections* [*ICTA 1988, ss 334–336*] contain longstanding provisions.

Section 334 charges to income tax Commonwealth and Irish citizens who have been ordinarily resident in the UK if they leave for occasional residence abroad. The Revenue attempted without success to use this *section* to charge a pop star who was absent in the USA for a whole tax year (*Reed v Clark Ch D 1985, 58 TC 528*) and it seems to have limited force.

181

19.4 *Residence, Ordinary Residence and Domicile*

Section 335 allows the residence of a person working abroad full time to be determined without regard to a place of abode maintained in the UK for his use or to incidental duties performed in the UK. The latter provision is not too helpful in the light of the decision in *Robson v Dixon Ch D 1972, 48 TC 527*, holding that 38 landings in the UK out of 811 in a six-year period were not merely incidental to an aircraft pilot's duties.

Section 336 effectively lays down the rule that six months' presence in the UK for any year of assessment constitutes residence for that year for income tax purposes. A long line of cases establishes the proposition that much shorter periods in the UK over a number of years for some continuing purpose can constitute residence. Concern was expressed by wealthy foreigners that they were being treated as resident in the UK by the Revenue because they owned property here, although they only stayed here for short and intermittent periods. To allay this concern *section 336(3)* was added by *FA 1993, s 208(1)*, providing that the question of residence for such individuals should be decided without regard to any living accommodation available in the UK for their use for 1993/94 onwards. See also the Inland Revenue's interpretation in the May 1994 issue of *Tax Bulletin* on this point.

The statutory code is supplemented by Revenue practice. The booklet IR20, 'Residents and Non-Residents—Liability to Tax in the United Kingdom' (revised in December 1999), is clear and helpful. It contains the important rule that a person going abroad to a job is normally regarded as non-resident for income tax purposes from the day following his departure until the day preceding his return. The rule is extended to capital gains tax by ESC D2, but will not be allowed in any case in which the Revenue considers it is being used for tax avoidance purposes (*R v CIR, ex p Fulford-Dobson QB 1987, 60 TC 168*). It is also now restricted by the provision in *FA 1998, s 127* preserving a charge to CGT on gains made by an individual who is non-resident for less than five complete tax years.

19.4 Where trustees are resident in the UK they are chargeable on the receipt of income, profits or gains (see e.g. *ICTA 1988, s 59* and *TMA 1970, s 13*). Surprisingly, the situation where a majority of the trustees are non-resident remained a grey area for income tax until the House of Lords finally decided in *Dawson v CIR HL, [1989] 62 TC 301* that a trustee resident in the UK was not liable to tax on its world-wide income in such circumstances. This decision was reversed with almost indecent haste by *FA 1989, s 110*. This provides that where a settlor was resident, ordinarily resident or domiciled in the UK at any relevant time, then if at least one trustee is resident in the UK, they are all treated as so resident. *FA 1989, s 111* extends the same treatment to personal representatives.

For capital gains tax there is a special rule. [*TCGA 1992, s 69*]. The trustees of a settlement are treated as being a single and continuing body of persons, distinct from the persons who may from time to time be trustees. This body is treated as being resident and ordinarily resident in the UK unless:

(a) the general administration of the trusts is ordinarily carried on outside the UK; and

(b) the trustees or a majority of them for the time being are not resident or not ordinarily resident in the UK.

There is some protection from this rigour in the case of a settlement made by a person not domiciled, resident, nor ordinarily resident in the UK, but the potential mischief of the *section* is illustrated by the decision in *Roome and Denne v Edwards HL, [1981] 54 TC 359*. In that case a settlement which had been divided into two funds was held to constitute still a single settlement and the trustees, resident and non-resident, to constitute a single body, so that gains which in fact accrued to Cayman Island trustees could be assessed on UK trustees.

The case highlights the extreme care which must be taken if trustees wish to carve a completely separate new settlement out of an existing one. It is likely to be a matter of general trust law, as applied to the specific terms of the deeds in question, as to whether this is in fact possible. See Inland Revenue Statement of Practice SP7/84 for the Revenue view on this matter (Appendix A).

Ordinary residence

19.5 This is not a concept which has often fallen to be construed on its own apart from residence itself. One area in which it has been of importance is in connection with 'exempt gilts', which are free of income tax while in the beneficial ownership of persons not ordinarily resident in the UK [*ICTA 1988, s 47*]. A leading case on the point is *Levene v CIR HL 1928, 13 TC 486*. The taxpayer had admittedly spent four or five months in the UK during the relevant years and lost his appeal with regard both to residence and ordinary residence, but on the latter point the Lord Chancellor, Viscount Cave, had this to say:

> 'The expression "ordinary residence" is found in the Income Tax Act of 1806 and occurs again and again in the later Income Tax Acts, where it is contrasted with usual or occasional or temporary residence; and I think that it connotes residence in a place with some degree of continuity and apart from accidental or temporary absences. So understood, the expression differs little in meaning from the word "residence" as used in the Acts; and I find it difficult to imagine a case in which a man while not resident here is yet ordinarily resident here'.

The practical importance of the distinction is that complete absence from the UK for an entire tax year will usually constitute non-residence for that year, but it would appear that this would only be a temporary absence for the purposes of ordinary residence, if a regular pattern of visits was resumed.

19.6 *Residence, Ordinary Residence and Domicile*

Domicile

19.6 In contrast to residence which is largely a question of fact and UK domestic law, domicile (or domicil) is a highly technical matter of private international law, or conflict of laws, rather than English common law. Its importance is immense, since non-domiciled individuals are taxed only on a remittance basis on their offshore income [*ICTA 1988, ss 65(4), 192*] and capital gains [*TCGA 1992, s 12*], while their offshore property is excluded from inheritance tax [*IHTA 1984, s 6*], (subject to the deemed domicile rules of *IHTA 1984, s 267*).

For trusts the significance of domicile is that a trust created by a non-domiciled individual will always retain that character. Equally a trust created by a domiciled individual will also retain that character. The residence of a settlement can change, but not its domicile, which remains that of the settlor.

Each individual must have a domicile, but only one domicile at any time, whereas multiple residence or ordinary residence is possible. Everyone starts life with a *domicile of origin*, which will derive from that of his parent, usually the father. This is also known as a *domicile of dependency*. At one time a married woman acquired her husband's domicile as a domicile of dependency, but this relic of the subordination of women was swept away by the *Domicile and Matrimonial Proceedings Act 1973*. However, it was held in *CIR v Duchess of Portland Ch D 1981, 54 TC 648* that where a wife had acquired her husband's domicile under the previous rules, this subsisted until she changed her domicile in accordance with general principles.

Each individual, on attaining the age of sixteen, can acquire a *domicile of choice*. The classic formulation of what is required to constitute a domicile of choice was made by Lord Westbury in *Udny v Udny HL 1869, 1 LR Sc & D 441* at p 458:

> 'Domicil of choice is a conclusion or inference which the law derives from the fact of a man fixing voluntarily his sole or chief residence in a particular place, with an intention of continuing to reside there for an unlimited time. This is a description of the circumstances which create or constitute a domicil, and not a definition of the term. There must be a residence freely chosen, and not prescribed or dictated by any external necessity, such as the duties of office, the demands of creditors, or the relief from illness; and it must be residence fixed not for a limited period or particular purpose, but general and indefinite in its future contemplation'.

It will be seen that the onus of proving that an individual has acquired a domicile of choice is a heavy one and there is a line of cases in which individuals who have lived in England for long periods have nonetheless retained their domicile of origin.

This is illustrated by the case of *CIR v Bullock CA 1976, 51 TC 522*. Group Captain Bullock was a Canadian, born in 1910, who served in the Royal Air Force from 1932 to 1959 and then retired in England. His wife refused to live in Canada but he retained the intention of returning there in the event of his surviving her. Along with other indications such as his maintenance of Canadian citizenship, this was held to be enough to rebut the contention that he had acquired a domicile of choice in England.

19.7 The Revenue are naturally unappreciative of the fact that wealthy foreigners can live here for decades and shelter most of their income and assets from UK tax. Some years ago they floated a consultative document suggesting that such people should be taxed on the basis of residence rather than domicile. The government, however, were alert to the damage which could be done to the British economy if wealthy foreigners were forced to leave these shores or face what they might regard as unacceptable taxation. Their rejection of the proposal was concurred in by the opposition, so that the retention of the tax advantages of non-domiciled residents of the UK seems to be assured.

However, the Revenue appear to be making an attempt to introduce the policy of the consultative document by the back door through attacking the domicile status of foreigners after they have resided in the UK for more than a decade. Basing themselves on the *Bullock* case (see 19.6 above), they ask for a specific event which would cause the foreign resident to return home. This line of reasoning is fallacious and should be resisted. The test to be applied was stated as follows by the Earl of Halsbury LC in *Winans v Attorney General HL, [1904] AC 287*:

> 'Now the law is plain, that where a domicil of origin is proved it lies upon the person who asserts a change of domicil to establish it and it is necessary to prove that the person who is alleged to have changed his domicil had a fixed and determined purpose to make the place of his new domicil his permanent home'.

Naturally the longer an individual resides here the easier it becomes to prove that point, and if he dies here, then it may be hard to resist the inference that the UK had become his permanent home. For example, in *re Furse (deceased) Ch D, [1980] STC 597*, a case which is an instructive contrast to *Bullock*, an American who came to England at the age of four and died here at the age of 80, having spent 58 out of the intervening 76 years here, was held to have died domiciled in England, despite a vaguely expressed intention to return to the United States when he was no longer able to live an active physical life on his farm.

At all events, links with the homeland should be maintained as firmly as possible—though there may be cases, such as those fleeing from oppressive or dictatorial regimes, where this may be impractical in the short or medium terms.

For those seeking to lose an English domicile of origin and acquire a foreign domicile of choice the law imposes a three year quarantine period

19.8 *Residence, Ordinary Residence and Domicile*

for inheritance tax purposes [*ICTA 1984, s 267*]. In view of the adhesive quality of the domicile of origin, the acquisition of a domicile of choice requires careful forethought and planning. The problems which can arise where this is not done is illustrated by the case of Sir Charles Clore (see *re Clore (deceased) (No 2) Ch D, [1984] STC 609* on the domicile point) which generated extensive litigation.

19.8 The Government announced in 1991 that it proposed to implement the Law Commissioners' joint report on the law of domicile (Cm 200). This would replace the concepts of domicile of origin and domicile of choice with a new rule that a child should be domiciled in the country with which he is for the time being most closely connected and that for the acquisition of a new domicile by an adult it should be sufficient to show that he intended to settle in the country in question for an indefinite period. However, by a Parliamentary written answer on 26 May 1993 (HC Debs, Vol 225, Col 600) the Prime Minister stated that the Government had no immediate plans to introduce legislation on this subject. Concern had been expressed on the damage that the proposed change might cause and this obviously had an effect on official thinking.

19.9 The Prime Minister's statement has been confirmed in another Parliamentary written answer on 16 January 1996 (Hansard written answers, Vol 269, Col 489) by the Parliamentary Secretary, Lord Chancellor's Department:

'The Government have decided not to take forward these reforms on the basis that, although they are desirable in themselves, they do not contain sufficient practical benefits to outweigh the risks of proceeding with them and to justify disturbing the present long-established body of case law on this subject'.

This put the matter at rest so far as the previous Government was concerned. So far, there is no indication that the Labour Government will change this policy.

19.10 One anxiety felt by expatriates in relation to domicile was removed by *FA 1996, s 200*. This provides that in determining a person's domicile for tax purposes no regard shall be had to any action taken by him to register as an overseas elector or to vote in an election. There is a proviso that the action can be taken into account for determining any person's liability to tax if that person so wishes. The domicile so ascertained applies only for that purpose.

Chapter 20

Income Tax

Liability to UK tax

20.1 The fundamental rule governing income tax in this area was stated as follows by Lord Wrenbury in *Whitney v CIR HL 1925, 10 TC 88* at p 112:

'The policy of the Act is to tax the person resident in the United Kingdom upon all his income wheresoever derived, and to tax the person not resident in the United Kingdom upon all income derived from property in the United Kingdom'.

20.2 Trustees resident in the UK are accordingly taxable on the worldwide income of the trust, while non-resident trustees are taxable on income arising in the UK.

The question of what is the trustees' income for this purpose came up for consideration in *Williams v Singer and others HL 1920, 7 TC 387*. A number of shares in the Singer Company of New Jersey were held by UK resident trustees for a beneficiary who was neither resident nor domiciled in the UK. The dividends on the shares were paid under mandate to a New York bank. The Revenue assessed the trustees on the dividends. At first instance Sankey J confessed that he appreciated the position of those persons who 'found no end in wandering mazes lost', but his decision against the Revenue was upheld in the Court of Appeal and the House of Lords. Viscount Cave founded his reasoning on what is now *ICTA 1988, s 59*, charging income tax under Schedule D on the persons 'receiving or entitled to the income':

'The fact is that, if the Income Tax Acts are examined, it will be found that the person charged with tax is neither the trustee nor the beneficiary as such, but the person in actual receipt and control of the income which it is sought to reach'.

A converse point arose in *Archer-Shee v Baker HL 1927, 11 TC 749*. Lady Archer-Shee was the UK resident beneficiary under an American will trust. The assets consisted of foreign property the income from which was paid by the trustees to Lady Archer-Shee's order at a New York bank. At that time there was a distinction between Case IV and Case V of Schedule D [*ICTA 1988, s 18*], tax under Case IV on offshore securities being charged on an arising basis, and under Case V on

20.3   Income Tax

offshore possessions being charged on a remittance basis. The case was decided against the appellant on the basis that English law applied. A second appeal was commenced for later years of assessment and expert evidence was led regarding the New York law which was applicable (*Garland v Archer-Shee HL 1930, 15 TC 693*). This evidence was that Lady Archer-Shee's life interest gave her no proprietary interest in the income arising from the securities, stocks and shares constituting the trust fund but rather a right of action against the trustees if they failed to carry out their duties. The case was finally decided by the House of Lords in favour of the appellant on the grounds that this right, technically a chose in action, was a possession.

The problem thrown up by the *Archer-Shee* cases remains of general significance. Although English common law has travelled widely, equity has been less successful in winning acceptance internationally. The distinction between legal and beneficial interests in property tends not to apply. Rather the property is vested in the legal owner, with the rights of the beneficial owner enforceable as a separate matter.

20.3   Rather different, but equally difficult, issues were raised in *Lord Inchyra v Jennings Ch D 1965, 42 TC 388*. Lady Inchyra had an interest in one quarter of the income from her mother's estate commencing in 1950 and an interest in the remainder from 1955. Additionally, from 1951 to 1970 inclusive or until her earlier death, she was to receive annually one per cent of the capital value of the estate excluding real property. The Revenue contended that the payments out of capital were to be treated as income and that each stream of payments was to be treated as a separate source. Under the rules for taxing new sources of income under Cases III, IV and V of Schedule D, which then applied, it was advantageous to the Revenue to adopt the latter treatment.

Although evidence was led that the payments out of capital were treated as capital under American law, the judge held that its character in Lady Inchyra's hands was to be determined in accordance with English law. The weight of the authorities led to the conclusion that a series of recurrent payments over a period related in some way to the life of a beneficiary must be treated as income. However, on the subsidiary issue he held that there was a single source of income, namely Lady Inchyra's interest in her mother's estate, together with the right to have the estate applied for her benefit in accordance with the will.

A case which fell on the other side of the line was *Lawson v Rolfe Ch D 1969, 46 TC 199*. Mrs Lawson was entitled to a life interest in half of a trust fund. The fund was invested in American shares. In 1962, 1963 and 1964 some of the companies declared stock dividends. The rule in the United States is that where such a stock dividend is paid for out of profits it does not affect the integrity of a trust fund and may be passed on to a beneficiary. The trustees did so. The Special Commissioners held that in view of this rule the stock dividends must be regarded as income.

In the High Court it was common ground that under Californian law, which was applicable, Mrs Lawson had an equitable right in possession to receive during her life the proceeds of specific stocks constituting her share in the trust fund, rather than an *Archer-Shee* right to have the trusts properly administered. The judge considered the *Inchyra* decision and concluded that the stock dividends lacked the character of recurrent payments over a substantial period of time. Their issue was fortuitous and not planned so far as the trust was concerned. There was no element of recurrence so as to implant on what was capital the imprint of income when they reached Mrs Lawson's hands.

20.4 It was established in *CIR v Regent Trust Co Ltd (Butt's 1970 Settlement Trustee) Ch D 1979, 53 TC 54* that the additional rate tax liability in what is now *ICTA 1988, s 686* applied to offshore discretionary trusts. Trust management expenses chargeable to income are apportioned *pro rata* between income liable to UK tax and that not so liable. [*ICTA 1988, s 686 (2A)* introduced by *FA 1993, 6 Sch 8(3)*]. Such expenses are set off primarily against UK dividend income. [*FA 1993, s 79(3)*]. The tax liability on any UK dividends received by offshore trustees is now computed by reference to a notional lower rate tax credit. [*ICTA 1988, s 233(1A)* introduced by *FA 1993, 6 Sch 8(2)*].

20.5 A distribution by offshore trustees from such income does not strictly carry a credit under *ICTA 1988, s 687* but under ESC B18 relief will be accorded on a concessionary basis, provided the offshore trustees have rendered tax returns to the Revenue, supported by tax vouchers where appropriate and paid all *section 686* liability. Other reliefs will be available to the beneficiary where appropriate.

Anti-avoidance

20.6 The decade of the *Singer* and *Archer-Shee* cases also saw the beginnings of large-scale tax avoidance using offshore trusts. One of the pioneers in this field was the Vestey family, which was to have a long-running battle with the Revenue (see 20.7 below).

The Revenue's difficulty arose from the fact that it is not possible for them to enforce an assessment on a non-resident. The decision of the government not to ratify a far-reaching OECD convention for the mutual enforcement of tax assessments indicates that this principle will continue to be observed in this country.

Foreign tax laws are naturally considered where a double tax treaty exists between the UK and an overseas jurisdiction and unilateral relief may be available against foreign tax under *ICTA 1988, s 790*. These provisions will usually be beneficial to the taxpayer.

20.7 *Income Tax*

Transfer of assets abroad

20.7 The prime anti-avoidance provision is now to be found in *ICTA 1988, s 739*. Before amendment following the *Vestey* case (see below) its main thrust was to treat income payable to persons outside the UK as being the income of an individual ordinarily resident in the UK, where that individual had made a transfer of assets, either directly or indirectly, with a tax avoidance motive. So, in *Lord Howard de Walden v CIR CA 1941, 25 TC 121* it was held that the income of some Canadian companies the shares of which the taxpayer had transferred many years previously to trustees for his children should be treated as his income.

Shortly thereafter the House of Lords made a fateful extension of the section in *Congreve v CIR 1948, 30 TC 163* to impose liability on individuals other than the transferor. This was used by the Revenue to impose tax, for example, on Rudyard Kipling's daughter as a result of transactions carried out many years before by her parents (*Bambridge v CIR HL 1955, 36 TC 313*). Many taxpayers felt a considerable sense of grievance, in view of positive assurances which had been given when the legislation was passed. Such assurances, if given in Parliament, may now be relied on, following the decision in *Pepper v Hart HL, [1992] STC 898*.

It was the Vestey family who brought this matter to a head in *Vestey v CIR HL 1979, 54 TC 503*. The real vice of the *Congreve* decision was that the statute provided no means of apportioning foreign trust income among discretionary beneficiaries. The Revenue claimed that they had a general administrative power to do this, a contention which Walton J found 'laughable'. Lord Wilberforce agreed, 'less genially' and held that the application of *Congreve* in the case of discretionary trusts produced a result which was 'arbitrary, unjust and in my opinion unconstitutional'. *Congreve* was overruled and the assessments on the Vestey family beneficiaries were quashed.

The Revenue returned to the attack in 1981 with amendments to *section 739* and what is now *ICTA 1988, s 740*. *Section 740* imposes a liability on non-transferors where they receive a benefit provided out of assets available in consequence of the transfer.

20.8 The ambit of *section 739* is still not entirely settled. It might be supposed that the transfer of assets triggering the operation of the section must be made by an individual ordinarily resident in the UK while so resident and that the transfer must be from the UK to an offshore jurisdiction. In *CIR v Willoughby, HL [1997] STC 995*, it was held that in view of the *Vestey* decision, *section 739* should not apply to transfers made by non-residents. The expatriate planning to return to the UK, or foreigners planning to sojourn here, could therefore make arrangements prior to their arrival which would not attract the unwelcome

Income Tax **20.9**

attentions of *section 739*. The position has now been altered to the taxpayer's disadvantage by *s 739(1A)*, inserted by *FA 1997, s 81* (see 23.8 below).

There is a statutory exemption in *section 741* where it can be shown that the transfer had no tax avoidance purpose or was a bona fide commercial transaction. However, this may well be difficult to demonstrate. In the *Willoughby* case, it was held that the rollover of offshore insurance policies after the return of the expatriate did not constitute tax avoidance at all, but was rather tax mitigation following the analysis of Lord Templeman in *Commissioners of Inland Revenue v Challenge Corp Ltd, PC [1986] STC 548*.

The most recent case on *section 739* is *CIR v Botnar CA [1999] STC 711*. The taxpayer transferred shares to a trust established in Liechtenstein. The Special Commissioners held that the section did not apply since Mr Botnar and his family were excluded from benefit under the trust. However, the Revenue's appeal was allowed in the High Court on the ground that the assets could be transferred to another trust from which Mr Botnar and his family might benefit. Mr Botnar was not represented at the appeal and died shortly thereafter. An appeal to the Court of Appeal by Mr Botnar's Swiss lawyer, at which full argument was heard, was dismissed.

Transactions in land

20.9 A special attack on artificial transactions in land is made by what is now *ICTA 1988, s 776*.

Section 776 applies when land is acquired with the object of realising a gain from its disposal or is held as trading stock or is developed with the object of realising a gain from its disposal when developed and a gain of a capital nature is obtained from the disposal of the land directly or indirectly. Such a gain is brought into charge to income tax under Case VI of Schedule D.

Although *section 776*, unlike *section 739*, is not exclusively aimed at offshore structures, it has been used extensively in this connection. The leading example of the section in this context is provided by *Yuill v Wilson HL 1980, 52 TC 674* and *Yuill v Fletcher CA 1984, 58 TC 145*. Mr Yuill was a builder whose family company owned some land with valuable development potential. The beneficial ownership of this land found its way into the hands of trustees of Guernsey discretionary settlements. There was never much doubt in the course of prolonged litigation that Mr Yuill had incurred a charge to income tax by transmitting the opportunity of making a gain to the trustees [*ICTA 1988, s 776(5)(a)*], the only real issue being the point at which the charge crystallised.

It has become clear that *section 776* can be used to penalise perfectly normal transactions in land entered into with no tax avoidance motive. In

20.10 *Income Tax*

Page v Lowther CA, [1983] 57 TC 199, a wholly commercial arrangement whereby the trustees of the Holland Park Estate were to participate in the premiums realised on a development was caught by *section 776*. To emphasize the point, the rubric 'artificial transactions in land', which had been carried by the original legislation in 1969 and the consolidation in 1970 was dropped in the 1988 consolidation.

The unification of the rates of income tax and capital gains tax [*TCGA 1992, s 4*] may reduce the possible impact of *section 776* on transactions without an offshore element, since it may not be so material whether a gain is realised as capital or income. However, where land is held in an offshore structure, commonly by a company owned by a trust, *section 776* continues to be of great and continuing relevance, since gains which might otherwise escape UK tax altogether (assuming none of the other anti-avoidance rules apply) may be subjected to the unfavourable regime of Schedule D Case VI. It should therefore be considered in any offshore transactions involving land in the UK.

Deduction of tax

20.10 Under arrangements effective from 6 April 1996 (*ICTA 1988, s 481* as amended by *FA 1995, s 86; Income Tax (Building Societies) (Dividends and Interest) Regulations 1990, SI 1990, No 2231* as amended by *SI 1996 No 223*) bank and building society interest may be paid without deduction of tax to the trustees of offshore discretionary trusts. This is subject to completion of a declaration in approved form that the trustees are not resident in the UK and do not have any reasonable grounds for believing that any of the beneficiaries of the trust is an individual who is ordinarily resident in the UK or a company which is resident in the UK.

Under *ICTA 1988, s 1A* introduced by *FA 1996, s 73* the tax charge on savings income, such as bank and building society interest, is reduced from the basic rate to the lower rate of 20%. Among a number of consequential amendments, *FA 1996, 6 Sch 16* introduces a new *ICTA 1988, s 689A*. This applies to trust management expenses incurred by the trustees where a beneficiary has an interest in possession but is not liable to tax on an amount of that income by reason of being non-resident in the UK for tax purposes. In such a case a proportion of the expenses is disregarded in computing the income of the beneficiary equal to the proportion which the untaxed income bears to all the income arising to the trustees to which the beneficiary is entitled. The disallowance is computed on the basis of income arising to the trustees net of any tax chargeable on them. 'Excluded income', as defined in *FA 1995, s 128(3)* on which the beneficiary pays no tax because no tax is deducted at source, is to be treated as income on which the beneficiary is not liable to tax by reason of being non-resident in the UK for tax purposes (see also 6.2 above).

Chapter 21

Capital Gains Tax

Introduction

21.1 The introduction of capital gains tax in 1965, coinciding as it did with the beginnings of a period of chronic inflation in this country, provided a powerful stimulus for removing assets from the UK tax regime. For 17 years, during which the retail prices index increased more than five-fold, tax was levied at 30% on gains which could be wholly illusory in real terms. In these circumstances it became almost the duty of trustees to seek ways of protecting the value of the assets under their charge in the interests of the beneficiaries.

A clear route was provided by the legislation, which still enacts [*TCGA 1992, s 2(1)*] that 'a person shall be chargeable to capital gains tax in respect of chargeable gains accruing to him in a year of assessment during any part of which he is resident in the United Kingdom, or during which he is ordinarily resident in the United Kingdom'.

The original legislation, now in *TCGA 1992, s 69*, hardly began to address the problem which migrating settlements were about to provide. Trustees were to be treated as being a single and continuing body of persons, and that body was to be treated as being resident and ordinarily resident in the UK, unless:

(*a*) the general administration of the trusts was ordinarily carried on outside the UK; and

(*b*) the trustees or a majority of them for the time being were not resident or not ordinarily resident in the UK.

The only anti-avoidance provision built into the original legislation related to non-resident trusts where the settlor was domiciled and either resident or ordinarily resident in the UK or had this status when he made the settlement. In such a case, any beneficiary with the same status could have the gains of the trust apportioned to him on a 'just and reasonable' basis, according to the respective value of his interest. [*FA 1965, s 42*].

The 1965 legislation as amended was consolidated (except for provisions relating solely to companies) into *Capital Gains Tax Act 1979*. Important changes with respect to non-resident trusts have been made by *FA 1981*, *FA 1991* and *FA 1998*.

21.2 Capital Gains Tax

The entire corpus of legislation relating to CGT and the related tax on companies' chargeable gains was consolidated into *Taxation of Chargeable Gains Act 1992*. [*TCGA 1992*]. The following discussion deals with the development of the legislation in sequence, since much of it does not have retrospective effect.

Exporting trusts

21.2 The 1965 legislation provided a powerful incentive to the export of existing trusts and the setting up of new trusts offshore. Until the abolition of exchange control in 1979, there were limits to what could be done in this direction, but the Channel Islands and the Isle of Man were within the sterling area and these jurisdictions soon built up the expertise required for trust administration.

One major difficulty was that few existing settlements contained a power to export them and to remove them from the jurisdiction of the English courts could be a serious breach of trust. If the beneficiaries were minors, it was requisite to seek the permission of the court. Ideally, to avoid the possible application of *FA 1965, s 42*, it was desirable to export the beneficiaries as well.

This was exactly what was proposed in *Re Weston's Settlements Ch D, [1968] 1 All ER 720; CA, [1968] 3 All ER 338* when approval to replace existing trustees with Jersey trustees was refused by the courts. The courts reacted with extreme hostility. At first instance, Stamp J described the application as a 'cheap exercise in tax avoidance', while in the Court of Appeal Lord Denning MR lamented the sad fate of the children, doomed to lose the benefit of being 'brought up in this our England, which is still "the envy of less happier lands"'.

The unfortunate position in which the Weston family found itself, having left these shores but denied the right to take its settlements with it, is less likely to occur today. The courts are now much more sophisticated and less likely to take umbrage at international tax planning. More importantly it is now common form in settlements to incorporate a specific power to move the administration to any jurisdiction and to appoint non-resident trustees.

The pre-1981 provisions

21.3 During the 1970s when the coincidence of high inflation and high tax rates made the entire system increasingly unfair, a vigorous tax avoidance 'industry' grew up and many of the schemes which were marketed involved the use of non-resident trusts. Indeed, the *Ramsay* case was heard in the House of Lords with *Eilbeck v Rawling HL 1981, 54 TC 101*, which included a sum of money being 'blasted into space' from a Gibraltar settlement to a Jersey settlement in order to create a tax loss in the former. *Eilbeck v Rawling* made its own way to the Lords, the taxpayer losing both at first instance and in the Court of Appeal, so that as with *Ramsay* the application of the 'wider approach' was not really necessary. The reverberations of *Ramsay* have not yet died away, and in the field of inheritance tax the litigation in *Countess Fitzwilliam and Others v CIR HL [1993] STC 502* has furnished important guidance on how far it is possible to go in multi-stage tax planning operations. The effect of the House of Lords decision is to confirm that strategic tax planning is permissible, provided the final outcome is not a foregone conclusion at the beginning.

Unlike the Weston family, most taxpayers do not wish to remove themselves physically from the UK in order to achieve tax savings and the schemes were directed to realising gains offshore which could not be charged on the resident beneficiaries. Two cases, *Chinn v Collins HL 1980, 54 TC 92* and *Berry v Warnett HL 1982, 55 TC 92*, were brought all the way to the House of Lords and in both the taxpayers, after fluctuating results in the lower courts, ultimately lost.

Other schemes failed at an earlier stage: *Bailey v Garrod Ch D 1983, 56 TC 695* and *Ewart v Taylor Ch D 1983, 57 TC 401* (although since both the taxpayer and the Revenue won, on different points, the latter case might be considered a draw). *Young v Phillips Ch D 1984, 58 TC 232* reached the wilder shores of tax avoidance by incorporating the device known as the 'Sark lark'.

21.4 The unfairness of the system was most clearly highlighted by *Leedale v Lewis HL 1982, 56 TC 501*, in which the parents of children who had a tiny actuarial interest in a settlement had large capital gains tax assessments raised on them. The Special Commissioners did not find this 'just and reasonable', but the judges preferred a broad brush rather than an actuarial approach.

The 1981 provisions

21.5 The key provision in the system introduced in 1981 (which still applies in most cases in addition to the 1991 provisions) is now contained in *TCGA 1992, s 87*. This applies to trusts with non-resident trustees where the settlor had been, when he made the settlement or during any year in which the trustees are at no time resident or ordinarily resident in the UK, domiciled and either resident or ordinarily resident in the UK. In such a case trust gains are to be treated as accruing to the beneficiaries, but only to the extent to which they receive capital payments from the trustees. The attribution of gains to beneficiaries is not to exceed the amount actually received by them.

The charge has now been extended to trusts set up by non-domiciled and non-resident settlors (see 21.19 below), but a non-domiciled beneficiary is still protected from charge by *TCGA 1992, s 87(7)*.

21.6 *Capital Gains Tax*

A settlement arising under a will or intestacy is to be treated as made by the testator or intestate at the time of his death. [*TCGA 1992, s 87(9)*].

21.6 The growing complexity of the system necessitated a raft of supplementary provisions, as follows:

(a) *TCGA 1992, s 89*. This deals with the position of 'migrant settlements', i.e. settlements which move in and out of the UK. A capital payment made to a beneficiary during a time when the trust was resident in the UK can be apportioned if it was made in anticipation of a disposal made by the trustees later when non-resident. Similarly, outstanding gains from the last year of a non-resident period can be attributed to capital payments made when the trust moves back to the UK.

(b) *TCGA 1992, s 90*. This was designed to prevent avoidance by transferring assets from one trust to another.

(c) *TCGA 1992, s 97*. This provides a wide definition of 'capital payment', to include any payment not chargeable to income tax, or, in the case of a non-resident, received otherwise than as income. The conferring of any benefit, including loans on favourable terms, is included in the charge to the value of the benefit. However, in distinction from the pre-1981 provisions, losses are permitted to be deducted from gains. [*TCGA 1992, s 97(6)*]. 'Capital payment' now does not include a payment under a transaction entered into at arm's length. [*TCGA 1992, s 97(1)(b)*]. It was held in *Billingham v Cooper Ch D [2000] STC 122* that an interest-free demand loan was caught by s 97.

(d) *TCGA 1992, s 98*. This confers on the Revenue the same wide information-gathering powers for the purposes of *sections 87–90* that they have under *ICTA 1988, s 745* in relation to *section 739*. A limited amount of protection is given to solicitors and banks, but the details which may be required from the latter trench deeply into traditional banking confidentiality (see *Royal Bank of Canada v CIR Ch D 1971, 47 TC 565* and *Clinch v CIR QB 1973, 49 TC 52*, concerning transactions with the Bahamas and Bermuda respectively).

(e) *TCGA 1992, s 13(10)*. This extends to non-resident trustees the provisions attributing gains made by non-resident close companies to shareholders resident or ordinarily resident (and in the case of individuals, domiciled) in the UK. Such gains realised by non-resident trusts are accordingly brought with the ambit of *section 87*. This provision is of some importance since a very common offshore structure is to hold assets in a company which is owned by a trust.

(f) *TCGA 1992, s 85*. This tackles the realisation of gains by disposing of interests in settlements. Under *TCGA 1992, s 76* the disposal of an interest in a settlement is exempted from CGT except where the interest has been acquired for value. This protection is withdrawn in the case of non-resident trusts. Where a disposal takes place which is protected by *section 76* and the trust subsequently emigrates, the gain is chargeable on the trustees, unless they have disposed of all the assets in the settlement before it emigrates. Tax not paid by the trustees can be charged on the disponor of the interest.

The tax in transition

21.7 The 1981 provisions had the serious defect from the Revenue's point of view that it was perfectly easy to avoid tax by exporting a trust and then disposing of assets so long as no capital payments were made to resident beneficiaries. In the analogous situation of companies, where migration without Treasury consent was a serious criminal offence under what became *ICTA 1988, s 765*, the European Court held that this last provision did not infringe Community law in its present state (*R v HM Treasury, ex p Daily Mail and General Trust Plc CJEC,* [1988] STC 787). In the meantime the government had imposed a charge to capital gains tax on a deemed disposal of assets when a company became non-resident [*TCGA 1992, ss 185–187*]. It was apparent that the same treatment would shortly be applied to trusts.

Meanwhile a further anti-avoidance provision was added to the 1981 code. Dual resident entities had been exploited for some time, since they opened the possibility of gaining tax allowances twice, a device known as 'double-dipping'. Also, the use of double tax treaties in tax planning had been realised. In *Padmore v CIR CA 1989, 62 TC 352* a Jersey partnership was used to shelter overseas income of UK residents, since it was held that it constituted a 'body of persons' for the purposes of the double tax treaty.

21.8 *TCGA 1992, s 169* was aimed at avoidance by dual resident trusts. A trust might attain this status if a majority of the trustees were resident in the UK but its general administration was carried on elsewhere. The trust would be resident in the UK under UK law [*TCGA 1992, s 69*], but a double tax treaty might provide that the trust would be treated as resident where the general administration was carried on. Use of the then existing general relief for gifts or the other rollover reliefs available allowed assets to be transferred into such trusts without tax. They could then be disposed of without triggering a charge under the shelter of the double tax treaty. *Section 169* strikes at this by denying holdover relief on the transfer.

The 1991 provisions

21.9 *FA 1991* introduced a triple attack on non-resident settlements. In outline, the three main new occasions of charge are as follows:

(*a*) a CGT exit charge when a trust becomes non-resident after 18 March 1991 [*TCGA 1992, ss 80–84*];

(*b*) a CGT charge on a settlor on the gains of a non-resident trust created after 18 March 1991 where he or his family retain an interest in the trust [*TCGA 1992, s 86, 5 Sch*];

21.10 *Capital Gains Tax*

(c) a supplementary charge on capital payments after 5 April 1992 to beneficiaries out of non-resident trusts in which the gains are not taxable on the settlor [*TCGA 1992, ss 91–95*].

Exit charge

21.10 *Section 80* provides that where after 18 March 1991 the trustees of a settlement become neither resident nor ordinarily resident in the UK, they are deemed to have disposed of all the assets of the settlement immediately prior to that time and reacquired them at market value. There are two exceptions to a *section 80* charge:

(i) where the assets are used or held for the purposes of a trade carried on by the trustees in the UK through a branch or agency (in such a case there is a continuing liability to capital gains tax under *TCGA 1992, s 10*);

(ii) where the trustees are protected by a double tax treaty (although in such a case they may be liable to charge under *TCGA 1992, s 83*— 21.11 below).

Roll-over relief under *TCGA 1992, s 152* is not available where the old assets are disposed of prior to the emigration of trustees and the new assets are acquired afterwards. This again does not apply where the trustees are carrying on a trade in the UK.

21.11 The basic provisions of *TCGA 1992, s 80* are supplemented by a number of additional provisions.

(a) *Death of a trustee.* A settlement may become non-resident or resident through the death of a trustee if in such a case the majority of the trustees become non-resident. It would be unjust in such a case for an adventitious charge to arise. Accordingly, *TCGA 1992, s 81* provides a period of grace of six months during which the trustees can take steps to become resident or non-resident again as the case may be. For temporarily non-resident trustees the relief does not apply to assets disposed of during the period of non-residence (although the trustees would almost certainly be chargeable in any case) nor to assets protected by a double tax treaty because this would open the door to tax avoidance. In the case of re-emigrating trustees, relief is denied where assets are acquired during the period of residence to which *TCGA 1992, s 165* (relief for gifts of business assets) or *TCGA 1992, s 260(3)* (gifts on which inheritance tax is chargeable) applies.

(b) *Past trustees: liability for tax.* It is one thing to impose a tax charge on non-residents, quite another to collect it. *TCGA 1992, s 82* attempts to give the charge some extra teeth by imposing a liability in certain circumstances on retired trustees. Where the exit charge is not paid within six months of the time when it becomes payable, the Revenue have three years from the time the amount of tax is

Capital Gains Tax **21.11**

determined to have recourse on anyone who was a trustee within the period of twelve months (but after 18 March 1991) before the emigration. A past trustee is exempt from charge where he can show that when he ceased to be a trustee there was no proposal that the trust might emigrate. It is difficult to prove a negative, and a trustee in circumstances where this provision might apply would naturally require a full indemnity. In view of the fact that the right of recovery he is given against the migrating trustees may be of limited value, he would be well advised to have documentary evidence showing that he did make the necessary enquiries at the time of his retiral.

(*c*) *Exit charge on trustees becoming dual resident. TCGA 1992, s 83* is the provision directed against the use of double tax treaties to avoid a CGT charge. In cases where trustees continue to be resident and ordinarily resident in the UK under UK domestic law but become exempt from capital gains tax on the disposal of assets because of the residence provisions of a double tax treaty, they are deemed immediately before the point of becoming dual resident to have disposed of the assets and reacquired them at market value. The charge applies where trustees become dual resident after 18 March 1991. It is unclear how far this has been a loophole in practice as the UK does not have double tax treaties dealing with capital gains tax with most of the territories which are usually regarded as tax havens. The basis of the Revenue's concern is *ICTA 1988, s 788(3)* which gives tax treaties primacy over 'anything in any enactment', even anti-avoidance provisions. This has been confirmed by decisions in *Lord Strathalmond v CIR Ch D 1972, 48 TC 537* and *Padmore v CIR CA 1989, 62 TC 352*.

(*d*) *Acquisition by dual resident trustees. TCGA 1992, s 84* continues on the theme of dual resident trusts by denying rollover relief under *TCGA 1992, s 152* where the new assets are acquired by such trustees after 18 March 1991. This mirrors the treatment under *TCGA 1992, s 80* where the new assets are acquired after the emigration of the trust.

(*e*) *Disposal of settled interest.* Finally, *TCGA 1992, s 85(2)–(9)* provides a relief from the charge under *TCGA 1992, s 85(1)* where an interest in a non-resident settlement is disposed of. In cases where there has already been a charge under *TCGA 1992, s 80* the base value of the interest concerned is increased to its market value at the time of migration, i.e. when the previous charge arose, so preventing the same gain from being taxed twice. This relief is modified where the trustees become dual resident in circumstances such that a charge under *TCGA 1992, s 83* was incurred before the *TCGA 1992, s 80* exit charge on full migration. If the interest disposed of was only created for or acquired by the beneficiary after the trustees became dual resident, there is no relief at all, i.e. no uplift in base cost to market value at the time of migration. If the interest disposed of was created or acquired before the dates of

21.12 *Capital Gains Tax*

becoming dual resident and becoming non-resident, there is partial relief with the beneficiary's cost base being uplifted to market value at the date the trust became dual resident.

Charge on settlor

21.12 This charge was evidently regarded by the government as the flagship of the *FA 1991* provisions, since it was dealt with on the floor of the House rather than 'upstairs' in Committee. The detailed provisions are in *TCGA 1992, s 86, 5 Sch*, but *FA 1991, s 89*, as well as introducing *Schedule 5*, made two amendments to the existing law:

(*a*) the first inserted *TCGA 1992, s 87(3)* to make it clear that gains deemed to accrue to the settlor under *TCGA 1992, s 86(4)* cannot also be trust gains chargeable on the beneficiaries for the purposes of *TCGA 1992, s 87(2)*;

(*b*) the second deals with the situation where gains are treated as accruing to a settlor both under *TCGA 1992, s 86(4)* and *TCGA 1992, s 77(2)* (gains of UK resident trust chargeable on settlor—see 4.16 above). Under *TCGA 1992, s 78* the settlor has a right of recovery for any tax paid by him. *TCGA 1992, s 78(3)*, in conjunction with *TCGA 1992, s 86(4)(b)* provides that the gains deemed to be those of the settlor as the highest part of the amount on which he is chargeable are those accruing under *TCGA 1992, s 86*, in priority to those under *TCGA 1992, s 77*.

21.13 The detailed provisions in connection with the charge are contained in *TCGA 1992, s 86, 5 Sch*. The charging section is *s 86(4)* which provides in effect that the chargeable gains of a qualifying settlement shall be treated as accruing to the settlor if he has an interest in it.

Where a charge under these provisions arises on a temporarily non-resident settlor under *TCGA 1992, s 10A*, inserted by *FA 1998, s 127*, this is reduced by the amount of the gains charged on UK-resident beneficiaries of the settlement during the non-resident period [*TCGA 1992, s 86A*, inserted by *FA 1998, s 129*].

Qualifying settlements

21.14 'Qualifying settlements' i.e. those which are potentially caught are defined in *TCGA 1992, 5 Sch 9*. Every settlement created on or after 19 March 1991 is a qualifying settlement. Settlements created earlier may also come within the qualifying settlement net if one of four conditions is satisfied.

(*a*) Property or income is provided directly or indirectly for the purposes of the settlement otherwise than under a transaction entered into at arm's length, and otherwise than in pursuance of a liability incurred by any person before 19 March 1991. However, payments

Capital Gains Tax **21.15**

towards meeting the trust's expenses relating to administration and taxation are ignored to the extent that these exceed its income.

(*b*) The trustees either become neither resident nor ordinarily resident in the UK or become dual resident for the purposes of a double tax treaty.

(*c*) The terms of the trust are varied so that any one of a range of persons becomes for the first time a person who will or might benefit from the trust. The persons include settlors, their spouses, children and stepchildren, *their* spouses, any company controlled by them and any associated company. 'Control' and 'associated company' are construed in accordance with *ICTA 1988, s 416*, but in deciding questions of control or whether companies are associated, no rights or powers of an associate of a person are to be attributed to him if he is not a participator in the company. 'Associate' and 'participator' are defined in *ICTA 1988, s 417*. This does something to prevent, say, a member of a family who is in the position of an innocent bystander from being sucked into charge by having shareholdings of relatives attributed to him when he himself has no personal interest in the company.

(*d*) One of the persons mentioned under condition (*c*) enjoys a benefit for the first time and is not one who, looking at the terms of the trust before 19 March 1991, would be capable of enjoying a benefit thereafter. This appears designed to catch what are sometimes known as 'limbo trusts', where perhaps the apparent ultimate beneficiary is a charity, behind wide discretionary trusts, but some operation takes place not amounting to a variation whereby benefits flow to the settlor or his family.

Meaning of 'settlor'

21.15 A settlor is chargeable if he has an 'interest in the settlement' [*TCGA 1992, 5 Sch 2*] and if the trust's disposals consist of or include those of property 'originating' from him. [*TCGA 1992, 5 Sch 8*]. However, the charge does not apply if the settlor is not domiciled in the UK during the year of assessment concerned. [*TCGA 1992, s 86(1)(c)*].

The test whether the settlor has an interest turns on whether property or income in the trust originating from him can be applied for his benefit or for the benefit of the same range of persons as in the qualifying settlements provision [*TCGA 1992, 5 Sch 2(3)*]. There are exceptions to this similar to those in *ICTA 1988, s 673(3)*. These deal with circumstances where the settlor's interest is contingent on the death or bankruptcy of someone else in specified circumstances. [*TCGA 1992, 5 Sch 2(4)–(6)*].

The charge is also excluded where the settlor dies during the year and where the life or marriage of some other person by reason of which the

21.16 *Capital Gains Tax*

settlor is treated as having an interest ends during the year. [*TCGA 1992, 5 Sch 3–5*].

There are extensive provisions [*TCGA 1992, 5 Sch 8*] expanding on the term 'originating' in relation to property or income in the trust. They are designed to prevent avoidance through the provision of funds under reciprocal arrangements or through a closely controlled private company (subject to a five per cent *de minimis* rule for any participator) or otherwise indirectly.

The settlor is given a right of recovery against the trustees for any amount charged on him. [*TCGA 1992, 5 Sch 6*]. On the authorities it is unlikely that he could enforce such a right against non-resident trustees and if he did perhaps such a payment could constitute another benefit under *Schedule 5*.

An extension of the ambit of 'settlor' has been provided by the House of Lords in *Marshall v Kerr HL*, *[1994] STC 638* (see 7.9 above). In the context of the 1981 provisions, it was held that a UK resident and domiciled beneficiary who executed a deed of variation altering the provisions of her non-resident and non-domiciled father's will did become a settlor of the trust created by the deed.

Information powers and requirements

21.16 It is one thing to create an elaborate structure for charging the gains of non-resident trusts, it is quite another to gather the information necessary to raise an assessment. In many cases property in the UK may be held, say, by a Cayman Islands trust through a British Virgin Islands company. The viability of such jurisdictions as commercial centres depends on their being 'black holes' into which assets can disappear from the ken of inquisitive tax authorities.

However, even in the case of British Commonwealth jurisdictions such as the Bahamas it has been possible in the past for the USA to extract information from an off-shore branch by way of levying penalties on its Miami branch until the required information was produced thereby circumventing the Bahamian secrecy laws *US v Bank of Nova Scotia, 691 F.2d 1384 (1982)*. A further possible inroad into the confidentiality of tax havens is sanctions against these areas in respect of monetary loss. This approach was taken by a private member's bill entitled Transactions with Tax Havens (Sanctions) Act 1993 which did not however become law.

To counter this, *TCGA 1992, 5 Sch 10* gives the Inspector powers to demand such information from trustees, beneficiaries and settlors as he thinks necessary for the purposes of *TCGA 1992, section 86* and *Schedule 5*. *TCGA 1992, 5A Sch* imposes reporting requirements for relevant occurrences in relation to the migration of trusts or the creation of non-resident trusts or the return to UK residence and domicile of a previously offshore settlor. These powers and requirements are backed by the penalty provision of *TMA 1970, s 98* (£300 initial penalty, plus £60 per day for continued non-compliance).

Obviously no professional person will want to run the risk of falling foul of these requirements. Even if he is non-resident, there is always the risk of harassment by the Revenue should he ever visit the UK. The parameters of the Revenue's powers in this area have been examined in *re Clore (deceased) (No 3), CIR v Stype Trustees (Jersey) Ltd Ch D,* [*1985*] *STC 394* and *re Tucker (a bankrupt), ex p Tucker CA,* [*1988*] *1 All ER 603*.

Supplementary charge

21.17 *FA 1991* introduced a new concept in UK tax law, in effect charging interest on beneficiaries who receive capital payments from offshore trusts. The idea appears to have been borrowed from the US tax code. The basic principle is that a 10% per annum surcharge on the CGT due under *TCGA 1992, s 87* will be charged in addition on delayed capital payments to beneficiaries, up to a maximum of 60%. An outline of the provisions, contained in *TCGA 1992, ss 91–95,* is as follows:

(*a*) where a capital payment is made on or after 6 April 1992 by trustees of a settlement to which *TCGA 1992, s 87* applies and the payment is matched with a gain of the trust for a previous year of assessment, then the tax payable by the beneficiary under *TCGA 1992, s 87* is increased by 10% per annum for the 'chargeable period';

(*b*) the 'chargeable period' is the period beginning on 1 December in the year of assessment following that in which the 'qualifying amount' is realised by the trust and ending on 30 November in the year of assessment following that in which the capital payment is made;

(*c*) capital payments are matched with gains on a first-in, first-out basis;

(*d*) gains made before 6 April 1990 are treated as accruing in the 1990/91 year of assessment.

Under these rules, no charge could arise before 6 April 1992, nor on a distribution made in the year of assessment following that in which a qualifying amount is realised. The Treasury is given power to vary by statutory instrument the percentage currently fixed at 10%.

Strengthening of 1981 provisions

21.18 The 1991 legislation also put additional teeth into the 1981 provisions. These amendments were in *FA 1991, 18 Sch*. The main changes were as follows.

21.19 *Capital Gains Tax*

(a) TCGA 1992, s 88 was inserted to apply the charge on beneficiaries under the 1981 code not only to non-resident settlements but also to resident settlements which are treated as non-resident because of the application of a double tax treaty;

(b) Payments received by beneficiaries for the purposes of *TCGA 1992, s 87* is extended by *TCGA 1992, s 96* to include:

   (i) payments from a company controlled by the trustees either alone or together with the settlor and persons connected with the settlor; and

   (ii) payments to a non-resident company controlled by beneficiaries.

These new provisions run very much in tandem with the other 1991 changes. They were given some mitigating treatment in Committee as regards the definition of 'control' (see 21.14(c) above).

The 1998 provisions

21.19 Yet another attack on non-resident trusts has been launched in *FA 1998*.

The first provision, regarded as so urgent that it came into effect ahead of Budget Day, on 6 March 1998, was to remove the exemption under TCGA 1992, s 76 for gains made on the disposal of an interest by a beneficiary in a trust where the interest disposed of is in, or originates from, a trust which has ever been an offshore trust. The provision covers cases where an interest in an offshore trust which has been transferred to the UK is subsequently moved to another trust which has always been resident in the UK prior to disposal. [*TCGA 1992, s 76* as amended by *FA 1998, s 128*]. This prevents a beneficiary in an offshore trust pregnant with capital gains from realising these gains tax free by disposing of his interest in the trust after it has been transferred to the UK.

The second provision brings gains made by an offshore trust set up by a person who is not resident or domiciled in the UK within the charge on UK beneficiaries who receive capital payments from the trust. [*FA 1998, s 130* amending *TCGA 1992, ss 87, 88*]. The charge applies for 1997/98 and subsequent years, but only in respect of gains and capital payments made on or after 17 March 1998. This measure, which followed on publicity regarding the financial affairs of a Treasury minister, is probably largely cosmetic, since the trustees will refrain from making payments to UK-resident beneficiaries.

The third provision extends the charge to tax on the settlor of an offshore trust to trusts from which a settlor's grandchildren, or their spouses, can benefit. [*FA 1998, s 131* amending *TCGA 1992, 5 Sch 2*].

Finally, and most importantly, the distinction between pre-1991 trusts and post-1991 trusts is prospectively abolished. [*FA 1998, s 132* amending

Capital Gains Tax **21.21**

TCGA 1992, 5 Sch 9]. This does not apply to 'protected settlements', defined as pre-1991 trusts where the beneficiaries are confined to children under 18, or future children; the future spouse of any child or the settlor; and persons who are not the settlor, his immediate family, or companies they control. A protected settlement will lose its exemption if any of the circumstances bringing a pre-1991 trust into charge previously is fulfilled (see 21.14 above).

Transitional provisions

21.20 The new charge on settlements for grandchildren exempts trusts set up before 17 March 1998, unless funds are added or the trust migrates. [*FA 1998, 22 Sch*].

The new charge on pre-1991 trusts applies to gains made after 5 April 1999. This allows a transitional period for those affected to re-organise their affairs if they so wish: for example, for the settlor, his immediate family and companies they control to exclude themselves as beneficiaries; or for the trust to be wound up or become resident in the UK. There are rules to prevent exploitation of the transitional period. Gains made during that period will be chargeable on the settlor in 1999/2000 where the trust does not fall within the charge on the settlor until the end of the transitional period. Gains will also be chargeable on the settlor where the trust assets are transferred to another settlement from which, at the end of the transitional period, the settlor, his immediate family, or companies they control, can benefit. It also applies where the trust assets are transferred in similar circumstances to a 'foreign institution', defined as any company or other institution resident outside the UK. There are exceptions where the only members of the settlor's family who can benefit are children under eighteen, future children and future spouses, or where the settlor is dead or where a beneficiary dies or ceases to be married. There are rules to prevent double charges from arising under these provisions [*FA 1998, 23 Sch*].

Application

21.21 The Revenue issued a Statement of Practice (SP5/92) on 21 May 1992 indicating how they will apply the 1991 provisions, particularly in relation to the charge on settlors. They issued on the same date ESC D40 relaxing the definition of 'participator' in a company to exclude individuals whose connection is only that they are beneficiaries of a settlement with an interest in the company. It should be borne in mind, however, that the Revenue will not permit a concession to be used for what they consider to be tax avoidance.

Further clarification on the interpretation of SP5/92 was given by the Revenue in the Issues 8, page 82, and 16, page 204 of its *Tax Bulletin*. There are a number of events which the Revenue may regard as 'tainting' a pre-1991 trust, and it is critical to ensure competent administration for an offshore trust so that the rules are not contravened.

21.22 *Capital Gains Tax*

The 1998 measures have prospectively closed the gap between trusts created before 19 March 1991 and those created after 18 March 1991, save in the case of 'protected settlements'. During the transitional period, thought will have to be given to appropriate action to keep pre-March 1991 trusts outside the ambit of the new charge. This will require careful consideration and expert advice so that the action taken does not itself trigger a charge to tax.

The 2000 provisions

21.22 FA 2000 contains further provisions impacting on tax avoidance through offshore trusts.

The first, contained in 26 Schedule, deals with offshore aspects of the device known as a 'flip-flop', whereby gains are extracted from a trust tax-free, or with a significant tax saving, using borrowed money. 25 Schedule deals with the flip-flop in relation to a UK-resident trust. 26 Schedule extends the anti-avoidance provision to offshore trusts by inserting new TCGA 1992 4C Schedule. The flip-flop works by the trustees borrowing money on the security of assets in the trust and advancing the money to another trust. The settlor then severs his interest in the first trust. In the following tax year the trustees of the first trust sell the assets and use the proceeds to repay the debt. Capital payments can then be made to UK-resident beneficiaries from the second trust without charge to tax. New TCGA 1992 4C Schedule charges beneficiaries in respect of gains accruing to offshore trustees by virtue of a transfer of value made by them which falls within 4B Schedule, inserted by FA 2000 25 Schedule.

The second is contained in FA 2000, s 94. This inserts a TCGA 1992, s 79 B to prevent double tax treaties being used to shelter gains realised by offshore companies owned by a trust. Such gains may be attributed to resident or non-resident trustees as participators in those companies.

The third is contained in FA 2000, s 95, which amends TCGA 1992, s 85 to block a device whereby a trust is brought onshore and then exported again. The gains on the trust property escape charge because they were realised while the trust was offshore, while the beneficiary pays little or no tax on the sale of an interest in the trust because of the rule providing for its value to be uplifted on the trust's exit from the UK. The amendments provide that there will be no uplift where the trust is pregnant with gains not attributed to beneficiaries or the trust has gains which are caught under the measures against flip-flop schemes in FA 2000 25 and 26 Schedules.

Finally, FA 2000, s 96 amends TCGA 1992, s 96(5) to eliminate the requirement that each of the persons controlling an offshore company to which payments are made by offshore trustees must be resident or ordinarily resident in the UK. The interposition of non-resident persons in the control of the offshore company has been used to frustrate the operation of TCGA 1992, s 96.

Chapter 22

Inheritance Tax

22.1 The important factor for offshore trusts in relation to inheritance tax is not residence or ordinary residence but rather the domicile of the settlor.

Excluded property

22.2 'Excluded property' is property excluded from the scope of an inheritance tax charge either for a lifetime disposition or for a deemed transfer on death. In relation to trusts, if the excluded property is settled property, the termination of an interest in possession in it is not taxable, nor is it relevant property for the purposes of the inheritance tax regime applied to discretionary trusts. [*IHTA 1984, ss 3(1)(2), 5(1), 53(1), 58(1)*].

The main provisions relating to excluded property and trusts are to be found in *IHTA 1984, s 48*, which makes certain interests in trusts and certain assets held in some trusts excluded property.

Settled property situated outside the UK

22.3 Under *IHTA 1984, s 48(3)(a)*, where property in a trust is situated outside the UK (but not a reversionary interest in the property—see below) it is excluded property unless the settlor was domiciled in the UK at the time the settlement was made.

This is a provision of the highest importance, since it confers a permanent exemption from IHT irrespective of the subsequent history of the trust, provided the property itself is situated outside the UK.

The settlor

22.4 It should be noted that *IHTA 1984, s 44(1)* provides a wide definition of 'settlor' to include 'any person by whom the settlement was made directly or indirectly, and in particular (but without prejudice to the generality of the preceding words) includes any person who has provided funds directly or indirectly for the purpose of or in connection with the settlement or has made with any other person a reciprocal

207

22.5 Inheritance Tax

arrangement for that other person to make the settlement'. Where this definition produces more than one settlor, the part provided by each can be treated as a separate trust. [*IHTA 1984, s 44(2)*]. This will catch arrangements where there is a dummy settlor and subsequently other property finds its way into the trust.

Situation of property

22.5 The situation, or 'situs', of property is, like the domicile of an individual, a question governed by private international law. In many cases there will be no real doubt regarding the situation of property. Land is obviously situated where it is located and shares in a company are situated where the register is kept. Sometimes points of greater complication arise, requiring reference to the general law, or to a double tax treaty.

The total number of double tax treaties covering IHT has remained small in comparison with the treaties dealing with income, corporation and capital gains tax. Those in force relevant to inheritance tax exist with eleven countries but since three of them (Canada, Pakistan and India) have abolished estate duty, there are only eight which are of practical significance, those with France, Italy, Ireland, South Africa, the USA, the Netherlands, Sweden and Switzerland. Although several important jurisdictions are included, none of the territories where offshore trusts are most likely to be located for tax planning purposes figure on the list.

An ingenious and successful attempt to use situs rules for tax avoidance was considered in *Kwok v Commissioner of Estate Duty PC,* [*1988*] *STC 728.* Mr Kwok, literally on his death bed, transferred shares situated in Hong Kong worth US$1.8m to a Liberian company in consideration of a non-negotiable promissory note, payable on demand after 60 days at Monrovia. The Privy Council could see no escape from the conclusion that the chose in action represented by the promissory note was situate in Monrovia, but their Lordships issued a warning that such transactions were vulnerable on *Ramsay* principles (this had not been raised as an issue in the case).

Reversionary interests

22.6 Reversionary interests are defined under *IHTA 1984, s 47* as future interests under a settlement, whether vested or contingent.

There is a general exemption for reversionary interests, except in three specific cases, under *IHTA 1984, s 48(1)*. The rationale for this is that a reversion will usually take effect after an interest in possession and the holder of an interest in possession is treated under *IHTA 1984, s 49* as beneficially entitled to the property in which the interest subsists. This is a legal fiction, since a life interest and a reversionary interest under a

Inheritance Tax **22.8**

trust have an actuarial value. Many tax avoidance schemes, notably that employed in the recent case of *Countess Fitzwilliam and Others v CIR HL 1993, 67 TC 614* (see 21.3 above), have exploited this anomaly. A reversionary interest is excluded property unless:

(*a*) it has at any time been acquired (whether by the person entitled to it or by a person previously entitled) for a consideration in money or money's worth, or

(*b*) for a settlement made after 15 April 1976, it is one to which either the settlor or his spouse is (or, for a reversionary interest acquired after 9 March 1981, has been) beneficially entitled, or

(*c*) it is the interest expectant on the determination of a lease treated as a settlement under *IHTA 1984, s 43(3)*.

[*IHTA 1984, s 48(1)(2)*].

If a reversionary interest is not already excluded property under the general rule of *IHTA 1984, s 48(1)* above, it may still be excluded property if the person beneficially entitled to it is an individual domiciled outside the UK. Reversionary interests in settled property situated outside the UK are prevented from being excluded property under *IHTA 1984, s 48(3)(a)* (see 22.3 above), but are brought back in as excluded property by *section 48(3)(b)* which provides that *IHTA 1984, s 6(1)* applies to a reversionary interest in the property but does not otherwise apply in relation to the property. *Section 6(1)* provides that property situated outside the UK is excluded property if the person beneficially entitled to it is an individual domiciled outside the UK. Therefore, for a reversionary interest in foreign property to be excluded property, the individual reversioner must be domiciled outside the UK.

Exempt gilts

22.7 Certain UK Government securities, commonly known as exempt gilts, which are held in trust are also excluded property if certain conditions are met. The securities in question are ones issued by the Treasury on terms giving exemption from taxation so long as the securities are in the beneficial ownership of persons neither domiciled nor ordinarily resident in the UK. [*IHTA 1984, ss 6, 48(4)*].

There is an attractive range of exempt gilts available, with maturities for most years running into the second decade of this century.

22.8 The conditions for exemption from inheritance tax for exempt gilts held by trusts, as set out in *IHTA 1984, s 48(4)* are as follows:

(*a*) a person neither domiciled nor ordinarily resident in the UK is entitled to a 'qualifying interest in possession' (see 22.2 above and Appendix A) in them; or

22.9 *Inheritance Tax*

(*b*) there is no qualifying interest in possession in them, but it is shown that all known persons for whose benefit the trust property (or income from it) has been or might be applied, or who are or might become beneficially entitled to an interest in possession in it, are neither domiciled nor ordinarily resident in the UK.

To facilitate the creation of a gilt strips market, the exemption from taxation for non-resident holders of exempt gilts is extended from income tax to capital taxes. Previously the latter exemption only applied where the holder was non-domiciled as well as non-resident. [*FA 1996, s 154, 28 Sch 7, 8*].

22.9 There has been some litigation in connection with these provisions, not surprisingly in view of their rather convoluted nature. *Von Ernst & Cie SA v CIR CA, [1980] STC 111* concerned a trust in what is a rather common form, with a discretionary class of individuals as primary beneficiaries and a final gift over to UK charities. Both of the individuals concerned were neither domiciled nor ordinarily resident in the UK. An interest in possession in exempt gilts was appointed to the two individuals and the trustees argued the securities were excluded property. The transaction was charged to CTT under the provisions of *FA 1975, 5 Sch 6(2)* as a capital distribution. The Court of Appeal held that what is now *IHTA 1984, s 48(4)(b)* did apply to exempt the securities as excluded property since a charity, because of its fiduciary nature, could never become beneficially entitled to its property.

A five-part scheme to use the exempt gilts provision to transfer assets tax free from a mother in the UK to her daughter abroad came to grief in *CIR v Brandenburg Ch D, [1982] STC 555*.

In *Minden Trust (Cayman) Ltd v CIR CA, [1985] STC 758*, exempt gilts were transferred from a trust which did not qualify under *section 48(4)(b)* to one which did and then appointed on to the beneficiaries. This arrangement succeeded, but the *Minden* route has since been closed by *IHTA 1984, s 48(5)* which requires the domicile and ordinary residence conditions of *IHTA 1984, s 48(4)(b)* to be satisfied by both trusts where there is a transfer of property from one trust to another.

The most recent battle on the exempt gilts front was in *Montagu Trust Co. (Jersey) Ltd v CIR Ch D, [1989] STC 477* in which trustees transferred exempt gilts to themselves as trustees of a second trust and then proceeded to appoint them to beneficiaries who had emigrated to Israel. This arrangement failed to meet the statutory requirements for excluded property as it was possible that people domiciled in the UK might benefit on the technical construction of the deeds, and tax was chargeable accordingly.

The *Von Ernst* case has supplied useful clarification on what is necessary to meet the requirements of *IHTA 1984, 48(4)*. *Minden* and *Montagu*, and the subsequent countervailing legislation in *IHTA 1984, s 48(5)* indicate the difficulty of using the exemption through a reconstruction of existing trusts. The only really provocative attempt to utilise the exemption was in *Brandenburg* and this failed.

Exempt gilts provide a means for non-ordinarily resident and non-domiciled individuals to benefit from UK gilts through a trust without incurring any charges to IHT. Other uses, or abuses, of the exemption, appear decidedly risky.

Domicile

22.10 In addition to the general law of domicile mentioned at 19.6 above, an individual may be treated under *IHTA 1984, s 267* for the purposes of IHT only as domiciled in the UK at a time (the 'relevant time') when he is domiciled elsewhere under general law. This applies where he was domiciled (under general law) in the UK at any time during the three years immediately preceding the relevant time, or he was resident in the UK in not less than 17 of the 20 years of assessment (i.e. ending on 5 April) ending with the year of assessment in which the relevant time falls. The income tax rules for determining residence apply (see 19.3 above).

This deemed domicile rule does not apply in the following circumstances:

(*a*) in determining whether exempt gilts which are in the beneficial ownership of a non-domiciled person (or are settled property to which such a person is entitled to a qualifying interest in possession) are excluded property;

(*b*) in determining whether certain savings to which persons domiciled in the Channel Islands or Isle of Man are beneficially entitled are excluded property;

(*c*) where the domicile of a person is determined under a double tax treaty having IHT effect;

(*d*) in determining whether settled property which became comprised in a settlement before 10 December 1974 is excluded property; and

(*e*) in determining the settlor's domicile for the purposes of *IHTA 1984, s 65(8)* in relation to property held on discretionary trusts which became comprised in the settlement before 10 December 1974.

Reporting obligation

22.11 The Revenue is obviously faced with difficulty in obtaining information on offshore trusts. Accordingly, *IHTA 1984, s 218* imposes a liability on any person, other than a barrister, who has been concerned with the making of a trust in the course of his trade or profession, and knows or has reason to believe that the settlor was domiciled in the UK and that the trustees are not or will not be resident in the UK, to report this to the Revenue within three months of the creation of the trust with the names and addresses of the settlor and the trustees.

For the purposes of the provision trustees of a settlement are regarded as not resident in the UK unless the general administration of the settlement is ordinarily carried on in the UK and the trustees or a majority of them (and, where there is more than one class of trustees, a majority of each class) are for the time being resident in the UK.

Failure to comply carries a penalty of £300 plus £60 per day if it continues after it has been declared by a court or the Special Commissioners. The reasonable excuse defence is provided. [*IHTA 1984, s 245A*]. The requirement to provide information in this way is important in alerting the Revenue to the existence of such trusts. It does not apply to will trusts or to a trust where an account has been delivered to the Revenue under *IHTA 1984, s 216*.

Executors and trustees

22.12 When an individual dies his estate vests in his personal representatives, i.e. his executors if he has made a will or his administrators if he has not (for convenience it is usual to employ the term executor). An executor is not exactly in the position of a trustee (although he does have fiduciary responsibilities) since his primary duty is to wind up the estate as quickly as possible. The will itself however may set up a trust and in such a case it is treated as operating from the death of a testator. [*IHTA 1984, s 83*]. Where the will provides for an interest in possession in all or part of the residue this too is treated as operating from the death. [*IHTA 1984, s 91*].

Personal representatives are defined to include any person by whom or on whose behalf an application for a grant of administration or for the resealing of a grant made outside the UK is made and also any person who takes possession or intermeddles with, or otherwise acts in relation to the property (known in Scotland as a vitious intromitter). [*IHTA 1984, ss 4(a), 272*].

In *CIR v Stannard* Ch D [1984] *STC 245* the executor was resident in Jersey. The Revenue raised a determination against him for £60,000 and sought an order for payment out of his own assets (technically *de bonis propriis*). The court refused to do this, holding that he was only liable to pay from the deceased's assets (*de bonis testatoris*). On appeal, the order was made in the *de bonis propriis* form and Scott J held that there was no difference in this regard between the liability of executors and the liability of trustees. [*IHTA 1984, s 204(1)(2)*].

Enforcement—the Clore case

22.13 The position of executors and trustees is illustrated by the prolonged litigation in the *Clore* case. Sir Charles Clore died in July 1979, having given up residence in the UK and made moves towards establishing domicile in Monaco. The major issue was whether Sir Charles died domiciled in England or in Monaco. It took until 1984 for the court to hold that he had never abandoned his English domicile of origin (*re Clore (deceased) (No 2) Ch D, [1984] STC 609*). The case is a salutary example of how not to go about things if intending to change domicile. The other, related, litigation serves to illustrate not only that the Revenue has extensive enforcement powers, from which non-resident executors and trustees are not exempt, but also that they will not hesitate to use those powers where there is sufficient tax at stake.

Chapter 23

The Use of Offshore Trusts in Tax Planning

23.1 *FA 1991* obviously dealt a severe blow to the emigration of trusts as a means to the avoidance or mitigation of capital gains tax. *FA 1998* extended the attack to trusts which were already non-resident prior to the 1991 measures. Non-resident trusts, however, may still have a part to play in tax planning in suitable cases. The trust itself remains a well-tried and flexible instrument by which an individual can make prudent and forward-looking dispositions of his property while he is still alive and retain some control over its disposal in the event of his death or incapacity.

A foreigner coming to live in the UK will be taxed on the remittance basis on his offshore trust income, in the same way as on his personal income. The trust can also be structured so as to protect his capital indefinitely, subject to the domicile rules (see 19.6 above). The emigrant from this country can achieve similar advantages once he has surmounted the three year quarantine period imposed for IHT under *IHTA 1984, s 267* (and even that provision can be bypassed if the trust assets are held in the form of exempt gilts). Domicile therefore remains of crucial importance in the use of offshore trusts.

Protection and establishment of domicile

23.2 It is vital for the individual coming to this country and wishing to maintain his domicile of origin to maintain as close links as possible with his homeland. Circumstances may render this difficult. Many who come to this country do so because of hostile regimes in their native land. In such cases the intention to return when circumstances improve will maintain the domicile of origin. However, where residence here is voluntary, there may be more room for arguing that there is an intention to remain here permanently. The Revenue now contend that this can be inferred unless there is a predictable event (other than the receipt of a massive assessment) which will cause the individual to leave this country. This contention is dubious on the authorities and should be resisted.

For the emigrant it is essential, given the adhesive quality of the domicile of origin, that the links with the domicile of choice should be made as firm and durable as possible and the intention to leave this country permanently evinced clearly. In this, as in so many other respects, the *Clore* case (see 22.13 above) is a prime example of how not to do it. Sir Charles had been given professional advice that for tax planning purposes, particularly in connection with his offshore trust, it was essential that he should establish a foreign domicile. He did in the main follow this advice. He took steps to associate himself with Monaco. Why then was he held to be still domiciled here? The reason was that four close friends provided evidence that he was profoundly unhappy in his self-imposed exile. On this basis there was not sufficient evidence to satisfy the conscience of the court that Sir Charles ever formed a settled intention to reside permanently in Monaco. Tax planning in this area can never be a mechanical exercise. The subjective intentions of an individual are all important.

The trust document and its contents

23.3 The principles of the English law of equity are so well defined in a long line of decisions that a trust deed need not be unduly complex. This is not so in other jurisdictions. Some favourite venues, such as the Cayman Islands, Jersey and Guernsey, have produced their own Trustee Acts, but for maximum flexibility the deed will usually provide for moving the trust elsewhere, particularly in case of emergency. It is also usual to spell out the powers of the trustees in some detail. Frequently the deed provides for a protector nominated by the settlor; the consent of the protector may be required for important dispositive, as distinct from administrative acts. The protector is largely unknown to English law except in the almost obsolete context of estates in tail.

Where the trust is discretionary in form, there will usually be a letter of wishes from the settlor, not binding on the trustees, but certain to be given due weight by them.

There may be dangers in attempting to tie things up too tightly. This was illustrated by a case in the Royal Court of Jersey, *Abdel Rahman v Chase Bank (CI) Trust Co Ltd 1991 JLR 103*, earlier proceedings in which are reported in *1983 JLR 1, 1984 JLR 127, 1985–86 JLR N–5, 1987–88 JLR 81* and *1990 JLR 59, 136*. It concerned a Jersey trust set up by a Lebanese national. After his death his widow commenced an action against the trustees, alleging *inter alia* that the trust breached the maxim of Jersey law *'donner et retenir ne vaut'*, which means, broadly, that the settlor cannot retain control of something he has given away. The court held that the maxim was applicable, but its decision on this point has been overtaken by an amendment to the *Trusts (Jersey) Law 1984* providing that *'donner et retenir ne vaut'* could not be applied to invalidate a trust.

However, the court took evidence on the actual operation of the trust and found that the settlor retained dominion and control over the trust fund during his lifetime. There were also provisions in the trust deed which aligned it more with an American grantor-controlled trust than a true discretionary trust. The court concluded that the settlement was a sham in the sense that it was made to appear what it was not.

The obvious lesson to be drawn is that in setting up an offshore trust it is essential to be sure that it will stand up under local law as well as English law. If the settlor is unwilling to relinquish effective personal control, it is better not to proceed. In the *Rahman* case, the trustee strongly recommended a discretionary trust with a letter of wishes, and it would have been well had this advice been heeded.

The family context

23.4 The main purpose of an offshore trust is likely to be for benefiting the family. To achieve this purpose effectively it is important to ensure that the family are fully in sympathy with the terms and objects of the trust. This appears to have been overlooked by Mr Rahman in the case mentioned in 23.3 above. It was also forgotten by Sir Charles Clore (see 22.13 and 23.2 above). His dispositions were attacked not only by the Revenue in England, but by his son in Jersey. The result was a sorry multiplicity of proceedings. Although there were half a dozen parties to the summons in the action to determine Sir Charles' domicile, not one was prepared to make a positive case for a Monegasque domicile.

Parallel proceedings were going on in Jersey regarding domicile, which might reach an opposite conclusion. This was a prospect that, as the judge remarked, 'although one which may to the uninitiated seem rather odd, I have to face with equanimity'. No doubt the members of the family did not share his sang-froid.

Where gifts to the family fail, there is sometimes a final gift over to charity. There are now few restrictions on gifts to charity for the purpose of exemption from tax, although it should be noted that:

(*a*) the charity must be subject to the jurisdiction of the UK courts (*Dreyfus (Camille & Henry) Foundation Inc v CIR HL 1955, 36 TC 126*);

(*b*) it must not run foul of the anti-avoidance provisions in *ICTA 1988, ss 505, 506 and 20 Sch*, introduced to counter abuses which the Revenue considered were exemplified in *CIR v Helen Slater Charitable Trust Ltd CA, [1981] STC 471*.

The security aspect

23.5 The powers of the Revenue in relation to the enforcement of tax, including the obtaining of information which they may require, are wide (see 20.4, 21.16, 22.11 and 22.13 above) but they are not unlimited. The decision in *Government of India v Taylor HL, [1955] AC 491* confirmed the long-standing rule that the British courts will not enforce directly or

The Use of Offshore Trusts in Tax Planning **23.6**

indirectly the revenue laws of a foreign state. This is likely to apply equally in any jurisdiction where an offshore trust is based.

The attitude to information-gathering is less definite. *Re State of Norway's Application (Nos 1 & 2) HL, [1990] 1 AC 723* concerned applications by Norway requesting the oral examination of two City bankers in connection with a large tax assessment on the estate of a wealthy shipowner. A key question was the identity of the settlor of a trust. The bankers objected to revealing this on grounds of their duty of confidentiality. The examination was allowed to proceed, but on the basis that the bankers were not required to reveal the identity of the settlor, unless it emerged from their evidence that the settlor was acting merely as the shipowner's agent or nominee in relation to the matters with which the Norwegian court was directly concerned.

The amendments to the law made by FA 2000, ss 146 and 147 providing for exchange of information with other countries under tax information agreements or double taxation agreements foreshadow increased official activity in this area.

Absolute confidentiality can no longer be relied on in all circumstances. The golden rule is that nothing should be advised or attempted which cannot be revealed in the last resort to the tax authorities of any relevant country.

The location of the trust

23.6 There are now a number of jurisdictions which actively compete for offshore trust business. In the days of the sterling area and exchange control the Isle of Man, the Channel Islands and, to a lesser extent, Gibraltar were frequently used. More recently it has been possible to move further afield. The Cayman Islands and the Bahamas offer great expertise and a reassuring background of English law. The Channel Islands and Gibraltar have recently seen increased activity in this area, no doubt to some extent in anticipation of the advent of the present Government.

There has been a trend towards the setting up of asset protection trusts. These originated in the desire of US professionals to protect their assets from malpractice suits. In the UK such a trust would be the subject of scrutiny where there appeared to be a possibility under *Insolvency Act 1986, s 423* of an intention to defeat creditors. Some jurisdictions, such as the Turks and Caicos Islands, now have a trust ordinance which protects the trust from a creditor unless the settlor was insolvent at the time of the transfer into the trust.

Very often an offshore structure will include companies owned by the trust and it may be desirable to incorporate these in other jurisdictions. This is also now a well-trodden route on which competent professional offshore trustees will be ready to advise.

23.7 *The Use of Offshore Trusts in Tax Planning*

Offshore structures have unfortunately been in the limelight as a means of 'laundering' money arising from drug trafficking and other criminal activities, and it may be necessary to demonstrate the innocent provenance of the funds.

Opportunities for non-domiciled individuals

23.7 A non-UK domiciled or resident individual should seriously consider setting up an offshore trust if he intends to re-establish residence here. It should also be remembered that the spouse of such an individual can now retain an independent foreign domicile. Income and gains arising on such trusts are taxable only on a remittance basis for a non-domiciled individual. [*TCGA 1992, s 12(1), ICTA 1988, s 65(4)*]. Care must be taken not to infringe the rules regarding constructive remittance. [*TCGA 1992, s 12(2), ICTA 1988, s 65(5)–(9)*]. Non-UK assets will remain outside the scope of inheritance tax. [*IHTA 1984, s 48(3)*].

A prime disadvantage is that the assets concerned will pass out of the control of the settlor to that of the trustees. The use of a side letter indicating the settlor's wishes is frequently used in the case of a discretionary trust, but the *Rahman* case (see 23.3 above) indicates the problems which may arise if the trustees are not accorded adequate discretion.

Gains made by offshore trusts set up by non-resident and non-domiciled persons are now chargeable on UK beneficiaries who receive capital payments from the trust (see 21.19 above).

A sting in the tail

23.8 Finally, it should be remembered that *ICTA 1988, s 739* may still be deployed by the Revenue to attack the best of structures. Although it was patently clear at the time of its origin that it was meant to counter transfers of assets offshore by individuals resident in the UK at that time, and despite the savaging which the Revenue received from the House of Lords in the *Vestey* case (see 20.7 above) they still attempted to use the old warhorse against non-domiciled individuals who set up offshore trusts before coming to reside in this country.

Comfort in this regard was given by *CIR v Willoughby, CA [1995] STC 143, HL [1997] STC 995* in which it was held that the overruling of *Congreve* by *Vestey* meant that *section 739* did not apply to non-residents, whether expatriates or foreigners, who made transfers of assets before taking up or resuming residence in the UK.

The anticipated unfavourable decision of the House of Lords in *Willoughby* was reversed by *s 739(1A)*, inserted by *FA 1997, s 81*, which provides that *s 739* is not confined to cases where the individual was ordinarily resident in the UK at the time when the transfer was made. It

The Use of Offshore Trusts in Tax Planning **23.8**

also widens the ambit of the section to cover transfers of assets where the purpose of the transfer is to avoid capital gains tax or inheritance tax but has the effect of avoiding income tax as well. These changes applied to income arising after Budget day, 26 November 1996.

Even after *Vestey* and *Willoughby*, the position remained unclear regarding transfers of assets already outside the UK by a UK resident. It is likely that such arrangements will be attacked by the Revenue.

Appendix A

Press Releases and Statements of Practice

1 November 1973, Inland Revenue Statement of Practice D10
Termination of life interest in settled property
(*TCGA 1992, s 71* and *TCGA 1992, s 72*)

1. Where a life interest in part of settled property terminates and the part can properly be identified with one or more specific assets, or where within three months of the termination the trustees appropriate specific assets to give effect to the termination, the Board will accept that the deemed disposals and reacquisitions under *TCGA 1992, s 71* and *TCGA 1992, s 72 (CGTA 1979, s 54 and 55)* apply to those specific assets, and not to any part of the other assets comprised in the settled property.

2. Where the benefit of this practice is claimed Inspectors of Taxes will require trustees to sign an undertaking, which will be binding on the Inland Revenue and the Trustees concerned as well as their successors in office, to the effect that the right to compute the gain or loss on any subsequent disposal on any other basis is given up. For the purposes of limiting the capital gains tax charged Inspectors will be prepared, in particular, to agree with trustees lists of assets properly identifiable with the release of a life interest, and any such agreement will be similarly binding on the Revenue and the trustees.

3. This practice applies on any act or event which terminates a life interest whether voluntarily or involuntarily.

Inland Revenue Statement of Practice E1
Accumulation and maintenance settlements: powers of appointment

1. It is not necessary for the interests of individual beneficiaries to be defined. They can for instance be subject to powers of appointment. In any particular case the exemption will depend on the precise terms of the trust and power concerned, and on the facts to which they apply. In general, however, the official view is that the conditions do not restrict the application of *IHTA 1984, s 71* to settlements where the interests of individual beneficiaries are defined and indefeasible.

2. The requirement of *IHTA 1984, s 71(1)(a)* is that one or more persons will, on or before attaining a specified age not exceeding twenty five, become beneficially entitled to, or to an interest in possession in, the settled property or part of it. It is considered that settled property

Appendix A

would meet this condition if at the relevant time it must vest for an interest in possession in some member of an existing class of potential beneficiaries on or before that member attains 25. The existence of a special power of appointment would not of itself exclude *section 71* if neither the exercise nor the release of the power could break the condition. To achieve this effect might, however, require careful drafting.

3. The inclusion of issue as possible objects of a special power of appointment would exclude a settlement from the benefit of *section 71* if the power would allow the trustees to prevent any interest in possession in the settled property from commencing before the beneficiary concerned attained the age specified. It would depend on the precise words of the settlement and the facts to which they had to be applied whether a particular settlement satisfied the conditions of *section 71(1)*. In many cases the rules against perpetuity and accumulations would operate to prevent an effective appointment outside those conditions. However the application of *section 71* is not a matter for a once-for-all decision. It is a question that needs to be kept in mind at all times when there is settled property in which no interest in possession subsists.

4. Also, a trust which otherwise satisfies the requirement of *section 71(1)(a)* would not be disqualified by the existence of a power to vary or determine the respective shares of members of the class (even to the extent of excluding some members altogether) provided the power is exercisable only in favour of a person under 25 who is a member of the class.

Annex to SP E1
Practical illustrations of *IHTA 1984, s 71*. The examples set out below are based on a settlement for the children of X contingently on attaining 25, the trustees being required to accumulate the income so far as it is not applied for the maintenance of X's children.

Example A
The settlement was made on X's marriage and he has as yet no children.

> *IHTA 1984, s 71* will not apply until a child is born and that event will give rise to a charge for tax under *IHTA 1984, s 65*.

Example B
The trustees have power to apply income for the benefit of X's unmarried sister.

> *IHTA 1984, s 71* does not apply because the conditions of *subsection (1)(b)* are not met.

Example C
X has power to appoint the capital not only among his children but also among this remote issue.

Appendix A

IHTA 1984, s 71 does not apply (unless the power can be exercised only in favour of persons who would thereby acquire interests in possession on or before attaining age 25). A release of the disqualifying power would give rise to a charge for tax under *IHTA 1984, s 65*. Its exercise would give rise to a charge under *IHTA 1984, s 65*.

Example D
The trustees have an overriding power of appointment in favour of other persons.

IHTA 1984, s 71 does not apply (unless the power can be exercised only in favour of persons who would thereby acquire interests in possession on or before attaining age 25). A release of the disqualifying power would give rise to a charge for tax under *IHTA 1984, s 65*. Its exercise would give rise to a charge under *IHTA 1984, s 65*.

Example E
The settled property has been revocably appointed to one of the children contingently on his attaining 25 and the appointment is now irrevocable.

If the power to revoke prevents *IHTA 1984, s 71* from applying, (as it would for example, if the property thereby became made subject to a power of appointment as at C or D) tax will be chargeable under *IHTA 1984, s 65* when the appointment is made irrevocable.

Example F
The trust to accumulate income is expressed to be during the life of the settlor.

As the settlor may live beyond the 25th birthday of any of his children, the trust does not satisfy the condition in *subsection (1)(a)* and *section 71, IHTA 1984* does not apply.

12 February 1976, Inland Revenue Press Release (now contained in Appendix A in leaflet IHT 16).
Interests in possession

The Board of Inland Revenue are aware that doubts have been expressed in the legal press and elsewhere concerning the precise scope of the term 'interest in possession' as used in *Part III* of the *Finance Act 1975* [now *Part III Chapter II IHTA*], and in particular about its application where an interest in settled property is subject to a discretion or power to accumulate the income of the property or to divert it elsewhere.

The Board therefore feel it appropriate, in view of the importance of the expression in *Schedule 5, Finance Act 1975* [now *Part III IHTA*], to make known their understanding of the meaning of the expression. This is that an interest in possession in settled property exists where the person having the interest has the immediate entitlement (subject to any prior claim

Appendix A

by the trustees for expenses or other outgoings properly payable out of income) to any income produced by the property as the income arises; but that a discretion or power, in whatever form, which can be exercised after income arises so as to withhold it from that person negatives the existence of an interest in possession. For this purpose a power to accumulate income is regarded as a power to withhold it, unless any accumulations must be held solely for the person having the interest or his or her personal representatives.

On the other hand the existence of a mere power of revocation or appointment, the exercise of which would determine the interest wholly or in part (but which, so long as it remains unexercised, does not affect the beneficiary's immediate entitlement to income) does not in the Board's view prevent the interest from being an interest in possession.

15 April 1976, Inland Revenue Statement of Practice E13
Charities

IHTA 1984, ss 23, 24 exempt from inheritance tax certain gifts to charities and political parties to the extent that the value transferred is attributable to property given to a charity etc. *IHTA 1984, ss 25, 26, 3 Sch* exempt in similar terms gifts for national purposes and for the public benefit.

Where the value transferred (i.e., the loss to a transferor's estate as a result of the disposition) exceeds the value of the gift in the hands of a charity etc., the Board of Inland Revenue have hitherto taken the view that the transfer is exempt only to the extent of the value of the property in the hands of the transferee. The Board wish it to be known that they are now advised that the exemption extends to the whole value transferred. *Section 26* was repealed from 17 March 1998.

15 August 1979, Inland Revenue Statement of Practice SP10/79
Inheritance tax: power for trustees to allow a beneficiary to occupy a dwelling house

Many wills and settlements contain a clause empowering the trustees to permit a beneficiary to occupy a dwelling house which forms part of the trust property on such terms as they think fit. The Board do not regard the existence of such a power as excluding any interest in possession in the property.

Where there is no interest in possession in the property in question the Inland Revenue do not regard the exercise of the power as creating one if the effect is merely to allow non-exclusive occupation or to create a contractual tenancy for full consideration. The Inland Revenue also take the view that no interest in possession arises on the creation of a lease for a term or a periodic tenancy for less than full consideration, though this will normally give rise to a charge for tax under [*IHTA 1984, s 65(1)(b)*]. On the other hand, if the power is drawn in terms wide enough to cover the creation of an exclusive or joint right of residence, albeit revocable,

223

Appendix A

for a definite or indefinite period, and is exercised with the intention of providing a particular beneficiary with a permanent home, the Revenue will normally regard the exercise of the power as creating an interest in possession. And if the trustees in exercise of their powers grant a lease for life for less than full consideration, this will also be regarded as creating an interest in possession in view of [*IHTA 1984, ss 43(3), 50(6)*].

A similar view will be taken where the power is exercised over property in which another beneficiary had an interest in possession up to the time of the exercise.

6 April 1982, Inland Revenue Statement of Practice SP1/82
The interaction of income tax and inheritance tax on assets put into settlements

1. For many years the tax code has contained legislation to prevent a person avoiding higher rate income tax by making a settlement, while still retaining some rights to enjoy the income or capital of the settlement. This legislation, which is embodied in *ICTA 1988, Part XV*, provides in general terms that the income of a settlement shall, for income tax purposes, be treated as that of the settlor in all circumstances where the settlor might benefit directly or indirectly from the settlement.

2. If the trustees have power to pay or do in fact pay inheritance tax due on assets which the settlor puts into the settlement the Inland Revenue have taken the view that the settlor has thereby an interest in the income or property of the settlement, and the income of the settlement should be treated as his for income tax purposes under *ICTA 1988, Part XV*.

3. The inheritance tax legislation ([*IHTA 1984, s 199*]), however, provides that both the settlor and the trustees are liable for any inheritance tax payable when a settlor puts assets into a settlement. The Board of Inland Revenue have therefore decided that they will no longer, in these circumstances, treat the income of the settlement as that of the settlor for income tax purposes solely because the trustees have power to pay or do in fact pay inheritance tax on assets put into settlements.

4. This change of practice applies to settlement income from 1981–82 *et seq.*

11 October 1984, Inland Revenue Statement of Practice SP7/84
Capital gains tax: exercise of a power of appointment or advancement over settled property

The Board's Statement of Practice SP9/81, which was issued on 23 September 1981 following discussions with the Law Society, set out the Revenue's views on the capital gains tax implications of the exercise of a Power of Appointment or Advancement when continuing trusts are declared, in the light of the decision of the House of Lords in *Roome & Denne v Edwards HL*, [*1981*] *STC 96*. Those views have been modified

Appendix A

to some extent by the decision of the Court of Appeal in *Bond v Pickford CA, [1983] STC 517.*

In *Roome & Denne v Edwards* the House of Lords held that where a separate settlement is created there is a deemed disposal of the relevant assets by the old trustees for the purposes of *Section 71(1), TCGA 1992* (formerly *Section 25(3), Finance Act 1965*). But the judgments emphasised that, in deciding whether or not a new settlement has been created by the exercise of a Power of Appointment or Advancement, each case must be considered on its own facts, and by applying established legal doctrine to the facts in a practical and commonsense manner. In *Bond v Pickford* the judgments in the Court of Appeal explained that the consideration of the facts must include examination of the powers which the trustees purported to exercise, and determination of the intention of the parties, viewed objectively.

It is now clear that a deemed disposal under *Section 71(1), TCGA 1992* cannot arise unless the power exercised by the trustees, or the instrument conferring the power, expressly or by necessary implication, confers on the trustees authority to remove assets from the original settlement by subjecting them to the trusts of a different settlement. Such powers (which may be powers of advancement or appointment) are referred to by the Court of Appeal as 'powers in the wider form'. However, the Board considers that a deemed disposal will not arise when such a power is exercised and trusts are declared in circumstances such that:

(*a*) the appointment is revocable, or

(*b*) the trusts declared of the advanced or appointed funds are not exhaustive so that there exists a possibility at the time when the advancement or appointment is made that the funds covered by it will on the occasion of some event cease to be held upon such trusts and once again come to be held upon the original trusts of the settlement.

Further, when such a power is exercised the Board considers it unlikely that a deemed disposal will arise when trusts are declared if duties in regard to the appointed assets still fall to the trustees of the original settlement in their capacity as trustees of that settlement, bearing in mind the provision in *Section 69(1), TCGA 1992* that the trustees of a settlement form a single and continuing body (distinct from the persons who may from time to time be the trustees).

Finally, the Board accept that a Power of Appointment or Advancement can be exercised over only part of the settled property and that the above consequences would apply to that part.

10 November 1986, Inland Revenue Statement of Practice SP8/86
Treatment of income of discretionary trusts

This statement sets out the Board's practice concerning the inheritance tax/capital transfer tax treatment of income of discretionary trusts.

Appendix A

The Board take the view that:

— Undistributed and unaccumulated income should not be treated as a taxable trust asset; and

— For the purposes of determining the rate of charge on accumulated income, the income should be treated as becoming a taxable asset of the trust on the date when the accumulation is made.

This practice applies from 10 November 1986 to all new cases and to existing cases where the tax liability has not been settled.

21 March 1990, Text of a letter addressed to the professional bodies by the Director, Capital and Valuation Division of the Inland Revenue
1. Section 40 IHTA 1984—partly exempt transfers

Section 40 directs that 'where gifts taking effect on a transfer of value take effect separately out of different funds'—for example where on a death there are gifts out of the free estate and out of settlements—then each fund is to be considered separately for the purpose of the allocation of exemptions under *Chapter III* including the grossing-up of the gifts. The rate of tax used by the Capital Taxes Offices to gross up separate gifts out of different funds has until now been the rate applicable to the total value of *all* property chargeable on the testator's death. The Board now accepts that the rate of the tax to be used for grossing up should be found by looking at each fund separately and in isolation.

2. Section 52(1) IHTA 1984—the coming to an end of an interest in possession in settled property

When an interest in possession in settled property comes to an end during the lifetime of the person entitled to it, *section 52(1)* states that the value for inheritance tax purposes is '... equal to the value of the property in which his interest subsisted'. Until now this value has been determined as a rateable proportion of the aggregate value of that settled property and other property of a similar kind in the person's estate. The Board now take the view that, in these circumstances, the settled property in which the interest subsisted should be valued *in isolation* without reference to any similar property.

These statements of the Board's position are made without prejudice to the application in an appropriate case of the *Ramsay* principle or the provisions of the *Inheritance Tax Act 1984* relating to associated operations. The changes of view will be applied to all new cases and to existing cases where the tax liability has not been settled. The operation of the legislation will be kept under review.

19 December 1990, Inland Revenue Press Release
New trust deeds: change of practice

The Inland Revenue have decided to change the way in which they handle new trusts for income tax and capital gains tax. From 6 April 1991 tax offices will in general no longer ask, as they do at present, for a copy

Appendix A

of every new trust document. Instead they will rely on the information shown by trustees, settlors and beneficiaries in their annual tax returns or repayment claims.

The Inland Revenue will seek further information only where necessary, and only exceptionally will they ask to see trust deeds, wills or other documents. That may happen if, for example, an inspector is not satisfied with a tax return or repayment claim, or if the taxpayer is unsure of the effect of the document and the issue cannot be resolved in some other way.

When a new trust is created, trustees will be sent a form which asks them to give some basic general factual information about the identities of the trustees and settlor and whether the trustees have power to accumulate income or to distribute it at their discretion.

The change of practice is concerned only with ordinary family trusts where the documents are currently sent to local tax offices. It does not affect any arrangements for special types of trust such as unit trusts, charitable trusts and employee trusts. Nor does it alter the examination of deeds for inheritance tax purposes by the Capital Taxes Office.

16 March 1993, Inland Revenue Statement of Practice SP4/93
Deceased persons' estates: discretionary interests in residue

Section 698(3) of the *Income and Corporation Taxes Act 1988* provides for discretionary payments out of the income of the residue of an estate of a deceased person, whether made directly by the personal representatives, or indirectly through a trustee or other person, to be treated as the income of the recipient for the year in which they are paid.

The Inland Revenue will apply *section 698(3)* whenever such discretionary payments are made, whether they are payments out of income of the residue as it arises or out of income arising to the personal representatives in earlier years, which has been retained pending the exercise of their discretion.

Where payments are made out of income of the residue of United Kingdom estates (as defined in *section 701(9)*) they are treated as received after deduction of basic rate tax. Recipients who are not liable to income tax on the payments, including charities, are entitled to claim repayment of this basic rate tax. Recipients who are higher rate taxpayers will be subject to a further tax charge to satisfy their liability at the higher rate.

Where payments are made indirectly through trustees, the trustees may be liable to an additional rate tax charge on the payments under *section 686* of the *Income and Corporation Taxes Act 1988*. Beneficiaries may be treated as receiving the payments after deduction of tax at the sum of the basic and additional rates. This tax may be repaid or further tax charged,

Appendix A

depending on the beneficiary's marginal rate. The trustees are not chargeable to income tax at the additional rate where a trust is established for charitable purposes only.

With effect from 16 March 1993 the Inland Revenue will apply *section 698(3)* in this way to all open cases whether this results in repayment of tax or an assessment to income tax at the higher rate. Claims for repayment of tax may also be made for years from 1986/87 onwards, including supplementary claims where an earlier claim was refused under the Revenue's previous practice. Claims for the 1986/87 tax year made after 5 April 1993 but before 6 April 1994 will be accepted notwithstanding that, in accordance with *section 43* of the *Taxes Management Act 1970*, they would, in strictness, be out of time.

Note: At the time of publication there was no lesser or savings rate or Schedule F ordinary rate of tax.

Appendix B

Extra-Statutory Concessions

B 18 Payments out of discretionary trusts (as amended by Inland Revenue Press Release on 1 April 1999)

UK Resident trusts

A beneficiary may receive from trustees a payment to which *TA 1988 s 687(2)* applies. Where that payment is made out of the income of the trustees in respect of which, had it been received directly, the beneficiary would have been entitled to exemption in respect of FOTRA Securities issued in accordance with *FA 1996 s 154*; or have been entitled to relief under the terms of a double taxation agreement; or not have been chargeable to UK tax because of their not resident and/or not ordinarily resident status the beneficiary may claim that exemption or relief or, where the beneficiary would not have been chargeable, repayment of the tax treated as deducted from the payment (or an appropriate proportion of it). For this purpose, the payment will be treated as having been made rateably out of all sources of income arising to the trustees on a last in first out basis.

Relief or exemption, as appropriate, will be granted to the extent that the payment is out of income which arose to the trustees not earlier than six years before the end of the year of assessment in which the payment was made, provided the trustees—

— have made trust returns giving details of all sources of trust income and payments made to beneficiaries for each and every year for which they are required, and have paid all tax due, and any interest, surcharges and penalties arising, and

— keep available for inspection any relevant tax certificates.

Relief or exemption, as appropriate, will be granted to the beneficiary on a claim made within five years and ten months of the end of the year of assessment in which the beneficiary received the payment from the trustees.

Non-resident trusts

A similar concession will operate where a beneficiary receives a payment from discretionary trustees which is not within *TA 1988 s 687(2)* (i.e. where non-resident trustees exercise their discretion outside the UK).

Appendix B

Where a non-resident beneficiary receives such a payment out of income of the trustees in respect of which, had it been received directly, it would have been chargeable to UK tax, then the beneficiary may claim relief under *TA 1988 s 278* (personal reliefs for certain non-residents); and may be treated as receiving that payment from a UK resident trust but claim credit only for UK tax actually paid by the trustees on income out of which the payment is made.

The beneficiary may also claim exemption from tax in respect of FOTRA securities issued in accordance with *FA 1996 s 154* to the extent that the payment is regarded as including interest from such securities.

A UK beneficiary of a non-resident trust may claim appropriate credit for tax actually paid by the trustees on the income out of which the payment is made as if the payments out of UK income were from a UK resident trust and within *TA 1988 s 687(1)*.

This treatment will only be available where the trustees—

— have made trust returns giving details of all sources of trust income and payments made to beneficiaries for each and every year for which they are required, and

— have paid all tax due and any interest, surcharges and penalties arising, and

— keep available for inspection any relevant tax certificates.

Relief or exemption, as appropriate, will be granted to the beneficiary on a claim made within five years and ten months of the end of the year of assessment in which the beneficiary received the payment from the trustees.

No credit will be given for UK tax treated as paid on income received by the trustees which would not be available for set off under *TA 1988 s 687(2)* if that section applied, and that tax is not repayable (for example on dividends). However, such tax is not taken into account in calculating the gross income treated as taxable on the beneficiary under this concession.

F8 Accumulation and maintenance settlements

The requirement of *section 71(1)(a)* of the *IHTA 1984* is regarded as being satisfied even if no age is specified in the trust instrument, provided that it is clear that a beneficiary will in fact become entitled to the settled property (or to an interest in possession in it) by the age of 25.

[See Appendix F for the text of *section 71*.]

Appendix C

Checking Liabilities and the Tax Pool, etc in 1999/2000

Basic data

The settlement was made in May 1979 for the benefit of such of the settlor's grandchildren as might attain the age of 25.

The grandchildren are:

	Date of Birth	Age in 1999/2000
Alice	6 April 1973	26
Belinda	6 April 1981	18
Cathy	6 April 1982	17

The *Trustee Act 1925, s 31* applies. This is not considered to be good drafting. As a result this is an accumulation and maintenance settlement with income vesting at 18. Alice is entitled to her third of the capital. However, one of the assets is a property which still has to be sold so that no distributions have been made so far.

In 1999/2000:

the trustees received:

	£
UK dividends (Net)	4,500
Building society interest (net)	450
Rent (gross)	3,000

they paid:

	£
professional fees for 1998/99	940
overdraft interest	100
interest on overdue tax	20
bank charges	50
tax – as assessed	

to beneficiaries £600 each in December 1999.

In July 2000 they paid fees for 1999/2000 amounting to £1,175. The rent of £3,000 was a pure profit rental.

Appendix C

On pages 3 and 4 of the return, the trustees will report:

	Gross	Tax	Net
Building society interest	563	113	450
UK dividends	5,000	500	4,500
			£4,950

The rent will be reported on the supplementary page for income from land and property.

On page 4:

1. Alice's and Belinda's interests will be mentioned at Q.13.
2. The management expenses will be noted as £1,345 at Q.13.19. This comprises:

fees	1,175
overdraft interest	100
interest on tax	20
bank charges	50
	£1,345

This is in accordance with the Guide, on page 18. That tells us to deduct the expenses paid out of the income of the year. The fees were accrued at 5 April 2000 and so were paid out of 1999/2000.

On page 7 the payment of £600 to Cathy, which was discretionary, will be reported at Q.14.

Because Alice is absolutely entitled there will be no deduction for expenses in calculating her income. Expenses will be deducted from Belinda.

Belinda's income is:

Net dividends	4,500	10% income
Net interest	450	20% income
Net rent	2,310	23% income
	7,260	
Expenses	1,345	
Net income	£5,915	
One third share	£1,972	

The expenses are set against the dividend income.

Therefore she has:

10% income	1052 net
20% income	150 net
23% income	770 net

Appendix C

and her tax voucher will be prepared accordingly. Alice's voucher will be based on:

	Net
10% income	1,500
20% income	150
23% income	770
Net share	£2,420

Cathy's income is the £600 paid out at Christmas and this will go on her tax voucher as:

Gross	909	
Tax	309	(= 34%)
Net	£600	

The liability of the trustees is:

1. The income

Gross Dividends	5,000
Expenses (1,345 grossed @ 10%)	(1,494)
	3,506
Gross BSI (= 20% income)	563
Rent (= 23% income) gross	£3,000

2. The tax

Rent @ 34%	1,020
Schedule F trust rate @ 25% less 10% tax credit = 15%	526
20% income @ 14%	79
Liability due 31.1.2001	£1,625

The tax pool will be:

Balance 5 April 1999		2,365
Add tax for 1999/2000		
10% income net of expenses	3,506	
20% income	563	
23% income	3,000	
@ 34%	7,069	2,403
		4,768
Less tax deducted from Cathy		309
Balance 5 April 2000		4,459

Appendix C

Notes

1. This is not an illustration of the calculations on the form for calculating tax. It is simply a convenient check on the figures which the Inland Revenue produce, coupled with detailed workings (as for instance, Alice's income) which should be kept on file.

2. Note that the 23% and 20% income have to be separate and that the dividend income where the 10% tax is *notional* is kept separate again. Note the order of set off which takes the expense from the least worthwhile income.

Appendix D

Statement of Practice SP8/94

SP8/94

Allowable expenditure: expenses incurred by personal representatives and corporate trustees

Expenses incurred by personal representatives

1 Following discussion with representative bodies, the scale of expenses allowable under *TCGA 1992 s 38(1)(b)*, for the costs of establishing title in computing the gains or losses of personal representatives on the sale of assets comprised in a deceased person's estate, has been revised. The Revenue will accept computations based either on this scale or on the *actual* allowable expenditure incurred.

2 The revised scale is as follows—

Gross value of estate	*Allowable expenditure*
A Up to £40,000	1.75 per cent of the probate value of the assets sold by the personal representatives.
B Between £40,001 and £70,000	A fixed amount of £700, to be divided between all the assets of the estate in proportion to the probate values and allowed in those proportions on assets sold by the personal representatives.
C Between £70,001 and £300,000	1 per cent of the probate value of the assets sold.
D Between £300,001 and £400,000	A fixed amount of £3,000, to be divided as at B above.
E Between £400,001 and £750,000	0.75 per cent of the probate value of the assets sold.

3 The scale does not extend to gross estates exceeding £750,000 where the allowable expenditure is to be negotiated according to the facts of the particular case by the inspector and the taxpayer.

4 The revised scale takes effect where death occurred after 5 April 1993.

Appendix D

Expenses incurred by corporate trustees

5   Following discussion with representative bodies, the Revenue have agreed the following scale of allowable expenditure under *TCGA 1992 ss 38, 64(1)(b)*, for expenses incurred by corporate trustees in the administration of estates and trusts. The Revenue will accept computations based either on this scale or on the *actual* allowable expenditure incurred.

6   The scale is as follows—

(*a*) *Transfers of assets to beneficiaries etc.*

    (i) Quoted stocks and shares

(A) One beneficiary	£20.00 per holding
(B) More than one beneficiary between whom a holding must be divided	As (A), to be divided in equal shares between the beneficiaries
(ii) Unquoted shares	As (i) above, with the addition of any exceptional expenditure
(iii) Other assets	As (i) above, with the addition of any exceptional expenditure

(*b*) *Actual disposals and acquisitions*

(i) Quoted stocks and shares	The investment fee as charged by the trustee
(ii) Unquoted shares	As (i) above, plus actual valuation costs
(iii) Other assets	The investment fee as charged by the trustee, subject to a maximum of £60, plus actual valuation costs

Where a comprehensive annual management fee is charged, covering both the costs of administering the trust and the expenses of actual disposals and acquisitions, the investment fee for the purposes of (i), (ii) and (iii) above will be taken to be £0.25 per £100 on the sale or purchase moneys.

(*c*) *Deemed disposals by trustees*

(i) Quoted stocks and shares	£6 per holding
(ii) Unquoted shares	Actual valuation costs
(iii) Other assets	Actual valuation costs

Appendix D

7 This scale takes effect for acquisitions and disposals, or deemed disposals, by corporate trustees after 5 April 1993.

Authors' Note: SP8/94 replaced SP7/81, to which earlier statement reference should be made in the case of deaths and acquisitions or disposals before 6 April 1993.

Appendix E

Trustee Act 1925, ss 31–33

Section 31: Power to apply income for maintenance and to accumulate surplus income during a minority

(1)   Where any property is held by trustees in trust for any person for any interest whatsoever, whether vested or contingent, then subject to any prior interests or charges affecting that property—

(i) during the infancy of any such person, if his interest so long continues, the trustees may, at their sole discretion, pay to his parent or guardian, if any, or otherwise apply for or towards his maintenance, education, or benefit, the whole or such part, if any, of the income of that property as may, in all the circumstances, be reasonable, whether or not there is—

   (*a*) any other fund applicable to the same purpose; or

   (*b*) any person bound by law to provide for his maintenance or education; and

(ii) if such person on attaining the age of eighteen years has not a vested interest in such income, the trustees shall thenceforth pay the income of that property and of any accretion thereto under subsection (2) of this section to him, until he either attains a vested interest therein or dies, or until failure of his interest:

Provided that, in deciding whether the whole or any part of the income of the property is during a minority to be paid or applied for the purposes aforesaid, the trustees shall have regard to the age of the infant and his requirements and generally to the circumstances of the case, and in particular to what other income, if any, is applicable for the same purposes; and where trustees have notice that the income of more than one fund is applicable for those purposes, then, so far as practicable, unless the entire income of the funds is paid or applied as aforesaid or the court otherwise directs, a proportionate part only of the income of each fund shall be so paid or applied.

(2)   During the infancy of any such person, if his interest so long continues, the trustees shall accumulate all the residue of that income in the way of compound interest by investing the same and the resulting income thereof from time to time in authorised investments, and shall hold those accumulations as follows:

Appendix E

(i) If any such person—

    (*a*) attains the age of eighteen years or marries under that age, and his interest in such income during his infancy or until his marriage is a vested interest; or

    (*b*) on attaining the age of eighteen years or on marriage under that age becomes entitled to the property from which such income arose in fee simple, absolute or determinable, or absolutely, or for an entailed interest;

the trustees shall hold the accumulations in trust for such person absolutely, but without prejudice to any provision with respect thereto contained in any settlement by him made under any statutory powers during his infancy, and so that the receipt of such person after marriage, and though still an infant, shall be a good discharge; and

(ii) In any other case the trustees shall, notwithstanding that such person had a vested interest in such income, hold the accumulations as an accretion to the capital of the property from which such accumulations arose, and as one fund with such capital for all purposes, and so that, if such property is settled land, such accumulations shall be held upon the same trusts as if the same were capital money arising therefrom;

but the trustees may, at any time during the infancy of such person if his interest so long continues, apply those accumulations, or any part thereof, as if they were income arising in the then current year.

(3)   This section applies in the case of a contingent interest only if the limitation or trust carries the intermediate income of the property, but it applies to a future or contingent legacy by the parent of, or a person standing in loco parentis to, the legatee, if and for such period as, under the general law, the legacy carries interest for the maintenance of the legatee, and in any such case as last aforesaid the rate of interest shall (if the income available is sufficient, and subject to any rules of court to the contrary) be five pounds per centum per annum.

(4)   This section applies to a vested annuity in like manner as if the annuity were the income of property held by trustees in trust to pay the income thereof to the annuitant for the same period for which the annuity is payable, save that in any case accumulations made during the infancy of the annuitant shall be held in trust for the annuitant or his personal representatives absolutely.

(5)   This section does not apply where the instrument, if any, under which the interest arises came into operation before the commencement of this Act.

Section 32: Power of advancement

(1)   Trustees may at any time or times pay or apply any capital money subject to a trust, for the advancement or benefit, in such manner as they

Appendix E

may, in their absolute discretion, think fit, of any person entitled to the capital of the trust property or of any share thereof, whether absolutely or contingently on his attaining any specified age or on the occurrence of any other event, or subject to a gift over on his death under any specified age or on the occurrence of any other event, and whether in possession or in remainder or reversion, and such payment or application may be made notwithstanding that the interest of such person is liable to be defeated by the exercise of a power of appointment or revocation, or to be diminished by the increase of the class to which he belongs:

Provided that—

(*a*) the money so paid or applied for the advancement or benefit of any person shall not exceed altogether in amount one-half of the presumptive or vested share or interest of that person in the trust property; and

(*b*) if that person is or becomes absolutely and indefeasibly entitled to a share in the trust property the money so paid or applied shall be brought into account as part of such share; and

(*c*) no such payment or application shall be made so as to prejudice any person entitled to any prior life or other interest, whether vested or contingent, in the money paid or applied unless such person is in existence and of full age and consents in writing to such payment or application.

(2) This section applies only where the trust property consists of money or securities or of property held upon trust for sale calling in and conversion, and such money or securities, or the proceeds of such sale calling in and conversion are not by statute or in equity considered as land, or applicable as capital money for the purposes of the Settled Land Act 1925.

(3) This section does not apply to trusts constituted or created before the commencement of this Act.

Section 33: Protective trusts

(1) Where any income, including an annuity or other periodical income payment, is directed to be held on protective trusts for the benefit of any person (in this section called 'the principal beneficiary') for the period of his life or for any less period, then, during that period (in this section called the 'trust period') the said income shall, without prejudice to any prior interest, be held on the following trusts, namely—

(i) Upon trust for the principal beneficiary during the trust period or until he, whether before or after the termination of any prior interest, does or attempts to do or suffers any act or thing, or until any event happens, other than an advance under any statutory or express power, whereby, if the said income were payable during the

Appendix E

trust period to the principal beneficiary absolutely during that period, he would be deprived of the right to receive the same or any part thereof, in any of which cases, as well as on the termination of the trust period, whichever first happens, this trust of the said income shall fail or determine;

(ii) If the trust aforesaid fails or determines during the subsistence of the trust period, then, during the residue of that period, the said income shall be held upon trust for the application thereof for the maintenance or support, or otherwise for the benefit, of all or any one or more exclusively of the other or others of the following persons (that is to say)—

   (*a*) the principal beneficiary and his or her wife or husband, if any, and his or her children or more remote issue, if any; or

   (*b*) if there is no wife or husband or issue of the principal beneficiary in existence, the principal beneficiary and the persons who would, if he were actually dead, be entitled to the trust property or the income thereof or to the annuity fund, if any, or arrears of the annuity, as the case may be;

as the trustees in their absolute discretion, without being liable to account for the exercise of such discretion, think fit.

(2) This section does not apply to trusts coming into operation before the commencement of this Act, and has effect subject to any variation of the implied trusts aforesaid contained in the instrument creating the trust.

(3) Nothing in this section operates to validate any trust which would, if contained in the instrument creating the trust, be liable to be set aside.

[N.B. The *Trustee Act 1925* does not override the provisions of the trust instrument. It applies only to the extent that it is not excluded by the trust instrument. It has no application in Scotland.]

Appendix F

Inheritance Tax Act 1984, s 71

Section 71: Accumulation and maintenance trusts

(1)   Subject to subsection (2) below, this section applies to settled property if—

(*a*) one or more persons (in this section referred to as beneficiaries) will, on or before attaining a specified age not exceeding twenty-five, become beneficially entitled to it or to an interest in possession in it, and

(*b*) no interest in possession subsists in it and the income from it is to be accumulated so far as not applied for the maintenance, education or benefit of a beneficiary.

(2)   This section does not apply to settled property unless either—

(*a*) not more than twenty-five years have elapsed since the commencement of the settlement or, if it was later, since the time (or latest time) when the conditions stated in paragraphs (*a*) and (*b*) of subsection (1) above became satisfied with respect to the property, or

(*b*) all the persons who are or have been beneficiaries are or were either—

   (i) grandchildren of a common grandparent, or

   (ii) children, widows or widowers of such grandchildren who were themselves beneficiaries but died before the time when, had they survived, they would have become entitled as mentioned in subsection (1)(*a*) above.

(3)   Subject to subsections (4) and (5) below, there shall be a charge to tax under this section—

(*a*) where settled property ceases to be property to which this section applies, and

(*b*) in a case in which paragraph (*a*) above does not apply, where the trustees make a disposition as a result of which the value of settled property to which this section applies is less than it would be but for the disposition.

Appendix F

(4)   Tax shall not be charged under this section—

(*a*) on a beneficiary's becoming beneficially entitled to, or to an interest in possession in, settled property on or before attaining the specified age, or

(*b*) on the death of a beneficiary before attaining the specified age.

(5)   Subsections (3) to (8) and (10) of section 70 above shall apply for the purposes of this section as they apply for the purposes of that section (with the substitution of a reference to subsection (3)(*b*) above for the reference in section 70(4) to section 70(2)(*b*)).

(6)   Where the conditions stated in paragraphs (*a*) and (*b*) of subsection (1) above were satisfied on 15th April 1976 with respect to property comprised in a settlement which commenced before that day, subsection (2)(*a*) above shall have effect with the substitution of a reference to that day for the reference to the commencement of the settlement, and the condition stated in subsection (2)(*b*) above shall be treated as satisfied if

(*a*) it is satisfied in respect of the period beginning with 15th April 1976, or

(*b*) it is satisfied in respect of the period beginning with 1st April 1977 and either there was no beneficiary living on 15th April 1976 or the beneficiaries on 1st April 1977 included a living beneficiary, or

(*c*) there is no power under the terms of the settlement whereby it could have become satisfied in respect of the period beginning with 1st April 1977, and the trusts of the settlement have not been varied at any time after 15th April 1976.

(7)   In subsection (1) above 'persons' includes unborn persons; but the conditions stated in that subsection shall be treated as not satisfied unless there is or has been a living beneficiary.

(8)   For the purposes of this section a person's children shall be taken to include his illegitimate children, his adopted children and his stepchildren.

Index

A

Absolute entitlement, capital gains tax, 7.6–7.8
Accounts for inheritance tax, 10.4, 14.2
Accrued income scheme, 6.5–6.17
  interaction with capital gains tax, 7.34
  interaction with ICTA 1988, s 686, 6.20
ACCUMULATION AND MAINTENANCE SETTLEMENTS, 10
  appointment from discretionary trust, 10.17, 15.23
  capital gains tax holdover, 7.15, 7.17
  definitions, 2.15–2.18, App B, App F
  income tax,
  —returns, 6.30, App C
  —tax pool, 6.27, 6.32, 6.36, 6.40, App C
  inheritance tax, charge to, 10.15
  introduction to, 1.3, 1.4
  payments to beneficiaries, 6.26–6.41
  potentially exempt transfers, 10.1, 10.4, 14.8
  qualifying conditions, 2.15–2.18
  settlements prior to 15 April 1976, 10.3
  use of, 10.7–10.14, 10.16
Accumulations, explained, 3.6
  income tax, 6.21–6.23, 6.37
  inheritance tax, 10.7, 11.7, 11.17, 11.34
Added property, 11.23–11.28, 12.17, 12.19
ADMINISTRATIVE MATTERS– INHERITANCE TAX, 14
Administration period, 2.4, 2.26, 6.21
Advancement,
  explained, 2.9
  —Trustee Act 1925, s 32, App E
  income tax consequences, 6.37, 6.39
Advance Corporation Tax, 4.9, 6.18
Age of majority, 2.8
Agricultural property relief, 1.3, 11.7, 11.8, 12.9, 14.6–14.9
  holdover for capital gains tax, 7.11
  valuation, 14.11

Alternative Investment Market (AIM), 7.11, 7.12, 7.21, 10.12, 14.6, 14.12, 14.14
ANTI-AVOIDANCE, 4
  'arrangement', settlor by, 4.7
  associated operations, 15.25
  capital gains tax, 4.12, 21
  charities, 17.9–17.14
  discretionary settlements, 11.31–11.33
  excluded property, 11.32, 11.33
  flip-flop schemes, 7.15, 21.22
  Furniss v Dawson, 15.26
  gifts with reservation of benefit, 8.8, 10.12, 11.37, 11.38, 15.8, 15.27
  income tax, 4.2–4.11
  inheritance tax, 4.13
  offshore trusts, 19.1, 21.22
  potentially exempt transfers, misuse of, 9.7, 9.8, 11.22
  property moving between settlements, 11.31
  settlements on children, 4.7
  transfer of assets abroad, 20.7, 20.8, 23.5
  transactions in land, 20.9
Appointment,
  capital gains tax, 7.36, App A
  discretionary trustees, by, 10.17
  explained, 2.9, App A
Artificial transactions in land, 20.9
Assessment, self, 18
Associated operations, 15.25

B

Bank interest, income tax, 6.22, 20.6
Bare trusts, 4.8
  capital gains tax, 2.28, 7.7
Basic rate income tax, 5.3–5.9, 6.1, 6.2
Beneficiaries,
  cash basis, 2.25
  date of entitlement, 7.6
  offshore trusts,
  income tax, 6.51
  —capital gains tax, 21.3–21.6, 21.17, 21.18
  —income tax, 20.7, 20.8
  payments to, 6.26–6.41
  —fixed interest, 6.42–6.46
  residence of, 5.13, 7.8, 7.19, 7.20, 19.3
  rights of, 3

Index

Benefit, gift with reservation of, 8.8, 10.12, 11.37, 11.38, 15.8, 15.10, 15.27
Board of Inland Revenue,
 annual report of, 1.2
 determination by, 14.5
 extra-statutory concessions, press releases and statements of practice, App A, App B, App D
 enforcement powers, 21.6, 22.11–22.13
 information powers, 21.16
Building society interest, income tax, 6.4, 20.6
Business property,
 holdover for capital gains tax, 7.11–7.14
 relief for inheritance tax, 10.12, 11.7–11.9, 12.9, 14.6–14.9, 15.12
 rollover relief, 7.11, 21.10, 21.11

C

CAPITAL GAINS TAX, 7 (UK), 21 (Offshore)
 absolute entitlement, 7.6–7.8
 accrued income scheme, 7.31
 anti-avoidance, 4.12
 bare trustees, 2.28; 7.7
 base values, 7.29–7.31
 beneficiaries, charge on, 21.3–21.6, 21.17, 21.18
 charities, 17.4, 17.8
 connected persons, 7.38
 deeds of variation, 7.9
 demergers, 7.38
 derived property, 4.11
 dual resident trusts, 21.8, 21.11
 Enterprise Investment Scheme, 7.28
 exemptions, 7.32
 expenses, 7.29
 general, 7.1, 7.2, 21.1
 half-gain rule, 7.23
 holdover relief, 7.5, 7.8, 7.10–7.22
 incidental costs, 7.29
 indexation loss, 7.2, 10.12
 instalments, 7.21
 interest in possession, 7.4
 'listed' shares, 7.42
 loss transfer, 7.40
 migration of trusts, 21.2, 21.10
 negotiated probate value, 7.29
 power of appointment and advancement, App A
 principal private residence, 7.26, App A
 probate costs, App D
 protective trusts, 7.37
 rates of tax, 4.11, 7.32, 7.33, 15.17
 remainderman, 7.3
 residence, 5.13, 7.19, 19.3, 19.4
 retirement relief, 7.24
 settled property defined, 5.2
 settlor, charge on, 4.11, 7.46, 21.12–21.16
 taper relief, 10.12, 16.3
 termination of life interest, 7.3–7.5
 trustees treated as one body, 5.2, 21.1
 valuation of building society shares, 7.29
 variation of trust, 7.48
 yield of, 1.2
Capital payments,
 as accumulations or advancements, 2.9, 6.39
 offshore trusts, 21.6, 21.7, 21.17, 21.18
 to settlor, 4.11
Capital transfer tax, 22.1
Certificates of discharge, 14.18
Certificates of tax deposit, 14.19
Channel Islands, 23.6
CHARITIES, 17
 anti-avoidance, 17.9–17.15
 contemplative order, 2.21
 definitions, 2.21, 2.22
 disaster funds, 17.19
 exemptions, 17.2–17.5, 17.8
 failure of family gifts, 23.4
 gift aid, 17.5
 Inland Revenue administration, 17.17
 shareholdings, transferred to, 17.6
 time charities, 2.22, 17.16
 VAT, 17.18
Children,
 accumulation and maintenance settlements, 10
 —defined, 2.21, 2.22
 outright gifts to, 6.22
 settlement for own children, 4.7
Class gifts, 2.12, 10.6, 10.9, 10.10
Company purchasing own shares, 6.23
Composite rate tax, 6.3, 6.4
Connected persons, 7.39
Constructive trust, 2.10
Contingent interest, 3.4, 3.5
Corrective affidavit, 2.26
Creditor protection, 23.6

Index

D

Death and resultant discretionary settlement, 11.5, 11.6, 11.22, 11.30
Declaration of trust, 2.7
Deductions for income tax, 6.2, 6.22, 6.27, App C
Deed of variation,
  anti-avoidance, 4.7
  capital gains tax, 4.14, 4.18, 7.9
  income tax considerations, 4.7
  inheritance tax, 10.13
Deemed chargeable transfer, *see* discretionary settlements and inheritance tax
Deemed cumulative total, *see* discretionary settlements and inheritance tax
Defeasible interests, 2.12
Deficiency of income, 5.8, 6.31, 6.44
Definitions,
  accumulation, 3.6
  accumulation and maintenance settlement, 2.15–2.18, App F
  administration period, 2.4
  advancement, 2.9
  appointment, 2.9
  charity, 2.21, 2.22
  —time charity, 2.22
  charities,
  —chargeable period, 17.9
  —non-qualifying expenditure, 17.9
  —qualifying expenditure, 17.9
  —qualifying investment, 17.9
  —relevant income and gains, 17.9
  constructive trust, 2.10
  contingent interest, 3.4
  disabled trust, 2.13
  discretionary settlement, 2.19, 2.20
  excluded property, 8.5
  gift with reservation of benefit, 8.8
  implied trust, 2.10
  interest in possession, 2.12, 8.3
  payment, 8.7
  potentially exempt transfer, 8.9
  protective trust, 2.14
  qualifying interest in possession, 8.4
  qualifying settlement, 21.14
  quarter, 8.7
  rate applicable to trusts, 6.19
  related settlement, 11.18
  relevant property, 2.20, 8.6
  relevant trustees, 5.18
  resulting trust, 2.10
  settled property, 5.2
  settlement, 4.3, 4.14, 8.2
  settlor, 4.3, 4.16
  spes, 3.2
  trust instrument, 2.3, 2.7
  'unlisted' shares, 10.12, 14.6
  vested interest, 3.3
Demergers, 7.38
Deposit, certificate of tax, 14.19
Deposit of tax, 14.20
Determinations, 14.5
Disabled trusts, 2.13
Disaster funds, 17.17, 17.19
Discharge, certificate of, 14.18
Discretionary interests in residue, App A
Discretionary payments, 6.23, 6.24, 6.25, 6.38, 6.41, 20.5
Discretionary settlements defined, 2.19, 2.20
DISCRETIONARY SETTLEMENTS AND INHERITANCE TAX, 11, 12, 13
  accumulations, 11.7, 11.17, App A
  added property, 11.23–11.28
  anti-avoidance, 11.31–11.33
  appointment on accumulation and maintenance trusts, 10.17
  commencement, 11.4
  death, 11.5, 11.6, 11.22, 11.30
  deemed chargeable transfer, 11.7, 11.11
  deemed cumulative total, 11.12–11.14
  effective rate, 11.10, 11.15
  excluded property, 11.32, 11.33
  holdover relief for capital gains tax, 7.15
  identification of property, 11.34
  leased property, 15.28
  non-relevant property, 11.20, 11.29
  pre-27 March 1974, 13
  proportionate charge, 12
  —added property, 12.17, 12.19
  —amount chargeable, 12.9
  —before first ten-year anniversary, 12.12–12.15
  —between ten-year anniversaries, 12.16–12.19
  —costs, expenses, 12.6
  —excluded property, 12.5
  —exemptions, 12.5, 12.7, 12.8
  —occasions of charge, 12.2, 12.3
  —rate of tax, 12.11, 12.14, 12.18
  rates of tax, 11.3, 11.10, 11.16

related settlements, 11.18, 11.19
ten-year anniversary, 11.4–11.6
ten-year charge, 11.1–11.3, 11.7–11.30
transitional charge, 13.2
undistributed income, 11.7, App A
valuation, 11.7–11.9
DISCRETIONARY SETTLEMENTS, USE OF, 15
introduction, 1.3, 1.5, 21.3
Dividend waivers, 4.9
DOMICILE, 19
generally, 19.6, 19.7
inheritance tax, 19.7, 22.10, 23.7
non-domiciled beneficiary, 21.5
protection of established, 23.2
reforms, 19.8, 19.9
Double tax relief, 20.6
Dual resident trusts, 21.8, 21.11
Dwelling house, 6.45, 7.36, App A

E

Effective rate, *see* discretionary settlements and inheritance tax
EIS Investments, 7.28
Emigration of trusts, 21.2, 21.10
Employee trusts, 2.20, 6.37, 12.8
Enterprise Investment Scheme, 7.25
Estate duty, 22.1
Estate in course of administration, 2.26
Excluded property, 8.5, 11.32, 11.33, 12.5, 16.11, 22.2, 22.6
Executor compared with trustee, 2.4, 2.6
Exempt gilts, *see* government securities
Exit charge, *see* proportionate charge
Exit charge on migration, 21.10
Expenses, income tax, 5.8, 6.2, 6.22, 6.30, 6.42
Export of trusts, 21.2, 21.10

F

Family companies, 4.9, 6.29, 7.11–7.13, 10.11, 10.12, 14.7, 14.14, 15.2, 15.9, 15.10
Family considerations, offshore trusts, 23.4
Family law reform, 2.8
Flip-flop schemes, 7.15, 21.22
Football club trusts, 2.20

Foreign dividends, 6.40, App C
Foreign income dividends, 6.20, 6.27
FOTRA, 6.42, 8.5, 11.33, 12.5, 22.8

G

Games trusts, 2.20
Gibraltar, 23.6
Gift aid, 17.5
Gifts,
adding property to settlements, *see* discretionary settlements and inheritance tax
class gifts, 2.12, 10.6, 10.9, 10.10
holdover relief, *see* capital gains tax
Insolvency Act 1986, effect of, 2.23, 23.6
reservation of benefit, with, 8.8, 10.12, 11.37, 11.38, 15.8, 15.27
separate funds, out of, 9.3, App A
Government securities, 6.5, 6.7, 6.8, 8.5, 11.33, 12.5, 19.5, 22.7–22.9, 23.1

H

Hague Convention, 2.24
Half-gain rule (capital gains tax), 7.23
Holdover relief (capital gains tax), 5.13–5.16, 7.5, 7.8, 7.10–7.22, 21.8
Husband and wife, *see* married couples

I

Identification of property, 11.34
Implied trust, 2.10
INCOME TAX, 6 (UK), 20 (Offshore)
accrued income scheme, 6.5–6.17
anti-avoidance, 4.2–4.11, 20.6–20.8, 23.5, 23.8
assessed on beneficiary, 5.7, 20.7
assessed on settlor, 4.2–4.11, 20.7, 20.9
assessed on trustees, 5.3, 5.4, 20.2, 20.3
bank interest, 6.1, 6.3
building society interest, 6.4
charities, 17.5, 17.8
dividend credits, 6.28, 6.29

Index

dividends, 6.1
expenses, 6.2, 20.4
foreign dividends, 6.1
Irish dividends, 6.1
land transactions, 6.47
liability to UK tax, 20.1, 20.5
mandated to beneficiary, 5.7
offshore income, 20.2
paying agent, 6.43
payments to beneficiaries, 6.37, 6.41, 6.42–6.46
rate applicable to trusts, 6.21–6.41
residence for, 19.3, 19.4
returns, 5.18, 6.28, App C
tax pool, 6.27, 6.32, App C
unit trusts, 6.1
Indexation losses, 7.2
Inheritance tax, *see generally* accumulation and maintenance settlements, discretionary settlements and inheritance tax
INHERITANCE TAX, ADMINISTRATIVE MATTERS, 14
accounts, 14.2
BES and EIS, 14.12
business tests, 14.6
certificate of discharge, 14.18
certificate of tax deposit, 14.19
deposits, 14.20
determinations, 14.5
due date for payment, 14.2
gilt strips market, 22.8
offshore, enforcement, 22.11–22.13
interest on tax overdue and overpaid, 14.3, 14.13, 14.20
liability, 14.17
payment by instalments, 14.13–14.14
quick succession relief, 14.10
returns (official requests for information), 14.4
yield of, 1.2
INHERITANCE TAX, DEFINITIONS, 8 (*see also* definitions)
INHERITANCE TAX, OFFSHORE TRUSTS, 22
Inheritance trust, 16.12
Inland Revenue, *see* Board of Inland Revenue
Insolvency Act 1986, 2.23, 23.6
Instalment payments, 7.21, 14.13–14.16
Instruments, trust, 2.3, 2.7, 2.8, 6.48, 23.3, App A

Interest,
accrued income scheme, 6.5–6.17
bank, 6.1, 6.3, 6.22
building society, 6.1, 6.4
certificates of tax deposit, on, 14.19
tax overdue or overpaid, on, 6.2, 6.22, 7.21, 14.3, 14.14, 14.21
Interest in possession, (*see also* life tenant and CGT, App B),
explained, 2.12, 8.3, App A
inheritance tax, 9
potentially exempt transfers, and, 8.9, 9.7–9.10
qualifying, 2.20, 8.4
Intermediate income, 3.5

J

Joint ownership, 7.44

L

Land transactions, 6.47, 7.9, 14.5, 20.9
Liabilities of settlors,
anti-avoidance, 4
capital gains tax, 7.46
Life tenant, (*see also* interest in possession) and CGT, App A,
income tax on payments, 6.40
termination of interest, 7.3–7.5
Loans, to settlor etc., 4.10
Location of offshore trust, 23.6
money laundering, 23.6
Losses, 5.5, 5.6

M

Majority, age of, 2.8
Married couples, 4.6, 15.6, 15.7
Management expenses, 5.8, 6.2, 6.22, 20.4, 20.7, App C
Mandating of income, 5.7
Migration of beneficiary, 5.13, 7.20
Migration of settlements, 21.2, 21.10

N

Newspaper trusts, 2.20
Non-domiciled individuals, 21.5, 23.7
Non-relevant property, 11.20, 11.29, 12.5

Index

Non-resident landlord's scheme, 5.11
Non-resident trusts, 21.19, 21.20
  attacks on, 21.19, 23.1, 23.7
  transitional provisions, 21.20

O

Offshore funds, 7.35
OFFSHORE TRUSTS, USE OF ETC., 23
Oral declaration of trust, 2.7
ORDINARY RESIDENCE, 19
Overdue inheritance tax, 14.3, 14.13
Overseas electors, 19.10

P

Payment: capital or income? 20.3
Personal representatives, 14.2, 18.19
Potentially exempt transfer,
  accumulation and maintenance settlement, 10.1, 10.4
  anti-avoidance, 9.7, 9.8, 11.22
  explained, 8.9
  failure of, 10.4, 10.14, 11.35, 11.36, 14.2, 14.7, 14.8
  holdover relief, 7.15, 7.16
  interest in possession, 9.7–9.9
  —termination of, 9.10
  misuse of, 9.7, 9.8, 11.22
Powers of advancement and appointment, 2.9
Powers of Attorney, 2.7
Pre-27 March 1974 settlements, 13
Principal private residence, capital gains tax, 7.26, App A
Probate value, 7.29, App D
Property moving between settlements, 11.31
Property occupied by beneficiary, 6.45, 7.26, 15.28, App A
Proportionate charge, 12
Protective trusts, 2.14, 7.37
  Trustee Act 1925, s 33, App E

Q

Qualifying interest in possession, 2.20, 8.4
Qualifying settlements, 21.14
Quarter, definition of, 8.7
Quick succession relief, 14.10

R

Rates of tax,
  capital gains tax, 4.12, 7.32, 7.33, 15.17
  effective, 11.10, 11.15, 13.4
  income tax, rate applicable to trusts, 6.21–6.41
  proportionate charge, 12.11, 12.14, 12.18
  ten-year charge, 11.3, 11.10, 11.16
Reinvestment relief, 7.27
Related settlements, 11.18, 11.19
Relevant property, 2.20, 8.6, 11.20, 11.29, 11.30, 22.2
Relevant trustees, 5.18, 6.47, 7.41
Remainderman resettlement, 2.27, 16.11
Remuneration, 10.12, 15.9
Reservation of benefit, 8.8, 10.12, 11.37, 11.38, 15.8, 15.27
RESIDENCE, 19
  of beneficiaries, 5.13, 7.8, 7.19, 7.20, 19.3
  of settlors, 19.3
  of trustees, 5.11, 14.4, 19.4
Resulting trust, 2.10
Retirement relief, 7.24
Returns of information, 5.18, 14.4, 21.6, 22.11
Reversionary interests, 9.5, 9.6, 22.6
Reversion to settlor, 4.12, 7.4
Revocation, 2.12, App A
RIGHTS OF BENEFICIARIES, 3
Rollover relief, 7.11, 21.10, 21.11

S

Scrip dividends, 6.18, 6.19
SELF-ASSESSMENT, 7.41, 18
  accounts, 18.17
  beneficiaries, 18.19–18.21
  —'applicable rate', 18.20
  —close of administration, 18.20
  —personal representatives, 18.19
  —tax vouchers, 18.21
  clearance, 18.16
  commencement, 18.1
  computation of tax, 18.3; 18.4
  de minimis, 18.11
  estates, 18.15
  estimates, 18.12
  interest and penalties, 18.13–18.15

Index

introduction of, 18.1
liability to notify, 18.7–18.9
life tenant's income, 18.19
payment of tax, 18.10
personal representatives, 18.18, 18.19
penalties and interest, 18.13–18.15
Schedule A, 18.3
Trust and Estate Tax Return, 18.24
trustees' duties, 18.2
trustees return, 18.17
trust income
—bank interest, 18.23
—preceding year basis, 18.23
—'relevant trustee', 5.18, 18.22
—transitional year, 18.23
Settled property,
absolute entitlement, 7.6
defined, 5.2
interest in possession in, 9, App A
outside UK, 22.3
Settlement,
definitions, 4.3, 4.13
general, 2.2
Settlor,
definitions, 4.3
liabilities of, 4, 6.22, 7.46, 21.12–21.16, 22.4
reversion to, 4.12, 7.4
shadow, 4.3, 4.16
SETTLOR, ANTI-AVOIDANCE PROVISIONS, 4
Shares,
buyback, 6.23
Shareholders, liability of, 2.23
Situs, 22.5
Spes, 3.2
Sports trusts, 2.20
Spouse,
benefits, 4.6, 4.11–4.12, 15.6, 15.7
surviving, 9.2
Stamp Duty, 15.15, 17.2
Statutory trusts for infants, 2.15
Trustee Act 1925, s 31, App E
Supplementary charge, 21.17

T

Taper relief, 10.11, 16.3
Tax deposit, certificate of, 14.19

Tax pool, 6.27–6.36, 6.40, App C
Ten-year anniversary, 11.4–11.6
Ten-year charge, 11.1–11.3, 11.7–11.30
Pre-27 March 1974 settlements, 13.3
Term assurance, 14.9
Termination of an interest, 7.3–7.5, 9.2–9.4
Time charities, 2.22, 17.16
Transactions in land, 20.9
Transfer of assets abroad, 20.7, 20.8, 23.5
Trust and Estate Tax Return, 18.24
Trustee Act 1925, ss 31–32, App E
Trust instruments, 2.3, 2.7, 2.8, 6.48, 23.3, App A
Trust or settlement?, 2.2
TRUSTEES, 5
assessments on, 5.3, 5.4, 6.48
declaration, 20.6
liability of, 5.12–5.17, 14.13, 14.16, 20.2–20.4, 21.10, 21.11, 22.12
professional, 5.19
'relevant trustees', 5.18, 18.20
remuneration of, 10.12
residence of, 5.11, 14.4, 19.4
Turks and Caicos Islands, 23.6
TYPES OF TRUST, 2
commencement, 2.26
deed, 2.25
infants, 2.26
intestacy, 2.24
remaindermen, 2.27
will, 2.25

U

USE OF DISCRETIONARY SETTLEMENTS, 15
Use of settlements, 1.3–1.6, 16

V

Valuation, 7.6, 7.29–7.31, 9.3, 9.4, 9.11, 11.7–11.9, 14.5
Value added tax, charities, 17.18
Value freezing, explained, 15.3

Index

Variation of trusts, 7.46
Vested interest, 3.3

W

Waiver of dividends, 4.9

Wills, 2.3, 2.4, 2.8, 2.23, 6.43, 11.6, 11.18, 11.22, 11.27
  variation of, 4.7, 4.14, 7.9, 10.13, 15.9
Woodlands, 8.9

Butterworths

21 Days Money Back Guarantee

The *only* book available on this subject

Purpose Trusts

By Paul Baxendale-Walker BA (Oxon)

Purpose Trusts introduces new perspectives on English and International Trust Law; facilitating new and advantageous practical Commercial and Family Trust Planning. This unique publication contains not only an authoritative statement of the present domestic and international laws of Purpose Trusts, but also presents a vital re-examination of precedents, which justifies a radical change in English and international trust law and practice.

What does the book do?

- Explains a method for constructing trusts which allows the solution of many modern commercial and family trust problems
- Allows powerful Off-balance Sheet arrangements
- Provides new Asset Protection arrangements
- Explains a completely new Commercial Benefits Trust
- Facilitates vital loan trust arrangements

Unique and innovative in its approach, **Purpose Trusts** gives analyses of twenty offshore trust regimes not available in any existing publication, as well as access to case reports not previously discussed in any other work. Numbered paragraphs, full case and statute indexes, and a full bibliography enable you to make quick and effective searches, while numerous case references give you the assurance of definitive answers.

Product Code: PTCP   **Price:** £130.00   **ISBN:** 0 40698 881 1

How To Order

To order, please contact Butterworths Tolley Customer Service Dept:
Butterworths Tolley, FREEPOST SEA 4177, Croydon, Surrey CR9 5WZ
Telephone: 020 8662 2000   Fax: 020 8662 2012

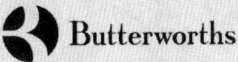

Butterworths

A member of the Reed Elsevier plc group
25 Victoria Street, London SW1H 0EX
VAT number: 730 8595 20
Registered Office Number: 2746621

NB: Your data may be used for direct marketing purposes by selected companies

Butterworths Tax Direct Service is the ultimate on-line service that provides you with instant access to the most authoritative information ... all via the internet.
For more information on all of our products, please visit our website at www.butterworths.com

The very best in specialist case law reporting....

International Trust and Estate Law Reports

An essential source of case materials for all trust and estate practitioners, this series, published bi-monthly, will provide you with full-text reports of major trust and estate cases from all over the world.

The series deals with such topics as:

- Actions to set aside trusts and procedural steps taken in litigation involving trusts
- The administration of estates (including cross-border administration)
- Taxation of trusts and estates and commercial matters of interest to persons acting as trustees or advising trustees.

Each issue includes approximately **seven significant cases** from around the world, reported **in full** with **concise headnotes and practical commentary** by the editor, Dr Philip Baker, highlighting essential points.

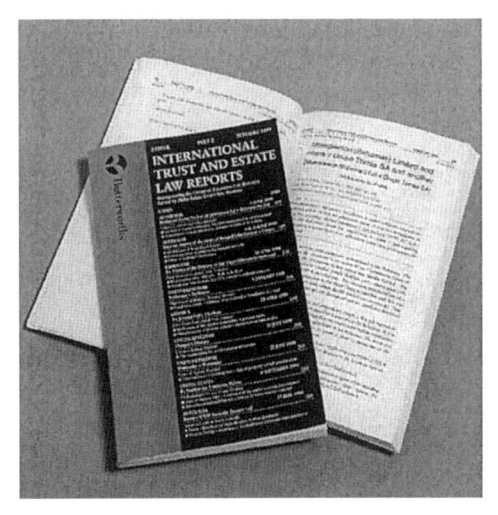

International Trust and Estate Law Reports
Product Code: ITELR   ISSN: 1464 - 7125
Price: £495

ORDER FORM

To order your copy now, please fill in this form and **post** it to: Alison O'Neill, Butterworths, FREEPOST (6983), London WC2A 1BR.
Alternatively you can place your order by
Fax: +44 (0)20 7400 2570
Tel: +44 (0)20 7400 2683.

☐ Please invoice me
My Butterworths account no is ....
☐ Please set up a new Butterworths account for me

Delivery Details

(Qty) Title ISSN Product Code	Unit Price
International Trust and Estate Law Reports Product Code: ITELR ISSN: 1464 - 7125 *Until further notice, continue to supply and charge for annually all future issues connected with this work.	£495
Total Amount due	£

Name: ....
Job Title: ....
Company: ....
Address: ....
....
....
....
Postcode: ....

Butterworths

OFFSHORE SERVICE / PSC / AO'N / IN-HSE / 5.2000

21 Days Money Back Guarantee

AVOID the pitfalls...
SEIZE the opportunities...
UNDERSTAND the new rules...

with

Butterworths Taxation of Offshore Trusts and Funds

Third Edition

(Previously Tolley's Taxation of Offshore Trusts and Funds)

This established guide has set a tradition of providing the most up-to-date information on the taxation of offshore investments. Covering all the latest developments in legislation and case law, this new edition is essential reading and reference for anyone needing reliable guidance on the taxation of offshore trusts and funds.

- The legislation is covered systematically, with separate treatment of Offshore Trusts and Funds.
- The pitfalls of each aspect are highlighted, so you can be confident in the advice that you give
- Opportunities and planning points are included throughout
- Worked examples, practical tables, appendices of official material, and tables of statutes and cases provide the necessary back up needed to unravel the issues in this complex area

Price: £75.00   Product Code TOF03   ISBN 0 75450 091 8

How To Order

To order, please contact Butterworths Tolley Customer Service Dept:
Butterworths Tolley, FREEPOST SEA 4177, Croydon, Surrey CR9 5WZ
Telephone: 020 8662 2000   Fax: 020 8662 2012

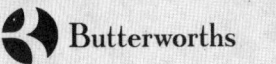

Butterworths   Tolley

A member of the Reed Elsevier plc group
25 Victoria Street, London SW1H 0EX
VAT number: 730 8595 20
Registered Office Number: 2746621

NB: Your data may be used for direct marketing purposes by selected companies

Butterworths Tax Direct Service is the ultimate on-line service that provides you with instant access to the most authoritative information ... all via the internet.
For more information on all of our products, please visit our website at www.butterworths.com

Tolley

NEW EDITION

Ensuring that you have the edge over your competitors

Tolley's Taxation in the Republic of Ireland 2000-01

Glyn Saunders, MA (Cantab)

"...packed with information for all those dealing with the Irish and their tax regime"
ACCOUNTANCY AGE

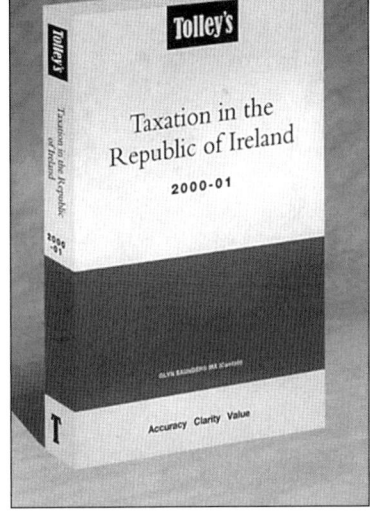

With Deloitte and Touche, Dublin, acting as consultants, **Tolley's Taxation in the Republic of Ireland 2000-01** is a detailed guide providing a comprehensive review of all the important legislative provisions across the wide range of taxes in Ireland.

This authoritative source of reference covers all major areas of taxation including income tax, corporation tax, capital gains tax and value-added tax. It also incorporates useful sections on social security and guidance on double taxation in relation to the UK.

Designed to save you time and effort, it features:

- A summary of the Finance Act 2000 provisions
- A full chapter devoted to over 225 Irish tax case summaries
- A table of income tax allowances and rate covering the last six years
- Coverage of double taxation in relation to the UK
- Text supported by full statutory authorities and references to Statements of Practice where relevant

All major changes resulting from the 1999 Finance Act are thoroughly covered by this new edition. They include: new employee savings-related share option scheme; major changes to the corporation tax rate structure; new company residence rules and new group anti-avoidance provisions. **Tolley's Taxation in the Republic of Ireland 2000-01** gives you comprehensive coverage of all recent pivotal developments and ensures you stay up-to date with this rapidly changing area.

Product Code: RI00   **Price: £49.95**   **ISBN: 0 7545 0273 8**

How To Order

To order, please contact Butterworths Tolley Customer Service Dept:
Butterworths Tolley, FREEPOST SEA 4177, Croydon, Surrey CR9 5WZ
Telephone: 020 8662 2000   Fax: 020 8662 2012

Butterworths   **Tolley**

A member of the Reed Elsevier plc group
25 Victoria Street, London SW1H 0EX
VAT number: 730 8595 20
Registered Office Number: 2746621

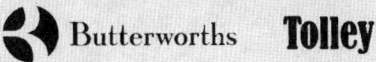

NB: Your data may be used for direct marketing purposes by selected companies

Butterworths Tax Direct Service is the ultimate on-line service that provides you with instant access to the most authoritative information ... all via the internet.
For more information on all of our products, please visit our website at www.butterworths.com